THE GODS IN THE FIELDS

Michael, Mary and Alice: Guardians of Enchanted Britain

By
Nigel Graddon

Adventures Unlimited Press

The Gods in the Fields

ISBN 978-1-948803-32-8

Published by:
Adventures Unlimited Press
One Adventure Place
Kempton, Illinois 60946 USA
auphq@frontiernet.net

AdventuresUnlimitedPress.com

10 9 8 7 6 5 4 3 2 1

CONTENTS

It was not yesterday what it is today, or what it will be tomorrow; but it does not the less hold us under its charm. "Qui d'elle pourrait se lasser? Toujours sa beauté renouvelle."

—Madame Michelet, *Nature, or the Poetry of Earth and Sea*

THE GODS IN THE FIELDS

Michael, Mary and Alice: Guardians of Enchanted Britain

By
Nigel Graddon

Adventures Unlimited Press

Other Books by Nigel Graddon:

JACK THE RIPPER'S NEW TESTAMENT
THE LANDING LIGHTS OF MAGONIA
U-33: HITLER'S SECRET ENVOY
OTTO RAHN AND THE QUEST FOR THE HOLY GRAIL

Other Books of Interest:

VIMANA
ARK OF GOD
THE LOST WORLD OF CHAM
OBELISKS: TOWERS OF POWER
ANCIENT TECHNOLOGY IN PERU & BOLIVIA
THE MYSTERY OF THE OLMECS
PIRATES AND THE LOST TEMPLAR FLEET
TECHNOLOGY OF THE GODS
A HITCHHIKER'S GUIDE TO ARMAGEDDON
LOST CONTINENTS & THE HOLLOW EARTH
ATLANTIS & THE POWER SYSTEM OF THE GODS
THE FANTASTIC INVENTIONS OF NIKOLA TESLA
LOST CITIES OF NORTH & CENTRAL AMERICA
LOST CITIES OF CHINA, CENTRAL ASIA & INDIA
LOST CITIES & ANCIENT MYSTERIES OF AFRICA & ARABIA
LOST CITIES & ANCIENT MYSTERIES OF SOUTH AMERICA
LOST CITIES OF ANCIENT LEMURIA & THE PACIFIC
LOST CITIES OF ATLANTIS, ANCIENT EUROPE & THE MEDITERRANEAN
LOST CITIES & ANCIENT MYSTERIES OF THE SOUTHWEST
YETIS, SASQUATCH AND HAIRY GIANTS
THE ENIGMA OF CRANIAL DEFORMATION
THE CRYSTAL SKULLS

Acknowledgements

There are a number of people to whom I must give grateful thanks for their gracious consent to quote from their work and to reproduce photographic or illustrative material.

Paul Broadhurst, co-author with Hamish Miller of *The Sun and the Serpent*, the book that in 1989 brought the St Michael ley and its dragon powers to the forefont of public attention, kindly gave me permission to quote from this seminal work.

Andreas Müller granted me permission to reproduce his images and graphics regarding his Turin Shroud analysis of the Wickham Green crop circles of 2010. Andreas founded in 1994 "ICCA - The International Crop Circle Archive," one of the world's most comprehensive databases on the subject. Andreas is proprietor of the crop circle site, www.kornkreise-forschung.de.

I am indebted to Bob Forrest for his permission to quote from his excellent statistical work in connection with his analysis of the late John Michell's findings concerning the St Michael line.

I was very pleased to receive permission from Gail Cornwell and Yuri Leitch to reproduce their wonderful representations of the Somerset Zodiac signs. To get an insight into their work, visit thealchemicaljourney.co.uk, www.yurileitch.co.uk and Donald Allen's victorialandscapezodiac.com/teachings-of-the-white-raven.

Jewels Rocka of Land and Spirit kindly allowed me to reproduce the graphic of the "Michael/Mary - Apollo/Athena" line See www.landandspirit.net for further information.

I am grateful to David Furlong for permission to quote from his 1997 work, *The Keys to the Temple* concerning the landscape circles of the Marlborough Downs (visit www.davidfurlong.co.uk for more information).

Ellic C. Taylor (ellisctaylor.com) was helpful in increasing my knowledge of the Oxford Henge and other handy tidbits. Ellis, I enjoyed our email exchanges about all things Carroll and Alice!

And, finally, a warm thank you goes to Roy Snelling for giving me leave to use extracts from his fascinating book, *The Planetary Matrix*, and his thought-provoking article, *The Atlantis Line*.

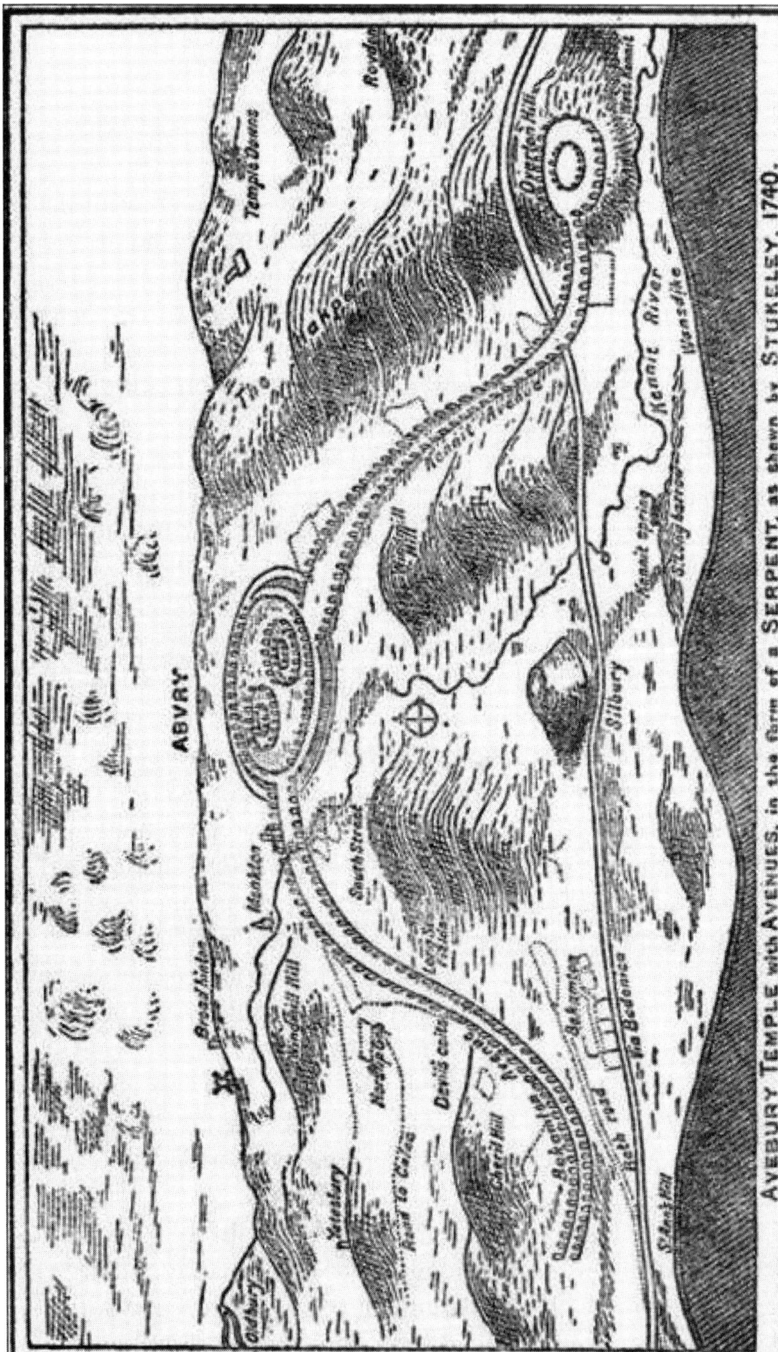

AVEBURY TEMPLE with AVENUES, in the form of a SERPENT, as shewn by STUKELEY. 1740.

William Stukeley's depiction of a serpentine Avebury complex in 1740

Chapter 1

Britain: Key, Lock and Door

> To the peoples of antiquity the isle of Britain was the very home and environment of mystery, a sacred territory, to enter which was to encroach upon a region of enchantment, the dwelling of gods, the shrine and habitation of a cult of peculiar sanctity and mystical power. Britain was, indeed, the *insula sacra* of the West, an island veiled and esoteric, the Egypt of the Occident.[1]

In 2001 I made a modest discovery concerning a hitherto unremarked feature of the St. Michael ley (also called the Serpent Line), which bisects southern England on a southwest-northeast alignment. For the purposes of consistency, throughout these pages I will refer to it as the St. Michael ley. It has been discovered that around the ley flow two terrestrial currents that resemble a double helix. The overall picture is of a straight staff, around which coil two serpentine energies mindful of the emblem of Asclepius, the Greek god of healing, and of Hermes' caduceus. It illustrates in the landscape the principle in Eastern medicine of vital currents that snake around the chakra points in the human body's invisible energy field; as above, as below.

The 21 nodal points where the two currents cross (see Tables on pages 49 and 255) define the relative straightness that distinguishes the St. Michael ley. I say "relatively" because the paths of these two sinuous waves, dubbed "Michael" and "Mary," can be visualised as if framed within an invisible *corridor* of complementary earth energies which extends from Land's End in Cornwall to Hopton-on-Sea in Norfolk. The widest distance between the pair along the route, approximately 10 miles in the Cambridgeshire region, determines the breadth of the overall corridor that contains the dragons' flight paths.

It is anyone's guess just how far the electromagnetic power of the two currents extends beyond the corridor boundaries. It could be just a hop, skip and a jump. On the other hand, Michael and Mary's overall

---

[1] Spence, L., *The Mysteries of Britain: Secret Rites and Traditions of Ancient Britain*, Sennet, 1994

field of influence could extend for many, many miles in all directions. The Michael and Mary route is also what one ends up with after being given a map and ruler and asked to draw the longest line in Britain without crossing water. Interestingly, the line is the exact axis along which the May Day sun rises over Britain. Doubly interestingly, esoteric writer Jiro Olcott has calculated its precise distance as 365.24 miles, comparing the number with a solar year of 365.242199 days duration.

There is no formal scientific consensus as to the existence of ley lines. Wikipedia says of them, for example:

> Ley lines are apparent alignments of landmarks, religious sites, and manmade structures. The pseudoscientific belief that these apparent lines are not accidental speculates that they are straight navigable paths and have spiritual significance.

Nigel Pennick and Paul Devereux define leys as "alignments of ancient sites stretching across the landscape."[2] The placement of key features along them is the art of geomancy: "the manipulation of structures and natural topography for reasons of secular harmony and concepts of sanctity."[3] Mathematically, one cannot reasonably argue against the laws of statistics, which state that the random distribution of a sufficient number of points on the earth's surface will inevitably generate measurably straight alignments among some of these points purely by chance. Nevertheless, one should be cautious of ceding absolute authority to the seemingly unarguable power of math. When in his inimitable fashion Mark Twain spoke of "lies, damned lies, and statistics," he was cautioning against over-reliance upon the illusory safety of numbers to support weak, unpopular or radical arguments. Personally, I believe that the evidence that supports the existence of a network of earth energies that covers the globe proves Twain's point, despite the efforts of intelligent yet unimaginative number-crunchers to pour scorn on the hypothesis. How might these invisible lines of force be generated? In a previous work for AUP,[4] I visited the topic.

It is known that the entire earth is charged with the invisible flow of ubiquitous electromagnetic energy. Its field is subtlely influenced by an array of factors, including the gravitational influence of near and far bodies in our solar system. It is also influenced by ground level factors such as the shapes and contours of landscape features, which also

---

[2] Devereux, P. & Pennick, N., *Lines on the Landscape*, Robert Hale, 1989

[3] ibid

[4] Graddon, N., *Otto Rahn and the Quest for the Grail*, Adventures Unlimited Press, 2008

influence the character of minerals deep underground. Rudolf Steiner discovered that cosmic influences affect the magnetic currents on the earth's surface. Not only that, they act upon the cycles of motion within the earth's minerals in relation to the orbits of the particular planetary body to which each most readily respond. At certain seasons they become charged with an energy that allows seeds to germinate.

Free thinkers and philosophers in the distant past, notably Pythagoras and, later, Plato, believed that the physical universe is composed of geometrical figures, among which the pentadodecahedron is identified as the "hull of the sphere." Plato refers in the *Phaedo* to a belief that the construction of the world is likened to the building of a ship by the use of geometric shapes. Consider the common saying: "the four corners of the earth," a reflection of the ancient belief that the earth is a vast stone. The pyramids in Egypt have a square base, signifying that man is foursquare, representing the four elements of the earth. Set upon that square base is the symbol of the spirit: the triangle, which represents the trinity of life: Father-Mother-Son, the three constituent parts of God, but also the life spirit which the ancients thought they had discovered in stone: life, spark and fire.

Scientific research appears to indicate that the earth resembles a gigantic crystal supported by a rigid skeletal structure beneath its surface. German scientist Siegfried Wittman claimed in 1952[5] that he and his study team had concluded that the earth has upon its surface a grid system consisting of a checkerboard pattern of positive and negative poles.

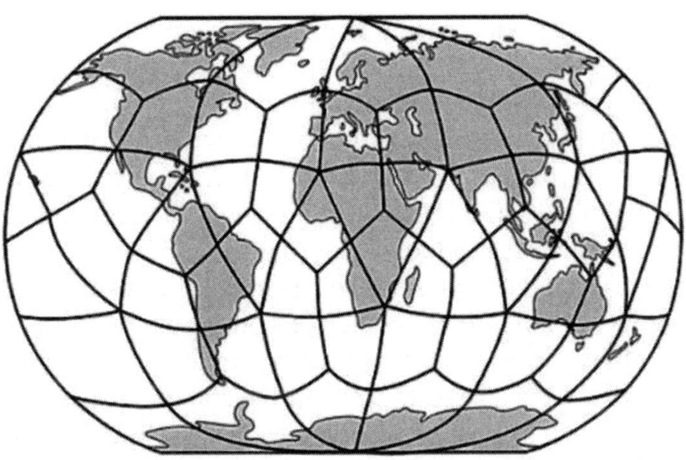

Morozov Planetary Grid System

[5] *Die Welt der geheimen Mächte* (*The World of the Secret Forces*)

The squared pattern has a centre pole surrounded by smaller poles within each section. The main pole concentrates energy through eight supporting poles. Four send pulses of energy skyward while the others send energy to the four points of the compass.

Ten years later, biologist Ivan Sanderson and colleagues, intrigued by geographical anomalies such as those portrayed in the Piri Reis map of 1523 and the Buache map of 1737 which suggest that pre-Egyptian civilizations possessed advanced mathematical and astronomical skills, set out to "pattern the mysteries." Sanderson's 1972 article, *The Twelve Devils' Graveyards Around the World*, plotted air and maritime disappearances worldwide. It focused attention on 12 areas, equally spaced over the globe, in which magnetic anomalies and other aberrations were linked to unaccountable physical phenomena.

Sanderson's investigations were the impetus for others to make a contribution to the study of electromagnetic aberrations upon the "planetary grid," the term coined by Christopher Bird writing in the *New Age Journal* of May 1975. In it Bird refers to the work of Russian researchers: historian Nikolai Goncharov, engineer Vyacheslav Morozov and electronics specialist Valery Makarov who had published in *Khimiya I Zhizn* (Chemistry of Life) in the *Science Journal of the USSR Academy of Life* an article: "*Is the Earth a Large Crystal?*"

The Russians' paper, which supports and builds on Sanderson's work, explores an idea that visualises the core of the Earth as a growing crystal that influences what occurs on the planet. The authors postulate that the earth projects from this inner crystal a dual geometrically regularised grid. The first grid layer consists of Sanderson's twelve areas that lie over the surface of the earth, which the Russians describe as pentagonal slabs (a dodecahedron) while the second is formed by twenty equilateral triangles (an icosohedron). The writers stated that the superimposition of the two grids over the globe's surface reveals a pattern of the earth's energy network. The lines tracing out the dual grid coincide with zones of active risings and depressions on the ocean floors, cave faults and mid-oceanic ridges such as in the Bermuda Triangle. The paper refers to twelve such areas.

In esoteric teachings these principle nodal points are described as the earth's etheric web points—gateways to other dimensions. The Russians theorised that these forms and their apexes possess qualities that can explain many unusual phenomena. They claimed that in these areas, viewed in conjunction with Sanderson's work, are to be found regions of seismic and volcanic activity, while magnetic anomalies are located at the vertices of the polygons. The grid nodes are said to denote centres of great changes in atmospheric pressures; hurricanes, for example, take shape in these areas. Prevailing winds and ocean currents also fit into the network as well as paths of migratory animals, gravitational anomalies and the sites of ancient cities.

The Russians' paper claims that if the grid was lined up on the surface of the globe so that all of the many factors could be correlated, the exact centre point is found to be Giza in Upper Egypt, the key being the "measure of Light." Researchers at the Earth-Life Science Institute at the Tokyo Institute of Technology similarly suggest that the power source for the Earth's magnetic field is the presence of crystallisation in the Earth's core.

Researcher Roy Snelling brings consciousness into the equation when he describes the powerhouse of the Earth as the presence of huge psychic crystals within its etheric body. Accordingly, our planet's true form, Snelling suggests, *is* its geometrical grid, the physical earth being a visible manifestation that could not exist in the absence of its etheric counterpart. This idea mirrors the esoteric belief that an etheric body is the magnetic field of a physical body (an example being the human aura), which contains a template of its idealised outer form.

> *The* [known] *laws of physics and nature... are only part of a broader spectrum of Cosmic laws, some of which relate to other dimensions, parallel universes, anti-matter, and also a universal energy field where science claims that there is only empty space.*[6]

Snelling suggests that the planetary matrix is defined by the perfect geometrical relationship of the five Platonic solids that constitute its geometrical form. In accordance with mathematical law, these five solids may be contained perfectly inside a sphere. Energy in the edge-lines of all five within the Earth radiates upwards to form lines of force on the surface: a projection by the Cosmos from its own substance, one of many levels of creation, each one descending in order of vibration-rate and coarseness of matter so that each level interpenetrates the level above and below without affecting the higher or lower levels.

Moreover, each form can transition into any other through a series of movements, including twisting, truncating, expanding, combining or faceting. Snelling speaks appreciatively of the mathematical beauty that binds the Platonic solids in a state of etheric perfection, the motivating power behind the earth's dynamic energy system.

---

[6] Snelling, R., *The Planetary Matrix*, Spiritual Genesis Books, 2013

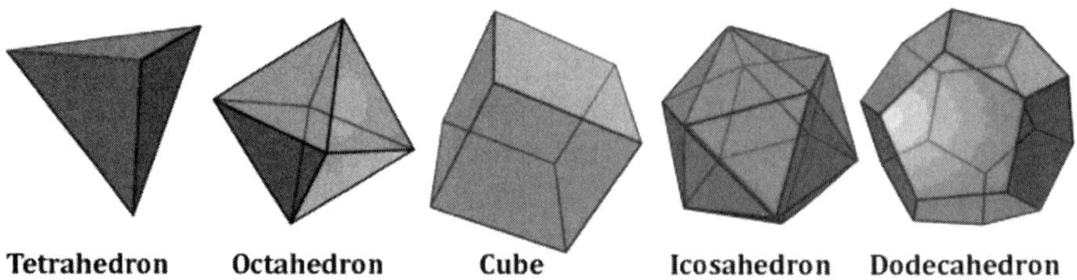

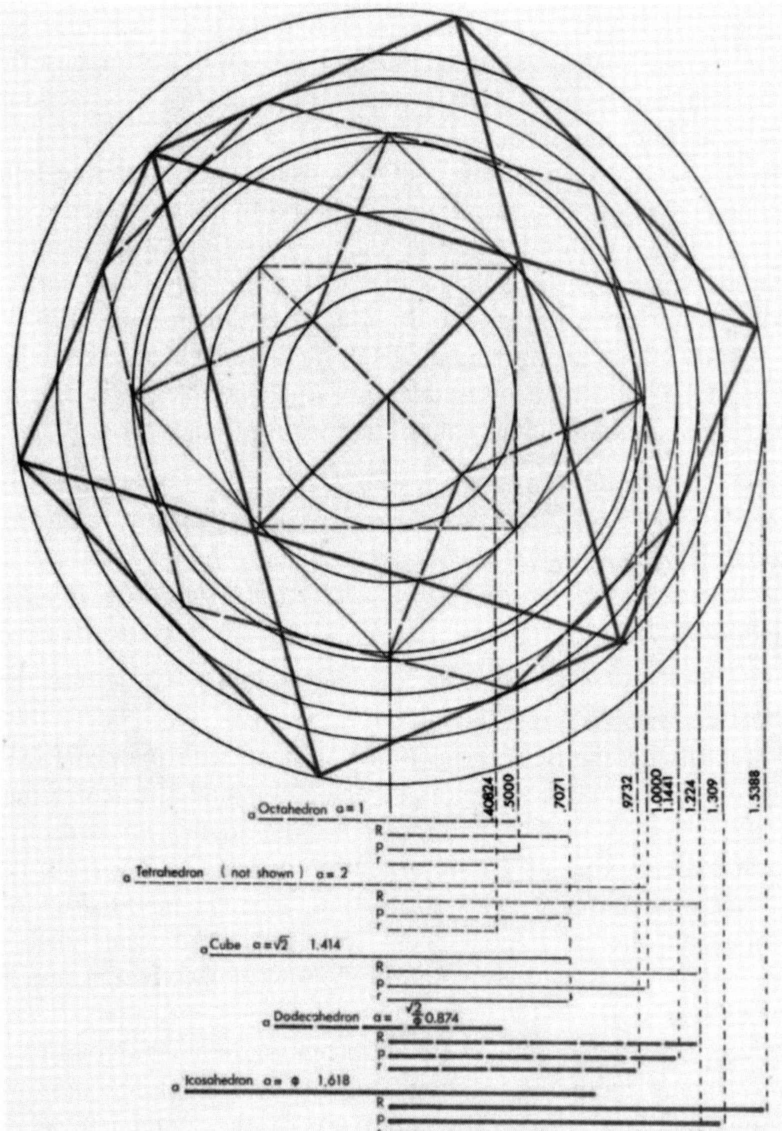

Top—the 5 Platonic Solids

Bottom—the energy grid: five Platonic solids nested perfectly inside a sphere.
Credit Robert Lawlor - *Sacred Geometry: Philosophy & Practice*

The 5-Platonic Solids and their Elements, Faces, Apexes and Edges			
	Faces	Apexes	Edges
Cube - earth	6	8	12
Icosahedron - water	20	12	30
Octahedron - air	8	6	12
Tetrahedron - fire	4	4	6
Dodecahedron - ether	12	20	30
	50	50	90

The five Platonic solids are the only shapes with equal side lengths, equal interior angles, faces made of the same regular shape which look the same from each vertex (corner point), and, crucially, all fit perfectly in a sphere with all points resting on the circumference.

Information about the Platonic solids has been taught since ancient times, particularly since the period of the Greek Mystery Schools approximately 2,500 years ago. They are called "Platonic" after Plato (427 – 347 BC) who, in the *Timaeus*, outlined a cosmology through the metaphor of planar and solid geometry. He associated the four elements with four of the Platonic solids: the tetrahedron as fire; the octahedron as air; the cube as earth, and the icosahedron as water. The dodecahedron represents the "fifth" element—the invisible ether.

> *Hence between fire and earth the god placed water and air, and he made them all stand in the same ratio to one another... so that as fire is to air, so air is to water, and as air is to water, so water is to earth, and so he bound together and structured the visible and tangible universe.*
>
> —Plato, *Timaeus*

Plato ascribes intelligence to the solids when he refers to the ability of the four elements to "transmute into each other" and how "they must be dissimilar to one another but capable of arising out of one another's disintegration." Cosmic Core, a web-based group that explores sacred geometry and the concept of twinning science with spirituality,[7] builds on Plato's ideas of intelligent design in describing the Platonic solids as not five separate shapes but five aspects of the same shape—the spinning torus. Cosmic Core views the torus as the embodiment of a principle of "Mater into Matter," in which Consciousness forms into Light, Light into Geometric Form, and Geometric Form into Matter.

[7] https://www.cosmic-core.org

The spinning torus in which Mater ("Mother") becomes Matter

The process begins when a sphere representing undifferentiated light polarises into opposites symbolized by two intersecting circles: the Vesica Piscis. We will later see an example of this at Avebury. The two poles swirl in opposite directions in rhythmic energy patterns, creating a toroidal flow. The building block of the torus is an "Aether Unit," a manifestation of the fluctuations of Consciousness. These units, Cosmic Core claim, are not "things" but an intelligent energy flow process that characterises and defines the planetary grid.

The planetary matrix comprises a network of 90 edgelines of all five Platonic solids. Snelling calls this the planet's Primary Leyline. At points on the Earth where some of these lines meet or cross at the apexes of the Platonic solids (which are all at the surface of the earth anyway), one is likely to find powerful vortices of energy. This was recognized long ago by our forebears. Many such sites became sacred and on them were built stone circles and other similar power structures.

> *The life of a region depends ultimately on its geological substratum, for this sets up a chain reaction which passes, determining their character in turn through its streams and wells, its vegetation and animal life, that feeds on this and finally through the type of human being attracted to live there. In a profound sense also the structure of its rocks gives rise to the psychic life of the land.*
>
> —Ithell Colquhoun, *The Living Stones*

Snelling asks how our forbears were able to create the secondary and tertiary ley-line networks from the primary-network defined by the Platonic Solids. He suggests that various topographical and geological features came into play such as fault lines in the Earth's crust where magnetic energies would be more concentrated, underground watercourses and mountain tops. By using standing stones where the qualities of the crystalline structure of the stone is known, together with dolmens and 'burial' mounds that act like electric accumulators, energy could be siphoned off from the primary-network to psychically irrigate the land for the benefit of humans, animals and crops.

Crystals are amazing things. Currently, scientists are exploring the possibilities to create time crystals such as those that power Doctor Who's TARDIS. A time crystal is a structure that repeats in time as well as in space. Normal crystals exhibit broken translation symmetry—they have repeated patterns in space and remain unchanged as time passes. Time crystals repeat themselves in time as well, leading the crystal to change from moment to moment. Physicists at the University of Maryland have made the first time crystal using ytterbium ions. According to *Popular Mechanics*,[8] time crystals incorporate spots at their edges that look different from others, thus breaking the symmetry of time.

Scale this up and one sees remarkable correspondences with the properties of the Earth's Platonic crystals and their ninety edge lines. It is certain that wise men of old were aware of these properties and incorporated them into certain structures to transcend the normal laws of physics. One such is the labyrinth in Chartres Cathedral, usually covered in chairs but observed one day in the summer of 1914 to serve as a time portal. A young Italian priest in France on papal business in the days before the outbreak of the Great War visited the cathedral. He thought he was alone but saw men enter the church and gather at the entrance to the labyrinth. The priest hid behind a pillar and observed what was happening. He saw the group trace a path round the labyrinth while chanting certain words. When they reached the centre the men disappeared one by one. The priest tried it for himself, having remembered the words. When he got to the centre he felt that he was stepping into wet sand, then immediately found himself standing in the labyrinth in Rheims Cathedral, 150 miles away. Then long retired, the priest related this story to a close friend of mind in Tuscany in 1977. He swore that it was true and said that he repeated the experience in other cathedrals in France. The world is truly a very mysterious home.

---

[8] https://www.popularmechanics.com/science/a30755983/time-crystals-time-travel/

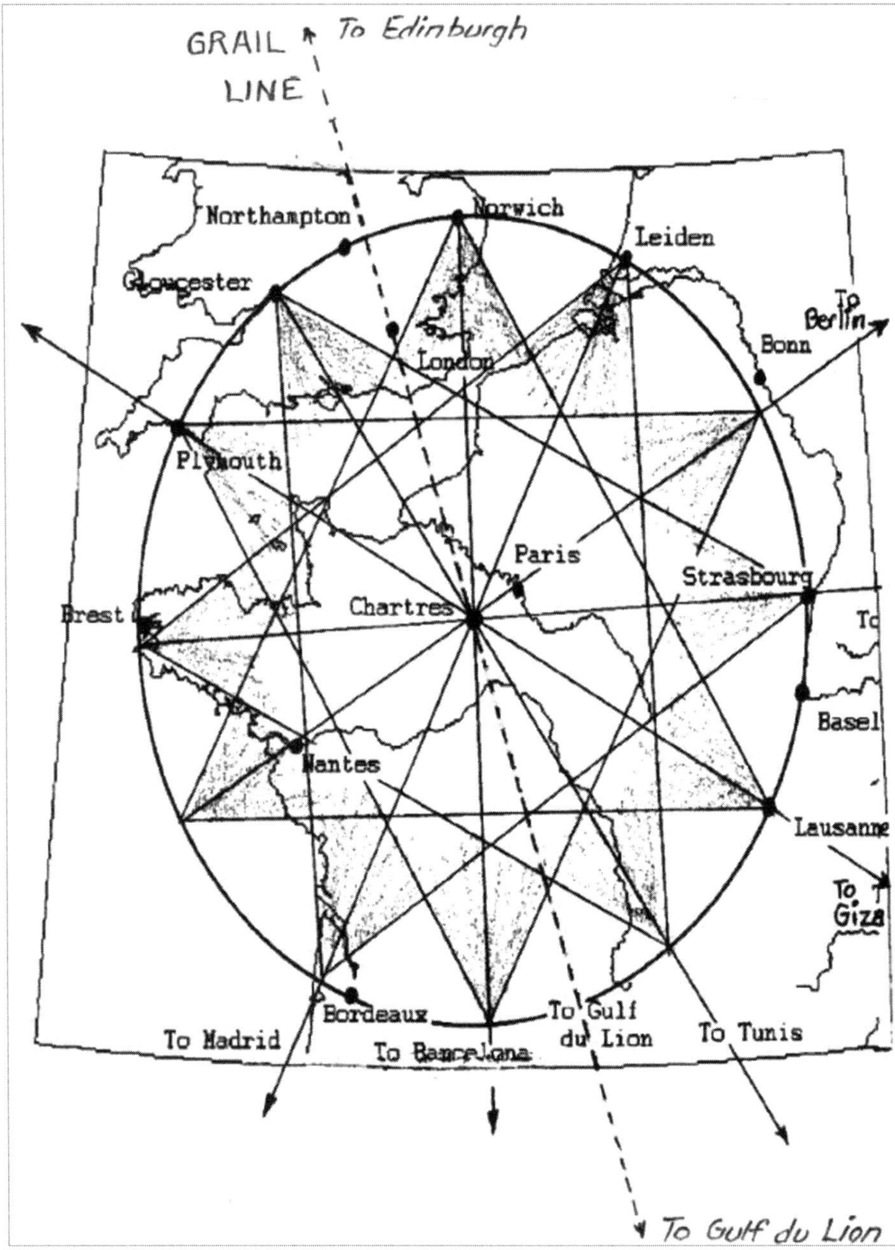

A view of one pentagonal face of the dodecahedron that covers much of Europe. Its dominant sacred site is Chartres Cathedral, a key part of a giant Earth-temple that extends into southern England. The line to Gloucester passes through Avebury. Credit Roy Snelling.

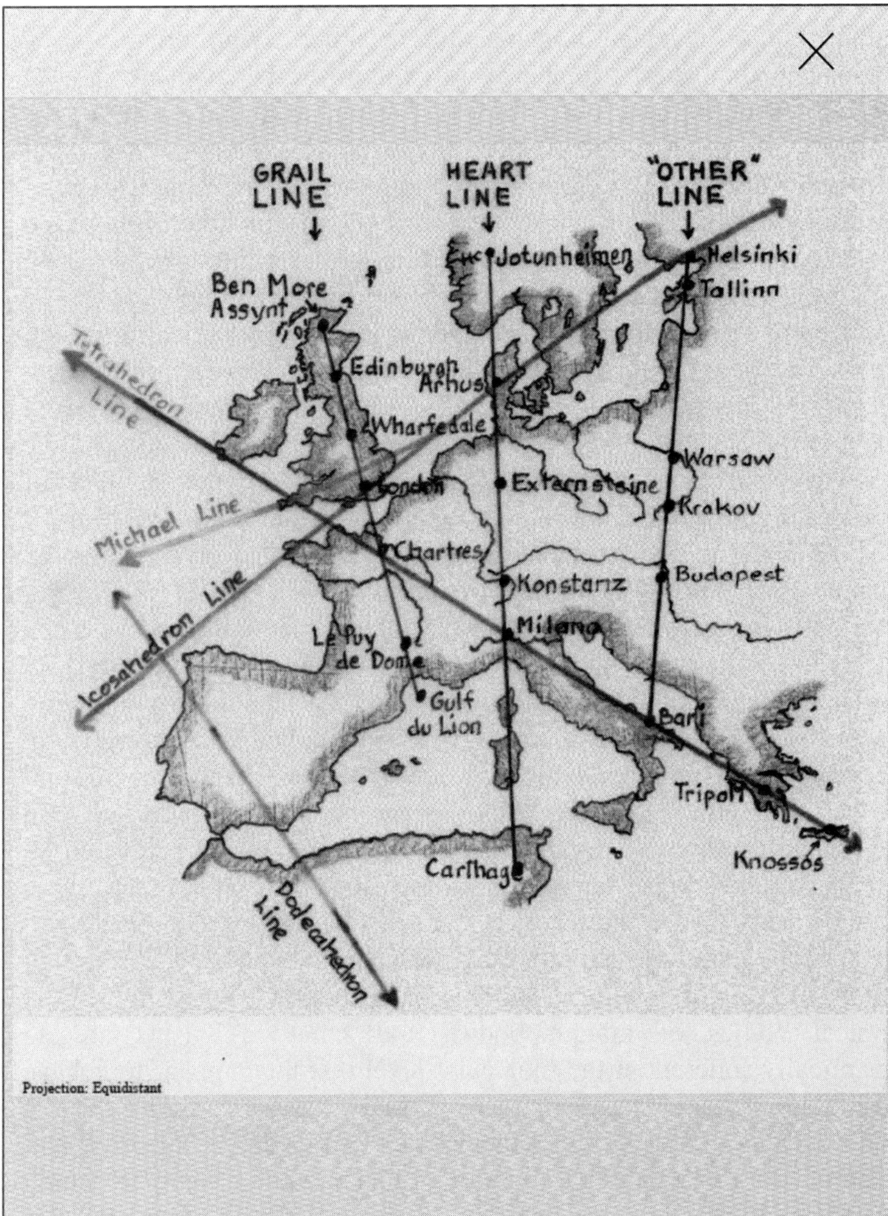

Key energy alignments lines in Western Europe, including the St Michael ley. Credit Roy Snelling.

The Michael and Mary currents are surface emanations from the edge-lines of the earth's toroidal geometry. At the microcosmic level, there is emerging evidence that these crystalline energies communicate at the cellular level in humans and in other living organisms, a relationship that goes a long way to explain the behaviour of the St Michael ley on human consciousness. A singular characteristic of the mineral world of crystal in all its forms is its pervasiveness throughout all parts of our physical earth. This ubiquitous crystal lattice structure provides great stability of structure and regularity of flow of any kind of electromagnetic energy that moves through it (which is why silicon chips are used in computers to provide memory, for example).

In particular, quartz crystal demonstrates the piezoelectric effect. The word "piezo" is Greek for push or press. Through the effect, mechanical energy can be transduced into electromagnetic energy, and vice versa. This property has long been put to good use in the deployment of quartz crystals in radios to ensure the stability of broadcasting channels and allow greater use of the radio spectrum. It does not take too many mental leaps to visualise that crystals may be capable of transforming or amplifying other energy forms not yet detected by scientific instruments but which human consciousness can detect, especially when facilitated by an appropriate form of crystal.

The structure of DNA reflects the essential crystallinity of living organisms. Each cell of a living organism contains a hexagonally shaped crystalline molecule of DNA, approximately 10 atoms wide and six feet in length. If the entire DNA in the human body was unfolded and strung together its length would be 125 billion miles, equivalent to seventy round trips between Saturn and the Sun. Yet these infinitesimally thin crystal lattice threads, too narrow to reflect light, are so strong that they have effectively carried the codes of life through billions of years of evolution. Biophysicists are now suggesting that the physical bodies of human bodies and other organisms are so dynamically coherent at the molecular level that they appear to behave like liquid crystals. The component particles (atoms or molecules) of liquid crystals tend to arrange themselves with a degree of order and exactitude far exceeding that found in ordinary liquids and approaching that of solid crystals. Consequently, every part of the organism is in communication with every other part through a dynamic, tunable responsive crystalline medium that pervades the whole body.

Anthropologist Jeremy Narby[9] explains that these living molecules of DNA emit light photons at regular intervals in a coherence strong

---

[9] Narby, J., *The Cosmic Serpent*, Weidenfeld & Nicholson, 1999

enough for them to be compared to an "ultra weak laser." This property is mindful of crystal radios and their energy-transducing properties. Narby has developed a hypothesis that DNA has its own consciousness, which he describes as the "mind of the biosphere" and that it is is related to crystals.

Dwelling on these startling new ideas and theories, crystallographers are posing the question as to whether our human cells each incorporate an actual laser and if excitation of the light-producing qualities of DNA account for the phenomenon of the human aura. And could exposure to certain crystals provide the necessary energy for influencing, altering and/or enhancing the human energy field?

These incredible crystal properties reveal that we are not so very different from the inorganic world of minerals. We ourselves are in a very real sense crystals composed of coherent structures approaching that of solid crystals, yet retaining the superior flexibility of liquid crystals. Consequently, it is not hard to imagine how an energy flow from a very large size crystal source (the massive Michael and Mary component of the earth's dodecahedral crystal lattice, for example) could be received and interpreted by one's own mind and body, analagous to the reception of signals from a broadcasting tower by a crystal radio set.

The corollary also holds true. If one focuses one's intentions on a piece of quartz one could potentially magnify the force of that intention, making our Michael ley serpent powers stronger and more energetic. Furthermore, the crystal may be capable of fixing the pattern of that intention, being "programmed" just like a computer chip. It follows that within this new framework of biophysical interactivity the crystals of the earth, as exemplified by the Michael and Mary piezo-currents, are wholly in tune with the crystal structure of the human body in an extremely powerful reciprocal sense of information receptivity, transmission and mutually assured evolutionary growth.

Rough piece of clear quartz crystal, "solidified light."

In 1958 Aimé Michel set out his ideas on the existence of fixed alignments of energy paths across the globe that are navigated by UFOs. Michael dubbed them "orthotenies." Bruce Cathie (1930-2013), a New Zealand pilot and pioneering researcher of earth energy science, returned to the theme in his descriptions of an all-encompassing worldwide grid, one whose interlocking lines correspond to the lines of flight of UFO appearances and whose properties are governed by the speed of light. The values of Cathie's grid reflect harmonic relationships with the acceleration and deceleration of light, gravity and the mass of the earth. Cathie's studies agreed with the Russians' findings that volcanic activity and earthquakes are connected to the grid structure but he additionally observed that atomic disruption (nuclear bomb blasts) is equally associated with the phenomenon.

The main plank of Cathie's work rested upon his observation that all major changes of physical state are caused by harmonic interactions of light, gravity and the mass of electrical and magnetic forces. The controlled manipulation of these resonant factors makes it possible to move mass from one point to another in space-time. Similarly, Cathie theorised, time can also be controlled by these manipulations of harmonic pulsations due to its relationship to the speed of light.

Adopting a mindset governed by an unyielding reliance upon mathematics to prove the empirically unprovable is to deny the active consideration of other, more metaphysically oriented theories in support of pan-global grid geometry. The component parts of the grid geometry—its shapes, forms and angles—are defined by a vast network of unseen lines, and, hence, it is a justly deserved tribute to the late Alfred Watkins, pioneer straight track investigator,[10] that we should call them by the name he coined in 1921—leys.

I use the term "empirically unprovable" because after forty years of reflection I am of the opinion that the answer to the riddle of the lines and associated phenomena such as crop formations lies in planes of reality far and beyond the limited perceptual scope of our physical senses. To accept confidently the existence of such realities is to take a contradictory stance in the face of mainstream scientific dogma. One must look with a different eye, the "third" one buried deep in our pineal gland for insights into the mysteries presented by the St. Michael ley and countless other incidences of high strangeness, phenomena that conventional science struggles to comprehend and therefore tends to disregard as legitimate areas of study.

---

[10] Watkins, A., *The Old Straight Track: Its Mounds, Beacons, Moats, Sites and Mark Stones*, 1925

I will turn in later pages to the specific nature of my discovery concerning Britain's most famous telluric alignment—the St. Michael ley and its impressive waymarkers—except to state that it concerns the country's ancient status as a place of especial favour to the Universal Powers, a privilege distinguished by these Isles' enduring reverence for the Mother Goddess and her gifts.

Information on Britain's mystical status is not to be found in historical records. Rather, one must turn to folklore, myth and esoteric sources for insight. A source that speaks powerfully of the most distant times in Britain's mythological history is "White Eagle," a genial spirit from the higher worlds, which conveyed its teachings through acclaimed medium, Grace Cooke (1892-1979). Cooke was a British seeress who began her calling in 1913 and used her phenomenal gifts to demonstrate evidence of survival after death. British Prime Minister Ramsay MacDonald was one among many of Grace's admirers who vouched for the accuracy of her spirit communications.

Together with husband Ivan, Grace founded the White Eagle Lodge in 1936. I have said elsewhere[11] that I find a depth of sincerity, insight and power in Grace's communications that are often lacking in other channelling sources. What are of relevance to this present work are the many commentaries that White Eagle provided in connection with Britain and its remarkable mystical beginnings. My source for these messages is two excellent books[12] produced by the White Eagle Publishing Trust, which I thoroughly recommend to those who wish to explore Cooke's teachings further.

Through Grace Cooke, White Eagle spoke of a sacred heritage secreted in Britain's ancient isles which only now is beginning to wake and give renewed vigour to the spiritual life force buried deep within its substance. This powerful legacy was bequeathed by the "Sun-Men," messengers from the higher realms who travelled all over the world to disseminate the "Ancient Wisdom" but who made their home in Britain, described by White Eagle as the Grail Chalice of the planet.

White Eagle described the "Ancient Wisdom" as the one true religion from which many others subsequently sprang in human history. It is the religion of the Sun or the divine principle, spiritual in essence with numberless manifestations.

---

[11] Graddon, N. *The Landing Lights of Magonia: UFOs, Aliens and the Fairy Kingdom*, AUP, 2018

[12] Cooke, G. & Cooke, I., *The Light in Britain*, The White Eagle Publishing Trust, 1971; and Cooke, G., *Sun Men of the Americas*, The White Eagle Publishing Trust, 1983.

The Sun-Men taught that the First Principle was God the Father (Power), the Second, the Mother Goddess (Wisdom), together giving birth to the Son (Love). Early man was blessed to receive these cosmic laws and expressed their thankfulness through worship of both the physical sun and the divine principle that it symbolised.

Esoteric tradition holds than human life on Earth is far, far older than archaeological evidence suggests. Plato dwelt on this in *Timaeus* and *Critias*. In his reflections on the cyclical tendency of history, he observed that civil life on Earth has been going on for "a vast and incredible length of time [during which] many thousands of cities have come into being and the same number have come to an end."

White Eagle taught that long ago, after a great deluge submerged much of the planet's landmasses (long before Atlantis, in the former eras of Mu and then Lemuria), the Sun-Men arrived in Britain as the messengers of the White Brotherhood, the ancient Brethren of the Sun who live and worship in the Sun temples and Sun cities of a "heaven world." This paradise realm is not to be found beyond the stars, said White Eagle, but in a world composed of finer ethers located just within our own "solid" world and which interpenetrates all physical life. Humans descend from these original "god-men." The Sun-Men came as an indescribably beautiful light: the spiritual Sun. Their purpose was to bring wisdom to humanity in its infancy so that it might learn the laws of God and eventually to break the bondage of physical matter and return to full spiritual awareness.

Esoteric records speak of successive Atlantean civilisations that came and went in a vast span of time after the destruction of Mu, the Motherland. Each ensuing civilisation was initially characterised by the universal practice of Sun worship. The theme was always the same. Manly P. Hall[13] describes a religion in which the solar deity was personified as a beautiful youth with long golden hair to symbolise the rays of the sun. In rituals and ceremonies this golden Sun God was slain by worshipers who personified the evil principle of the universe. By means of certain rites, symbolic of purification and regeneration, this Solar God was brought back to life and became the Saviour of His people. The ceremonies' secret processes symbolised the means by which man is able to overcome his lower nature and give expression to his higher self. Eventually, though, man's alliances with the Sun God falter. His efforts to tame his baser drives and instincts become insufficient for the task. Ruin follows, age after age.

Greek myths can be notoriously difficult to fathom but Hesiod's

---

[13] Hall, M., *The Secret Teachings of All Ages*, Philosophical Research Society, 1928

tale in the *Theogony* of the Five Races of Mankind corresponds closely with the esoteric tradition. Hesiod tells of how a golden race of men (White Eagle's Sun-Men) was created by the gods of Olympus. In their time, life was perfect. All were happy, no one needed to work, old age was unknown, and men and women lived happily ever after until death took them peacefully in their sleep.

The second, silver race that followed was inferior. Evidently, the ensuing generations of the golden race became successively more primitive in character and in its application of wisdom and intelligence. They existed as babies for one hundred years and on reaching maturity lived brief lives distinguished by arrogant pride, recklessness and stupidity.

Next came bronze era humanity, which bore witness to even greater levels of deterioration. Hesiod speaks of the third race's puzzling relationship with ash trees. Curiously, it appears that members of the bronze race were either made of ash wood, mated with ash-tree nymphs, or were "made of ashen spears." Their thirst for violence precipitated their ruin. Hesiod's description of a race that mated with unusual forms chimes with other sources, one of which is the work of renowned psychic Edgar Cayce (1877-1945). Cayce's readings complemented the esoteric records when he said that there were three destructions of Atlantis, occurring circa 50,000 BC, 28,000 BC and 10,000 BC.

> But afterwards there occurred violent earthquakes and floods; and in a single day and night of misfortune all your warlike men in a body sank into the earth, and the island of Atlantis in like manner disappeared in the depths of the sea—Plato, *Timaeus*.

Cayce described the events that preceded the final cataclysm. Atlantis by 10,000 BC had become a morass of violence and depravity. What finally undid this civilisation was its exploitation of genetics. Man-animal hybrids were bred for sexual gratification. Human sacrifice was rampant. Worse was to follow. Tasked by power-crazed rulers to manufacture the perfect man, scientists grew laboratory-bred humans but no one understood the metaphysical consequences of making disease-free, superperfect human clones. No spirit would choose such a vehicle for incarnation because evolutionary growth may only be achieved through experiencing a degree of physical imbalance. This left the door open for earthbound spirits and negative energies from other dimensions to inhabit the immaculate host bodies. Those in power were not entirely blind to the consequences of their actions. Atlantis's leaders knew what was coming and also knew that it could not be stopped. The extent to which the Atlanteans' science, technology and occult practices infringed upon the natural world and so alarmed the cosmic powers that caretake our planet had, just as on previous occasions, commenced an irreversible countdown. The poles switched, the waters rose, the continents were submerged. There were survivors. Channeling sources indicate that between 20,000 and 30,000 people, situated in the right place at the right time, were on safe ground when the waves struck.

From fossil studies of the Ahmarian, Bohunician and Aurignacian cultures, palaeontologists date the appearance of European early modern humans as roughly 48,000 years ago in the Upper Palaeolithic period, a date that tallies closely with Cayce's date of 50,000 BC for the date of the first destruction of Atlantis. It is ironical how the term Upper Palaeolithic conjures images of cave-dwelling savages but reflect on the facts. A more popular description for European early modern human is Cro-Magnon. The Cro-Magnon era, characterised by the first appearance of anatomically modern humans according to fossil studies, corresponds closely to the timespan defined by the three destructions of Atlantis, a 40,000-year period during which flourished civilisations seemingly more technologically advanced than our present day society.

One might expect as a consequence of cataclysmic upheavals that knowledge of the Ancient Wisdom would be lost, its priests and teachers taking the secrets to watery graves or to bottomless earth fissures. That is not the case. Esoteric and psychic records indicate that each occasion of destruction is marked by a dispersal of survivors seeking a new home. These are the members of Hesiod's fourth race, noble heroes who were allowed to live on the Isles of the Blessed (often associated with Avalon) after they died. Consequently, on each occasion, survivors who the day before were enjoying the technological trappings of an advanced society became Cro-Magnon hunter-gatherers the next. In, for example, the period separating Cayce's date of 50,000 BC and the emergence of early modern humans 48,000 years ago, one can visualise the gradual influx into Europe of survivors seeking a new home after massive global displacement.

The wise and spiritually developed, those who had formed a deep and loving kinship with nature and those entrusted with the ancient laws of God, organise themselves quickly. They re-align themselves with a very different kind of natural world (esoteric records speak of continual rain and cloud over the planet for two hundred years after the last cataclysm), and set to work to preserve the spiritual welfare and development of future generations of humankind. Nevertheless, among the descendants of the first wave of survivors are those that degenerate quickly into a tribal way of living and, over time, devolve physically and mentally. Paradoxically, their fossils will eventually tell a story in which future scientists cannot possibly conceive that what lies under the microscope is a bone from an individual that had *regressed* from modern human form tens of thousands of years in the past.

Together, these ensuing generations comprise the fifth race, that of iron—our present era and a time, according to Hesiod, of toil, grief and death in which might will be right, morality will dissipate, and evil will gain the upper hand. One only has to glance at a media story today to conclude that Hesiod's prophetic words are rapidly gaining traction.

In light of the foregoing, one may conclude that there is little mystery in the sudden appearance of modern day humans. In fact, one can go a little further and suggest that from the time of the Motherland, the time of White Eagle's "god-men," there have always been anatomically recognizable humans. In this model of thinking, the presence of humankind on Earth from the far past to the present is the rule rather than the exception. It is my considered belief that for Cro-Magnon man, read Atlantean survivors and their descendants.

Moreover, Britain appears to have been the sanctuary of choice for informed survivors. There is something embedded deep within the fabric of these isles that consistently pulls men and women of wisdom to its shores. Folklorist and occult scholar Lewis Spence described Britain as a "country of almost unique sanctity in the ancient world."[14]

The survivors that may have reached Britain in the years following the demise of the second Atlantis civilisation circa 28,000 BC would have soon been confronted by extremely challenging weather conditions. Geological evidence shows that between 26,500 to 18,000 years ago Britain suffered severe climatic deterioration at a time when much of North America, Northern Europe and Asia were covered in ice sheets. It is known that early modern humans at the end of the Aurignacian period (around 26,000 years ago) were still visiting these isles. However, their periods of occupation were necessarily brief and intermittent due to a climate which swung between low temperatures with a tundra habitat and severe ice ages (Britain's "Dimlington Stadial" period) that made the isles nigh on uninhabitable. Evidence suggests that people only began to return in numbers in the period 12,000 BC to 10,000 BC, a date once again that corresponds with an

[14] ibid

perfect adepts of their art make a voyage thither (Britain) to learn it" from the Druids and the seminaries, the most renowned of which was a large college on the Isle of Mona (Anglesey) in Wales. Caesar said that the Gauls believed that they were descended from Dis, a tradition shared by the Druids. Dis is the Latin form of Hades or Pluto, god of the dead, a term that evokes associations with initiation rites in which students die a symbolic death in order to be reborn as enlightened souls. In Britain, Dis is the Celtic god, Llyr or Bran.

The Celts' primal deity was the earth goddess, the Mother, whom was known by many names according to different sites with which she was associated. One such was Minerva who came to be known in Britain as Brighd or Brigit and who represented the virgin aspect of the Great Goddess. In Aqua Sulis (modern day Bath in Avon and Somerset) a perpetual fire was maintained in honour of Minerva. Brighd, a goddess of poetry and divine inspiration, was the patroness of the celebrated Druid bard, Taliesin.

Corresponding male gods were also worshipped, Belenos (the Greek Apollo) being held in special reverence. In the British Christian tradition, Belanos became conflated with St. Michael. The forest deity Cernunnos the Horned God, depicted with the antlers of a stag and known also as Hu or Hesus, was the Celtic god of the underworld, the gatekeeper to the invisible companion dimensions to Earth. Acting as a psychopomp (a guider of souls and spirits), Cernunnos escorted the dead to the afterlife. He also served as a god of fertility, life, animals and wealth. The Horned God is born at the winter solstice, marries the goddess at Beltane, and dies at the summer solstice. The Celts also worshipped totem animals, each associated with an important god or goddess, a fact to recall when we examine the Glastonbury Zodiac.

There is no common agreement as to the origin of Druidism. Spencer relates their emergence in Britain to the "Iberian" or "Mediterranean" race with origins in North-West Africa, perhaps the Sahara region. He notes that there were further influxes of incomers from other parts of Europe, notably the Celts, but confidently states that it was the Mediterraneans' religious and mystical ideas that dominated in these isles and, thus, Britain was to remain Iberian in the religious sense. Spencer theorised that when the Celts arrived they found a readily available system of mystical philosophy, Druidism, and so adopted it as their own. Manly P. Hall referred to the Druids as the Celts' Order of Literati.

White Eagle pushes back the origins of Druidism to the Atlantean era, in which time they were the continent's Sun-priests. He revealed that the Druids of Britain were the guiding force behind the planning and construction of Stonehenge, a project designed to replicate the Sun-worship practices of their ancient Motherland.

The origin of the word Druid is disputed. German scholar Max Müller believed that like the Irish word Drui it means “the men of the oak trees,” highlighting his theory by referring to the dryades, the forest gods and tree deities of the Greeks. (In Sanskrit the word dru means "timber”.) Others believe it to be a word of Teutonic origin, others Welsh. A few trace it to the Gaelic druidh, which means “a wise man” or “sorcerer.”

At the time of the Roman conquest, the Druids were thoroughly embedded in Britain and Gaul. Such was the respect and reverence with which they were esteemed that opposing foes about to attack each other would lay down their arms on the orders of the white-robed druids. No undertaking of any importance was undertaken without the assistance and blessings of these priests, who stood as mediators between the gods and men and whose understanding of Nature and her laws was unrivalled.

Having appropriated Druidism into their own culture, the Celts in Britain associated their religion with the sanctity of the land and the power of certain key locations within it, usually represented as a natural shape or alignment in the form of a goddess to demonstrate their reverence for nature and its manifestations. Pennick, one of Britain’s foremost authorities on geomancy, sacred geometry and associated topics, underscores the significance of these ancient beliefs when he writes:[15] “We connect with the ‘genius loci,’ the spirit of a place, the mother goddess of the landscape.”

Indeed, the Celtic tradition, from which we infer so much that rewards those who study the Ancient Wisdom, makes no distinction between mythology and history, religion and daily living; all was one sacred entity. Pennick reminds us that: “myths are primordial truths expressed at the highest level comprehensible to human beings.”[16] Despite the lack of consensus on the Druids’ origins, it is evident from Britain’s mystical traditions and from White Eagle’s revelations that the Druids of Britain were only the latest in a very long line of guardians of the Ancient Wisdom stretching back to the teachings of the Brethren of the Sun in the original Motherland. Hall wrote that in the time of the ancient philosophers there was a commonly held belief that no man could live intelligently who did not have a fundamental

---

[15] Pennick, N. *Celtic Sacred Landscapes*, Thames & Hudson, 1996

[16] ibid

knowledge of Nature and her laws. The Mysteries were devoted to instructing man on the operation of divine law on earth.

The Druids, custodians of the Ancient Wisdom and possessed of vast knowledge and understanding, were fundamental in the dissemination of these teachings. Reiser[17] writes of the Druids' claim that they possessed extraordinary powers inherited from their ancient mystical forebears: the ability to fly, to raise the dead, to control the weather, to move invisibly and to travel back and forth in time.

Hall believed that the Druids were initiates of a mystery school that dated back to the Bacchic and Eleusinian rites of Greece and the Egyptian rites of Isis and Osiris. The Eleusinian rites, established by Eumolpos 1400 years before Christ in dedication to Ceres and her daughter Persephone, were the most esteemed of all the ancient religious ceremonies.

At the heart of the Eleusinian mysteries is the interpretation of the secrets of Nature. Artemidorus, a second century AD diviner from Ephesus, wrote that Ceres and Persephone were worshipped in Britain or on an island close to it. Its doctrines were taught to students in forests and dark caves. Students were instructed in the creation of the universe, the mysteries of celestial bodies (including the zodiac), the secrets of occult medicine, and the rudiments of magic and sorcery. Initiations took place at the times of the two annual equinoxes and solstices. The birth of the sun god was celebrated on 25 December. They also had a Madonna or Virgin Mother with a Child in her arms who was sacred to their Mysteries. Its deepest teachings are said to have been founded on aspects of Pythagorean philosophy, especially regarding the concepts of reincarnation and metempsychosis.

> *The earth is not a dead body, but is inhabited by a spirit that is its life and soul. All created things, minerals included, draw their strength from the earth spirit. This spirit is life; it is nourished by the stars, and it gives nourishment to all living things it shelters in its womb. Through the spirit received from on high, the earth hatches the minerals in her womb as the mother the unborn child. This invisible spirit is like the reflection in a mirror, intangible, yet it is at the same time the root of all the substances necessary to the alchemical process or arising therefrom.*
>
> —15th century alchemist, Basilius Valentinus

---

[17] Reiser, O., *This Holyest Erthe: The Glastonbury Zodiac and King Arthur's Camelot*, Perennial Books, London, 1974

Roman mosaic at Littlecote House near Hungerford by the River Kennet. The mosaic depicts the story of Orpheus who is associated with the myth of the capture of Persephone by Hades, king of the Underwiorld

Marie O'Farrell Carr[18] believes that the St Michael ley is largely intact because of the work of the Druids. She suggests that after the destruction of Atlantis these alchemists made their way into Europe and Egypt and, over time, instituted monastic centres. The most prolific among these survivors from Atlantis' priesthood were the sects in Britain and France. By the use of magical powers, including the deployment of the anti-gravity qualities of sound vibrations these initiates built the stone circles.

Fourth century BC Greek historian, Hecataeus, referred to the gods appearing at Stonehenge: "On this island (Britain) is a remarkable temple, circular in shape, adorned with many consecrated gifts… It is said that in this island the moon appears very near to the earth, that certain eminences of a terrestrial form are plainly seen on it, that Apollo visits the island once in the course of nineteen years, in which period the stars complete their revolutions and that for this reason the Greeks distinguish the cycle of nineteen years by the name of the 'great year.' During this season of his appearance the god plays upon the harp and dances every night from the vernal equinox until the rising of the Pleiads, pleased with his own successes."

Some historians have suggested a link between the Celts and the semi-mythical Indo-Europeans ("Aryans"), the peoples of Eastern Europe and Asia Minor. Isabel Hill Elder enlarged on this thinking when she proposed that the original church of Britain was founded by Judean refugees, whom she described as the Culdees ("certain strangers").[19] Elder held that the Druids were Culdee priests. In this viewpoint, Elder was partly sharing the earlier opinions of Glastonbury Zodiac re-discoverer, Mrs Katherine Maltwood,[20] who, however, believed the Culdees (whom she termed Khaldis or Chaldees) to be of Iberian origin.

Maltwood believed that there were thousands of Chaldee Druids at work in Britain to satisfy what must have been a high demand for architect-priest-astrologers during a very lengthy time span for the design and placement of so many earthworks, effigies, dolmens and the like. Spence advanced similar ideas, writing that despite the Romans' efforts to wholly suppress Druidism, the priests continued their religious work under the guise of the Culdees who practised an eccentric style of Christianity.

---

[18] http://www.okinhealth.com/articles/arachangel-michael-leyline-skellig-island-ireland

[19] Elder, I.,*Celt, Druid, and Culdee*, London, 1962

[20] Maltwood, K., *Enchantments of Britain*, Victoria Printing and Publishing Co., 1944

The Druids' mystery ceremonies were presided over by the goddess Keridwen, her son Avagddu and servant Gwion. These supernatural figures feature heavily in Celtic mystery rites. A useful source is Taliesin who, according to legend, was the bastard son of Ceridwen, the goddess of the cauldron of Pwyll. Just as in the tales told of Merlin's birth, Taliesin had no father because he had been born from sorcery and enchantment. When Ceridwen gave birth she resolved to kill her son but she repented and, reminiscent of the Moses story, placed him in a stream to be found by some stranger.

In his poem "The Spoils of Annwn," Taliesin describes in allegorical fashion the initiate's journey from *Abred* (Welsh for earth-plane) into the lowest plane of the circles of *Annwn*, the underworld (in this context a companion dimension to Earth), to recover the cauldron whose fires beneath are kindled by the breath of nine maidens or Druidesses. The cauldron of Pwyll, which will not boil the food of a coward, is none other than the Grail vessel containing the blood of Christ, which after the crucifixion was brought, according to legend, from the Holy Land to Britain by Joseph of Arimathea accompanied by twelve holy men from the East. More than once White Eagle spoke of the arrival of Joseph and his mission to sew the seeds of mystical Christianity in Britain.

Taliesin said that the Grail could be found at Caer Sidi or Cair Pedryyan, "the Four-cornered Castle" in the mysterious Isle of the Active Door. Caer Sidi, sometimes interpreted as Annwn itself, means the Circle of Revolutions, suggesting a synchronous connection with the Glastonbury Zodiac, a doorway to the underworld.

During their ordeal the initiate is secured by a heavy blue chain, seemingly a reference in esoteric philosophy to the silver chord that secures a person's astral form to their physical body during out-of-body journeys. Once an initiate has recovered the cauldron, they return to the surface world nourished by the mystical secrets of enlightenment. Taliesin's description tallies with the mythical accounts of other renowned initiatory journeys, such as those undertaken by Osiris to the Egyptian underworld of Amenti and by Arthur to the Isle of Avalon at Glastonbury. There is no evidence for a royal historical personage named Arthur except in storytelling. The main source for the legend is Geoffrey of Monmouth's twelfth-century book, *The History of the Kings of Britain*, which chronicles the lives of the earliest British rulers. Although there are a few references to an "Arthur" figure in documents from the ninth and tenth centuries, Geoffrey gives the first extensive account of King Arthur's life and exploits.

The story begins when Arthur is conceived at Tintagel Castle, where Merlin transforms King Uther Pendragon into the likeness of Gorlois, the Duke of Cornwall, so that Uther can spend an evening of love with Gorlois' wife Ygerna. While many familiar aspects of King Arthur's story are included in Monmouth's version, he does not mention Camelot, Lancelot, the Holy Grail, Excalibur or the Knights of the Round Table. In fact, Monmouth's account of Arthur is frequently derided by today's historians. At best, Geoffrey is chastised for getting his facts wrong; at worst, he is accused, not least by contemporary chroniclers, of inventing the entire tale, cobbling together various different ancient tales, characters and episodes to create the heroic figure of Arthur. Monmouth himself claimed to have simply translated a very ancient book into Latin, a source that has never been identified.

Furthermore, no proof of Arthur's existence has been uncovered, even at Tintagel. It is not an entirely original story as it borrows heavily from the exploits of other well-known legendary rulers, especially Ambrosius Aurelianus, another British warlord who won a decisive battle against the invading Anglo-Saxons. Modern historians believe that Geoffrey used a variety of sources, including folklore, chronicles, king lists, dynastic tables, oral tales and bardic praise poems, in order to create a patriotic British narrative. Scholarly opinion has it that Arthur is an amalgam of at least five characters: in effect, a composite Celtic superhero and the ultimate warrior for the Britons.

Bellever Tor, Dartmoor National Park, Devon

Spencer argues that Arthur and Osiris are one and the same mythic personification, both associated with the cult of the bull. The glass-boat that conveyed Arthur's body to Avalon is synchronous with the barque of Osiris used to navigate the waters of Amenti.

Reiser[21] thought along similar lines but went further when he suggested that there were three iterations for the personality of Arthur: i) a mythic Sun-King figure deriving from a conflation of Ar-Thor of Atlantean mythology, the Persian god Ahura Mazda (the Assyrian god Assur), and Osiris; ii) the Zodiacal Arthur—King Arthur of the Round Table—arriving in Britain 500-600 AD, and whose adventures, Katherine Maltwood suggested, were modelled after the sequence of events depicted in the celestial zodiac, and; iii) the Arthur of the Troubadour Grail romances. In the next chapter we will explore a fourth alternative.

In Britain's ancient mystical tradition, the divine Sun is symbolised as in Reiser's Arthurian model by the white bull. Hu occupies a throne in the hub of its golden wheel. Hu's demiurge Keridwen (symbolised as the white cow) is the Mother Goddess of material creation and of the earth. In this symbolism, the earth is the Cauldron of Keridwen, Mother Nature. The bull and cow myths are directly associated with the Aurignacian period, a time of great transition when successive waves of survivors from the Atlantean lands were seeking sanctuary to escape Nature's fury.

Celts in ancient Britain saw in the sun's passage through the heavens a symbolic representation of an individual's mystical passage through life. At dawn the sun appeared to rise from Annwen, the underworld. In the daylight hours, it traversed Abred, the physical plane, the world of trial, test and experiment, the university of the physical curriculum from which man must continually strive to evolve. At night it sank into Gwynvyd, the sphere of the conscious and wholly developed spirit in perfect man. Britain's esoteric tradition makes it clear that the goal of man was to attain a passage into Gwynvyd by an initiatory process while still living to find the Cauldron of Inspiration and to drink from its magical waters.

Druidic sources indicated that a man was not expected to attain the initiate state until he was advanced in years, having "grown a long beard" after a lengthy period of tutelage and instruction. Ultimately, an individual, drawn to their mystical fulfilment by the power of one's inner and outer landscapes, has no choice other than to follow the solitary path of the initiate. Carl Jung summed it up succinctly when he

[21] ibid

wrote: "There is an unknown topographical law that rules man's disposition."[22]

There is something uniquely powerful and magical about the British landscape. Those who seek enlightenment have only to look about them to find the signs and symbols by which to facilitate their personal journey to the caverns of Pwyll. Through trial, tribulation and, ultimately, victory they find Ceridwen's cauldron and quaff its three drops of inspiration, symbolised by three golden apples.

The *key* to enlightenment as revealed in Britain's ancient and mystical landscape is the inner qualities of the truthseeker: unswerving belief, courage, insight, wisdom, patience, humour, a healthy sense of quest adventure, and an empathy with Nature. These are the essential ingredients by which one forges one's own personal key that will unlock the mysteries.

The *lock* represents certain components of Britain's physical landscape, not only those created by wise men long ago but also those of today in the shape of the marvels in the fields. These are the stones, circles, alignments, zodiacs, serpentine labyrinths, hills, mounds, faerie paths and magical rabbit holes that will respond to the insertion of a key honestly wrought.

The *door* is the portal to the companion planes of the earth, those enchanted realms of finer ethers "located just within our own 'solid' world," and which in Britain, according to esoteric tradition, are closer at hand than on any other place on earth.

The presence in the British landscape of Michael, Mary and Alice in their visible and invisible manifestations is an integral part of the magical process by which key, lock and door are forged, wrought and opened. We begin with Michael and Mary in our quest to unlock Britain's enchanted secrets.

---

[22] Jung, C. *The Spirit in Man, Art, and Literature*, Princeton University Press, 1966

A fairy fort at Littlecote House, Hungerford, near River Kennet

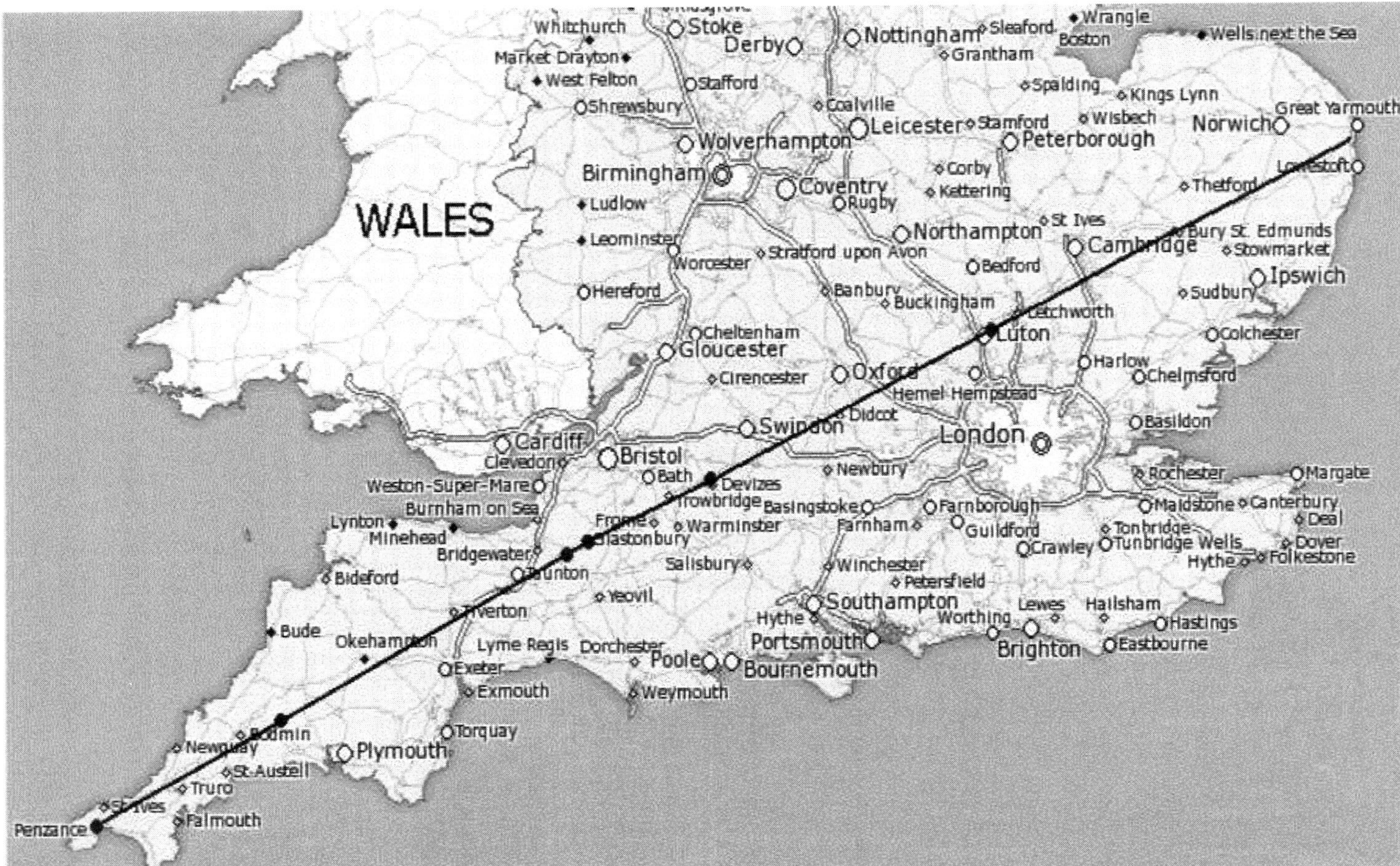

The St Michael ley, a straight line of best fit between the Michael and Mary energy currents

Chapter 2

Michael, Mary and Merlin

"All the country is lay'd for me."
—William Shakespeare, *2 Henry VI*

"Thus saith the Lord. Stand ye in the ways, and see, and ask for the old paths, where is the good way, and walk therein, and ye shall find rest for your souls."
—*Jeremiah,* vi, 16.

"We shall show them Our signs on the horizons and within themselves until it will be manifested unto them that it is the Truth."
—*The Koran* (XLI, 53)

It fell to the late John Michell to re-discover Britain's most celebrated ley. In a moment of inspiration experienced in the manner of past visionaries, notably ley pioneer Alfred Watkins, Glastonbury Abbey seer Bligh Bond and Somerset Zodiac visionary Katherine Maltwood, Michell received a revelation that he intuitively felt was part of a much bigger picture. In his groundbreaking work, *View Over Atlantis*,[23] Michell described his findings. One day in the late 1960s he stood on the summit of Glastonbury Tor. From his vantage point, Michell saw the prehistoric mound Burrowbridge Mump overtopped by a ruined church dedicated to St. Michael and known locally as King Alfred's Fort. He observed that the axis of the Tor seemed to point directly towards the Mump.

This observation triggered a vivid mental process in which Michell visualised a great line stretching across the countryside from St. Michael's Mount in Cornwall to the Mump via the Cheesewring, a towering stack of massive granite slabs balanced one on top of another on Stowe's Hill on the southeast edge of Bodmin Moor. It continues through the Mump before travelling onwards over the Somerset levels

[23] Michell, J., *View Over Atlantis*, Abacus, 1969

to the Tor. It then extends northeast through the megalithic complex at Avebury in Wiltshire before completing its land route on the east coast via the abbey site of Bury St. Edmunds. This alignment has become known as the St. Michael ley.

Making a closer study of his line on a map, Michell found other startling alignments, which he outlined in detail in a subsequent work.[24] St. Michael's church at Othery is situated very close to the line between Glastonbury and the Mump. Arrowing forwards on its northeast path, the line passes through Stoke St. Michael Church and then the southern entrance at Avebury Henge. It next passes through Ogbourne St George and, 27 miles later, St. Michael's Church at Clifton Hampden in Oxfordshire. Finally, the St. Michael ley flows firstly through the cathedral at Bury St. Edmunds in Suffolk and then the east coast town of Hopton-on-Sea between Lowestoft and Great Yarmouth.

If the ley is more accurately described as a "corridor of incidence" and a tolerance of 550m is allowed on each side, 63 churches fall within its boundary: 10 dedicated to St. Michael or St. George, and 23 to St. Mary. The Mary aspects of the alignment indicate the presence of a second component of the energy line, Mary being the Christianized Mother Goddess of ancient times.

Bromlow Callow in Shropshire. Photo courtesy of www.thebiggestlittlehills.com

[24] Michell, J., *The Earth Spirit: Its Ways, Shrines and Mysteries*, Thames and Hudson, 1975

Watkins, a 66-year-old antiquarian and businessman of Hereford, had made the momentous discovery of the "Old Straight Tracks" on a Summer Solstice day in 1921. Standing in the afternoon heat on a high hilltop near the Herefordshire village of Blackwardine, Watkins saw in the landscape something not seen by human eyes for perhaps thousands of years. His son, Allen, described the event in his biography of his father.

> Then without warning it all happened suddenly. His mind was flooded with a rush of images forming one coherent plan. The scales fell from his eyes and he saw over many long years of prehistory, all trackways were in straight lines marked out by experts on a sighting system. The whole plan of the Old Straight Track stood suddenly revealed… 'The whole thing came to me in a flash,' he told me afterwards.[25]

Others before Watkins had seen glimpses of it. In his 1846 book "*The Druid Temples of Wiltshire*," Rev. Edward Duke said that there once existed an "axis of power" between Stonehenge and Avebury, along which each prehistoric site on the line represented one of the seven astrological planets. Some years later William Henry Black, a member of the British Archaeological Society, enlarged on Duke's ideas and said that all ancient sites in Britain and possibly the world over could be linked by "Great Circle Lines," (these days referred to as a planetary grid or matrix). Alfred Watkins became a member of Black's study circle, which met at the Green Dragon Hotel in Hereford.

A couple of years before Watkin's "Eureka" moment, poet "A.E." (pen name of George Russell) in his *Candle of Vision* had spoken of seeing in his cherished hills and ancient sanctuaries of Ireland, "the many coloured land… I knew the Golden Age was all about me, and it was we who had been blind to it, but that it had never passed away from the world." Watkins described his hilltop vision in *The Old Straight Track*:

> Imagine a fairy chain from mountain peak to mountain peak, as far as the eye could reach, and paid out until it reached the 'high places' of the earth at a number of ridges, banks and knowls. Then visualise a mound, circular earthwork, or clump of trees, planted on these high points, and in low points in the valley other mounds ringed round with water to be seen from a distance. Then great standing stones brought to mark the way at intervals, and on a bank leading up to a mountain ridge or down to a ford the track cut deep so as to form a guiding notch on the skyline as you come up. In a

[25] Watkins, A., *Alfred Watkins of Hereford*, Garnstone, London, 1972

> *bwlch* or mountain pass the road cut deeply at the highest place straight through the ridge to show as a notch afar off. Here and there, at two ends of the way, a beacon fire used to lay out the track. With ponds dug on the line, or streams banked up into 'flashes' to form reflecting points on the beacon track so that it might be checked when at least once a year the beacon was fired on the traditional day. All these works exactly on the sighting line.

Watkins set to work marking out the churches and ancient sites on a 1-inch Ordnance Map and before long his vision was validated. Often he found nine or more sites aligned across relatively short stretches of countryside. Extending these to neighbouring maps, Watkins traced lines for miles, many ending on a high peak or hill.

He called his alignments "leys," describing them as the vestiges of Neolithic traders' routes that criss-crossed the countryside and were marked with standing stones and mounds of earth or cairns. These marked lines ran from hilltop to hilltop like "a fairy chain." The hilltops were marked with earthworks or were traditional beacon sites, locations ideally placed for line-of-sight communication. Often, when one peak was invisible to a neighbouring one stone pillars, earthworks, mounds, cairns, notched ridges, moats, ponds, crosses, holy wells, ancient crossroads, tree groupings, old moats, noteworthy boulders, pre-Reformation churches and other distinguishing natural "markstones" were placed clearly on the line to emphasise the arrow-straight alignment.

Because beacon fires are associated with the countrywide communication system developed by the Elizabethans, Watkins believed that their equal usefulness as surveying instruments had been overlooked. These surveyors' beacons, he suggested, were later enshrined in traditions such as the Beltane Fire festivals. He called such hilltops "initial points" and found that holy wells often fulfilled this function too. These old straight tracks were further delineated during the Bronze Age but the knowledge and usage of them gradually decayed.

Intuitively, Watkins associated leys with Hermes (the Roman Mercury, the Norse Woden, the Egyptian Thoth), the guide to wayfarers on unknown paths. Hermes carried a rod, a word that long ago meant road. Hermes is associated with the Celtic God Tout. Many mounds are called Tot, Toot, Tout, Tute and Twt. The Welsh word Llan, a prefix meaning church-place, has the same etymological origin as the Saxon word ley. "Ley" is also connected with the English archaic word laia, meaning a roadway in a wood.

Three months after experiencing his vision at Blackwardine, Watkins gave a lantern lecture to the local Woolhope Club in which he claimed to have discovered a fundamental principle behind the arrangement of ancient sites. His proposition was that prehistoric monuments and shrines were originally sited in relation to each other on a series of straight lines. In explanation, Watkins suggested that leys were archaic trackways and that the features aligned on them originally served to guide travellers on the "old straight track." The purpose of leys, he suggested, was both secular and sacred for traders and pilgrims alike. At their intersections were held markets and festivals. The sanctity of these places extended to the other sites in line with them and to the leys themselves. Finally, Watkins concluded, albeit somewhat reluctantly, that the underlying principle behind the ley system was deeply mystical and related to a system of ancient magic and religion whose traces are found in traditional folklore.

Very few amateur enthusiasts after Watkins' death in 1935 appear to have advanced his investigations into leys and earth energies. One notable exception was surrealist painter and mystic, Ithell Colquoun. Not only did Colquoun echo the essential aspects of Watkins' findings in her own discoveries but she also wrote about the existence of a trans-England St. Michael Line.

In 1949 Colquoun came to live in the idyllic Lamorna Valley near Penzance in west Cornwall. In her 1957 work, *The Living Stones*, she referred to a line of magnetic energies that extends from the east coast of England to the tip of Cornwall, passing close to Lamorna Cave where she lived. She believed it to be a pre-Christian Michael-force energy line and that it connected with both Arthur and the Knights Templar who, she said, were both aware of its power and wove it into their actions and adventures.

Colquoun believed that megalithic stones around the valley were powerhouses of vital energy that in some way invigorate the landscape. She said, "The earth is a being and certain places on its surface are conducive to different kinds of esoteric perception, these places are the mundane chakras of the earth itself (and) draw upon a 'Fountain out of Hecate,' an uprush of force from the macrocosmic underworld which focused by ceremony may coincide at precise times with the microcosmic unconscious." Dowser Andrew Davidson found evidence to support Colquoun's beliefs when he discovered that each stone in a megalithic structure is electrically charged, its polarity being the opposite of its neighbour. The polarity will change every 6 days after the new moon. The change on these occasions takes 7 minutes.

Ideas such as Colquoun's were still regarded as very radical. Watkins had instigated the discussion on the leys but Colquoun's startling contribution was to add to it a psychic and magical dimension. She spoke of the power of these stones travelling in lines upon the land. Where the earth current meets the sea current, "a whirlpool develops which stimulates health and visionary capacity." It would be another twelve years before John Michell, a gifted investigator from outside the rarified circle of academic geographers, would make his own profound discoveries concerning the St. Michael Line.

Meanwhile, archaeologists scoffed at Watkins' ideas, regardless of the fact that anyone taking the time to trace the alignments on a map must seriously consider that they were constructed by those who possessed a remarkable understanding of the countryside's hidden character. Bear in mind, however, that in 1921 archaeologists still believed in the veracity of the Piltdown Man discovery; its hoax status would not be confirmed until 1953. Archaeologists' professional instincts were obviously vulnerable to error and so their judgements about new discoveries should be seen in this context.

Mainstream archaeological opinion held that megalith builders were savages utterly incapable of surveying. It followed, therefore, that the whole concept of leys was an entirely absurd notion. Watkins' findings were dismissed out of hand. One archaeologist called the idea of leys a "damned nonsense." Nevertheless, not all professionals were dismissive of Watkin's findings. In 1938 German geographer Dr. Josef Heinsch presented a paper, "Principles of Prehistoric Cult-Geography," to an International Congress at Amsterdam.

In his address Heinsch spoke of a magic principle, now lost, by which sites of holy significance had been located in the distant past. He maintained that they had been placed along lines of great geometrical figures constructed relative to the positions of heavenly bodies. The units of measurement used in this terrestrial global geometry were based on simple fractions of the proportions of the earth. Heinsch concluded that the achievement attested to the former existence of a universal civilisation with an advanced knowledge of science and magic. Through the adept application of these now forgotten principles, this past race had enhanced the lives and spiritual substance of its citizens by means of a force activated through the correct geographical relationship of sacred centres.

It was not until the 1960s that interest in leys resurfaced. New findings led to marked changes in what has been described as the traditional "woad and skins" attitudes amongst establishment archaeologists. In particular, Professor Alexander Thom's scientific studies of stone circles provided fresh vigour to archaeologists' inquiries into prehistoric Britain's astronomical and metrological knowledge. Subsequent archaeological discoveries have indicated that prehistoric societies were much more complex than previously considered. Additionally, prehistorian Professor R.J.C. Atkinson proved that the laying out of an accurate straight line on the landscape was well within the capabilities of the megalithic builders.

Moreover, since Watkins's death paths of power and the geomantic tradition have been recognized all over the world. Long Island University scholar Dr Paul Kosok discovered in 1939 the enigmatic straight tracks at Nazca in Peru, Forty years later zoologist Tony Morrison reported on the tracks in the altiplano region of western Bolivia. The Bolivian tracks, set out by by unknown surveyors, correspond most closely to Watkins' ideas of leys. Some are 30 km in length and stretch from hilltop to hilltop like Watkins's "fairy chain" vision. Regarded locally as holy sites, the lines are marked by Indian cairn shrines and Spanish churches.

The Aborigines of Australia preserve their ancestral memories in their native countryside marked by songlines, mythological routes that relate to the "Dreamtime," an unseen world of endless time whose features, contours and alignments were shaped and modelled by elemental beings which existed in a primordial era. Once a year these magical lines, regarded also as fairy paths, are re-animated by a vital force that enriches the earth and brings new life to plants and animals. One undertakes a journey along the dream track in which each feature is imbued with sacred significance—hills, ridges, trees, rocks, caves, waterfalls and waterholes—each charged with a magical, numinous power (the Aboriginal "djang"). The tributaries of the dreaming track comprise a "knowledge network," which can be maintained and recharged through ceremonial actions such as singing, dancing and painting. Spiritually charged people, shamans and wise ones can convey information telepathically along them. American Indians, especially the Hopi of the Southwest, use similar invisible paths as power lines to enhance mental communication. The Irish associate leys with fairy paths. The Druids called terrestrial currents "Wouivres," channels of invisible force that flow through the earth, crossing at special places and nodes. In the early part of the 20th century, scholar J.D. Evans Wentz travelled far and wide in the Celtic regions collecting fairy stories. In answer to his question concerning an explanation for fairy paths, an Irish mystic, echoing the Druid belief, told Evans Wentz that they were lines of magnetic current whose precise nature had been forgotten. In Wales, the sacred paths are under the protection of Elen, the goddess of dawn and dusk. In the *Mabinogion,* Helen becomes the bride of Maxen Wledig, the emperor of Rome who searched far and wide for Helen for a year after seeing her in a vivid dream. The story reveals that Helen, a princess of Anglesey, constructed a system of roads running straight from castle to castle across Britain.

Clearly, it is not the mental or skills abilities of the megalith builders that are under question regarding the ley phenomenon but rather its technical issues. A common objection is that lines on the plane surface of a map cannot accurately represent alignments on the curved surface of the Earth. However, this factor is only relevant for lines longer than approximately 40 km, as the variation is so small on shorter distances that the error on the ground is far less than the sizes of an alignment's waymarkers. This negligibility is demonstrated in the well-known example of drawing the famous ley that runs south from Stonehenge through Old Sarum, Salisbury Cathedral, Clearbury Ring and Frankenbury Camp. One can then stand on Old Sarum, look south and see Salisbury Cathedral and Clearbury Ring aligning with it exactly as on the map.

A more significant objection concerns the fact that leys incorporate marker locations that can vary significantly in age. A line that may include a circle of dolmens and a pre-Reformation church presents a time span of more than 3,000 years. Naturally, this begs the question as to how the markers were set out deliberately. Watkins and successive ley hunters answered this by referring to the practice of adapting sacred sites in the interests of the evolving traditions of religious and social cultures. Often churches are built on earlier, pagan sites, St Swithins in Lincoln and Wells Cathedral being prime examples. Throughout the centuries Popes have instructed missionaries to convert pagan sites of sanctity for church building rather than destroy them.

And then there are the sceptics that dismiss the existence of leys as statistically improbable. However, the problem is not easily resolved mathematically. While it may be the case that some investigators over the past one hundred years have been hunting chance alignments, there are certainly leys that do prove to be statistically significant, one of which, for example, is the Craigearn line discovered by John Michell. Michell identified the ley among the standing stones and stone circles marked on the 1-inch Ordnance Survey Map of the Aberdeen area. At first sight there is little to suggest that Michell's discovery is not a series of chance connections but closer investigation identifies a tetrad (a group of four markers), 5½ cm long on the map (about 3½ km on the ground), which clearly stands out from the rest and whose straightness cannot be refuted in statistical terms.

Cambridge mathematician Michael Behrend derived an ingenious formula to demonstrate that sites will align by chance more often than one might expect. That being the case, Behrend was equally open to the existence of true leys. An admirer of Heinsch's studies, Behrend claims to have found across the British countryside vast networks of alignments, statistical analysis of which indicates that they were set out in accordance with two fixed distances equivalent to 295.3m and 464.1m. Interestingly, these added together total 759.4 and 759.4/464.1 = 1.6164, a close approximation to the Golden Mean. The Golden Mean will be a key factor that will come under scrutiny in later pages in the context of the "Alice" component of the St. Michael ley enigma.

The St. Michael ley is one such alignment; in fact, it is the longest in Britain and by far the most well known. Archaeological researcher Paul Devereaux and mathematician Robert Forrest have observed that it is basically a work of nature.[26] Many of its waymarkers such as Glastonbury Tor and St. Michael's Mount are natural features. However, the characteristics of the line strongly suggest that at some period of prehistory the line was made precise and formal. This is demonstrated most evidently in its central section, beginning at Burrowbridge Mump southwest of Glastonbury. A ringed island hill with a ruined church of St. Michael on its summit, the Mump is effectively a smaller twin of the Tor. From its summit the Tor is visible on the far horizon.

As observed by Michell, the axis of the Mump is aligned on the Tor. Its extension follows the old Pilgrims' Way along the Tor's ridge and forms the axis of its labyrinth. Projecting eastwards, the line runs precisely to the main southern entrance to Avebury temple, a manmade prehistoric complex. This straight line continues beyond Avebury to a former monastic site, the church at Ogbourne St. George, St. George being an earthly representation of St. Michael.

In 1983 Devereux and Forrest found themselves on the receiving end of criticism from ley sceptic, Martin Whittle of Manchester University. In a letter to the *New Scientist* published in January 1983, Whittle complained that the pair's article ("Straight lines on an ancient landscape," 23 December 1982) expressed ill-founded statistical arguments regarding the existence of leys. It went on to accuse the pair of erroneously applying Michael Behrend's formula to an alignment in

[26] Article by Paul Devereux and Robert Forrest in *New Scientist* 23/30 Dec 1982

a 10 km square on a map, which, in Whittle's opinion, was too small upon which to make a legitimate statistical evaluation. He said that the correct approach was to examine by "scouring the whole country" many 10 km squares and compare the total number of leys of a particular order with the statistical prediction.

Forrest responded but for some reason the *New Scientist* did not print his letter. He pointed out that any statistical model must stick as closely as possible to the process it is designed to model. It therefore follows that the ley hunter cannot investigate the whole of the British Isles without being constrained by the confines of the various O.S. Map sheets one uses. Since one can study Britain in its entirety only as a series of "packages," a realistic model of ley hunting must reflect this.

Forrest added that in statistical terms ley hunting is a game of chance alignment played with randomised map symbols within specified map boundaries. Consequently, each potential ley is related to a specific context, that context being the area of map sheet on which the alignment was first discovered rather than the total area of the British Isles. The only way a "scouring the whole country" argument can work is when the whole country is seen as a piecemeal collection of map sheets from which the ley bearing sheets are reported but the non-ley bearing sheets ignored. Forrest stressed that in their article they had been careful to acknowledge this argument, which is why they had been careful to state that "the statistical wheel is still in spin."

John Michell (left) and Robert Forrest conducting fieldwork

In a subsequent expert assessment of the St. Michael Line, Forrest adopted a somewhat more sceptical approach when he referred to it as an "alleged alignment of ancient sites." His note of caution, struck possibly in an attempt to deflect any further peer criticism, should be considered in context. In his paper Forrest is assessing the particulars of a supposed *line* (as distinct from any other kind of quality that might be discovered regarding the true characteristics of an alignment, a corridor arrangement, for example). Forrest goes on to highlight the difficulties of establishing any precise degree of straightness for the line or to determine accurately where it actually goes. These issues arise because of the challenges of tracing a geodesic across a map. For a set of sites on a map to align, they must all fall on a single line-of-sight, extending from one site to the next. Such a sightline is known as a geodesic. Forrest points out that over relatively short distances, such as for example the 40 km width of a 1:50,000 Ordnance Survey Map, a line-of-sight is a straight line and thus fulfils the definition of a geodesic. Over longer distances the natural curvature of the earth rules out the establishment of longer, true geodesics. In making a statistical and mathematical analysis of the St. Michael Line, Forrest addressed the question of what the actual geodesic looks like and how far it diverges from the straight line drawn across the map sheet. Because of these issues, Forrest found discrepancies between map-line and true geodesic, although they are much smaller than one might expect for a line covering such a long distance. One reason for this is that the line runs west to east (north to south lines tend to suffer relatively greater geodesic challenges). Neverthelesss, other deviations found by Forrest convinced him that "the St. Michael line as originally proposed [by John Michell in *View Over Atlantis*] is really not a line at all, either on the map or on the ground." However, Forrest then draws attention to some later aspects of Michell's thinking regarding a key section of the line as defined by Burrow Mump, Glastonbury Tor, Avebury and Ogbourne St. George. Forrest agrees that these four sites are "indeed aligned," the maximum deviation appearing to be no more than 31 metres. It appears, therefore, that the question of relative "straightness" along the alignment is a tricky one to address.

Subsequent chapters will explore the line's features in depth but David Furlong has provided a useful summary of significant sites, running southwest to northeast, with corresponding map references:

- St. Michael's Mount where the archangel Michael is said to have appeared to fishermen in the 8th century AD, Grid Ref:

SW 52456 29857

- Carwynnen or Giant's Quoit, Grid ref: SW 65006 37187, thought to be a late Neolithic or early Bronze Age dolmen tomb
- Ladock Church, Grid Ref: SW 9446 51062
- Bofarnel Downs (Tumuli), Grid Ref: SX 11817 63367
- The Hurler's Stone Circle, Grid Ref: SX 25837 71298, an early Bronze Age monument comprising three circles
- The nearby Cheesewring, Grid Ref: SX 25762 72478
- Great Links Tor, Grid ref: SX 55073 86753, one of the most impressive Tors on Dartmoor. From its summit at 586m there are excellent views over Cornwall and parts of Dartmoor.
- Cosdon Hill (Dartmoor), Grid Ref: SX 63598 91553
- West Buckland Church, Grid Ref: ST 17324 20518, a Norman church dedicated to St. Mary
- Burrowbridge Mump, Grid Ref: ST 35920 30528
- Glastonbury Tor, Grid Ref: ST 51180 38603.
- Oliver's Castle, Grid Ref: SU 00098 64687, an Iron Age hill fort on the edge of the escarpment, just to the north of the market town of Devizes
- Beckhampton Long Barrow, Grid Ref: SU 08704 69107, a notable Neolithic barrow dated to 3000+ BC. The barrow is aligned approximately to the orientation of the St. Michael line with a northeastern entrance pointing to Avebury.
- The Avebury Henge, Grid Ref: SU 10269 69957
- Temple Farm, Grid Ref: SU 14849 72362, once owned by the Knights Templar
- Pitstone Church, Grid Ref: SP 94224 14929, the Church of St Mary the Virgin
- Ivinghoe Hills, Grid Ref: SP 96219 16209, one of the highest points of the Chiltern escarpment, which stretches from Goring Gap in Oxfordshire to Royston in Hertfordshire
- Bury St Edmunds Abbey, Grid Ref: TL 85905 64254, formerly incorporating St. Margaret's and St James churches. The projected line passes into North Sea at southern end of Hopton.

Each of these locations sits on a dragon's flight path. In correspondence with Robert Forrest, John Michell introduced what I believe is the key to a more complete understanding of the Michael alignment when he said that deviations (which, according to Forrest, are a maximum of 1792 metres between St. Michael's Mount and Bury St. Edmunds) are not amiss if one regards the line as a "pilgrim route." Forrest examined this suggestion and remarked that it affects the "Michael-ness" of the line, pointing out that in making allowances for deviation tolerances, the result is that there are actually *more* churches along the route dedicated to St. Mary, St. Margaret or Mary Magdalene. These supportive factors, contrary from raising fundamental objections concerning the mathematical integrity of a St. Michael line phenomenon reinforce its true nature, which is better described as representing a *corridor* of male (positive electromagnetic polarity) and female (negative polarity) energies that twist around a spinal axis.

On 1 February 1987 Miller and Broadhurst commenced tracking the energies of the St. Michael ley. Their investigations added significant new knowledge that substantially complemented both Michell's initial identification of the ancient alignment and Forrest's remarks about its pilgrim-route nature. The pair published their findings in *The Sun and the Serpent*,[27] in which they describe their detection of a unique energy that winds around the straight axis of the Michael line. Initially, the pair traced it from Land's End as far as Avebury. At that point, the energy began to describe a more complicated pattern. Following it with his dowsing rod, Miller was surprised to learn that the current crossed another energy channel of a different quality. The new current was of opposite negative charge and, therefore, the polar counterpart of the first, positive channel.

Further investigation confirmed to the investigators' satisfaction that there was in fact a double line of serpentine energies in the form of the rod of Asclepius, the Greek god of healing, ravelling around the St Michael ley. Armed with this exciting new knowledge, Miller and Broadhurst went back to Land's End and retraced their entire journey to Avebury, tracking the path of the second channel. They then completed their task by following and mapping the routes of both energy lines eastward to the North Sea.

Guy Underwood discovered[28] that the geographical arrangement of prehistoric Britain coincides with the lines and centres of subterranean

[27] Miller, H. & Broadhurst, P., *The Sun and the Serpent,* Pendragon Press, Launceston, Cornwall, 1989

[28] Underwood, G., *The Patterns of the Past*, Abelard-Schuman Ltd, 1973

terrestrial currents. He distinguished three different forms of current: aquastats, track lines, and those that emanate from underground flowing water. These frequently follow the course of old tracks, linear earthworks, ancient banks and boundaries. Their direction of flow varies with the phases of the moon. Ley lines and dragon currents are terms synonomous with the lines of the earth current.

John Michell had also associated sacred paths and shrines with ways of the earth spirit: natural channels of energy that he believed were first traced out by the creative gods. He described the serpentine nature of these energies:

> …the serpent represents the mercurial currents of the earth spirit gliding in serpentine channels through the earth's crust—the yin force of nature… When the serpent current of the earth spirit is transfixed by the lance of the dragon killer, it can no longer move freely about the earth, for its energies are now fixed and concentrated in one spot… For many years, experienced dowsers… have observed the fact that every megalithic site is over a centre or channel of the terrrestrial current whose emanations are detected by the dowser's rod. All ancient tombs and stones were placed so as to coincide with and accumulate the flow of the earth's vital energy, its "Spirit." [29]

These serpents represent the vital energies that course around the spine of the human body. It is evident that the architects of the Michael and Mary currents intended to convey a similar meaning. The line delineates the backbone of southern England, energized by the vital currents of the earth. The sanctuaries along its length, distinguished by Michael and Mary in so many place names such as Glastonbury and Avebury, can be regarded as the "chakras" in Gaia's landscape.

In an article,[30] Roy Snelling describes an "Atlantis Line," which originates in the Azores. He restates a belief that the Azores are the remains of a mountain chain that once lay to the north of one of the large islands of Atlantis. One of the Azores islands, Pico, is thought to have been sacred to the priests of Atlantis and that it was here where they built a Sun-Temple. Snelling reviews the purported discovery by Portuguese yachtsman Diocleciano Silva between the islands of Miguel and Terceira of a stone pyramid of similar shape and size to the Great Pyramid. Snelling has calculated that its coordinates place it exactly on the edge-line of the hexahedron earth line. Moreover, he states that if the Michael and Mary line is projected southwestwards into the Atlantic it meets this earth line precisely. After the Atlantis Line's passage into

---

[29] ibid

[30] Snelling, R., *The Atlantis Line*, 2017

Cornwall, to all intents and purposes it "becomes" the St Michael ley, formerly christened the Michael line in 1969 by John Michell but later renamed by Miller and Broadhurst because of the preponderence of churches dedicated to these saints along is length, and also because they discovered during their investigations that they were actually dowsing two powerful energies, male and female. Snelling argues that although by his reckoning there are 83 churches dedicated to either Michael or Mary along the corridor alignment (I count 85, see table on page 255), there are similar concentrations in other parts of England, which, for Snelling rules out making a special virtue of a male-female quality along the Cornwall to Norfolk ley. I can appreciate the time and effort that Snelling has put into his calculations and conclusions. However, I believe there are good reasons for retaining the Michell-Miller-Broadhurst nomenclature, not least because the ley is a dual-polarity Nature force, a vital feature that cannot be ignored in the overall cosmological interpretation of its function in the English countryside. The "Michael-Mary" descriptor recognizes the ley's dipole nature and, thus, reinforces the principle perfectly.

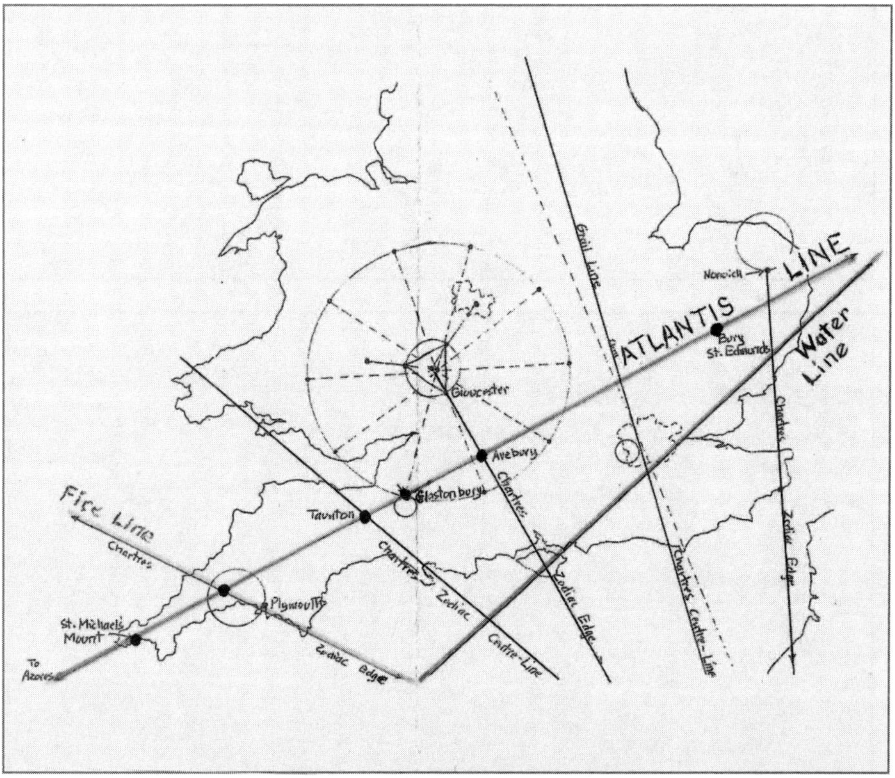

Snelling's "Atlantis Line" in conjunction with the Perpetual Choirs Decagon and other significant energy lines from Europe through and across southern England

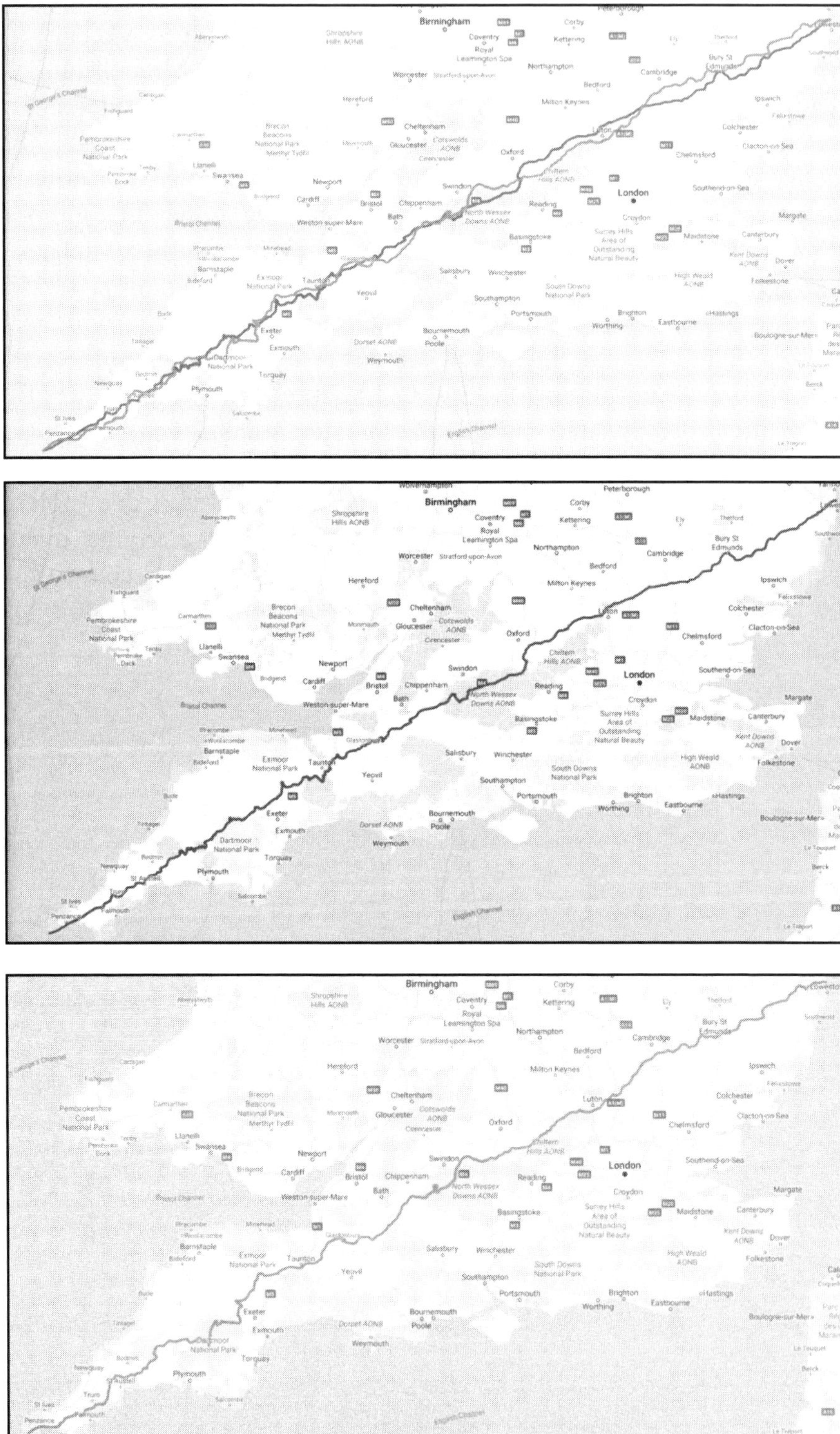

Michael and Mary currents, Michael, and the more sinuous Mary current (bottom)

English Counties	Michael Current Locations	Mary current locations
Cornwall	**Carn-Lês-Boels**, Penlee, **St. Michael's Mount**	**Carn-Lês-Boels**, Ailsa Holy Well
	Leedstown, Truro, St Michael Penkevil	**St. Michael's Mount**
	Resugga Castle, St Austell	**Resugga Castle**, Germoe, Old Kea
	St Neot, **Lostwithiel**, Ley	**Lostwithiel**, Roche Rock, St Clear
	The Hurlers at Cheesewring	Trevethy Quoit, **The Hurlers at Cheesewring**
Devon	**Brentor**, Lydford, Yes Tor	**Brentor**, Milton Abbott, Mary Tavy
	Belstone Tor, Ninestones	Throwleigh, Gidleigh, Spinster's Rock
	Hittisleigh, **Crediton**	**Crediton**, Prestonbury Castle, Dunsford
	Cadbury Castle, Tiverton	Tedburn St Mary, Holcombe Regis
Somerset	Wellington Monument, **Creech St Michael**	**Creech St Michael**
	Corfe, St Michael's Church North Newton	St Michael's Church Trull
	Burrow Mump, St Michael's Othery, **Chalice Well**	Small Knowl Down
	Street, **Glastonbury**, Pilton, Shepton Mallet	**Burrow Mump**
	Stoke St Michael, Devil's Bed and Bolster	**Glastonbury, Chalice Well**
Wiltshire	Trowbridge, **Bowerhill**, **Oliver's Castle**	**Bowerhill**, **Oliver's Castle, Windmill Hill**
	Windmill Hill, The Avebury Complex	**The Avebury Complex**, **Ogbourne St Andrew**
	Ogbourne St Andrew	**The mound at Ogbourne St George**
	The mound at Ogbourne St George	Ogbourne St George Church
Oxfordshire	Aldbourne (Berkshire), **Sinodun Hill**, Cuddesdon	**Sinodun Hil**l, Uffington, East Lockinge
	St Michael's Church Clifton Hampden	East Hendred, Dorchester
Bedfordshire & Hertfordshire	Dinton, Aylesbury (Buckinghamshire), Mentmore	Chinnor, Ivanhoe Beacon
	Dunstable, Luton (Waulud's Bank)	**Royston**, Whipsnade
	Baldock, **Royston**, Ickleton	Wandlebury Rings, Kirtling, **Bury St Edmunds**
Suffolk and Norfolk	**Bury St Edmunds**, Woolpit, Eye, Hoxne, Beccles	Stowlangtoft, Ditchingham
	Somerton, **St Margaret's Church Hopton**	**St Margaret's Church Hopton**

St Michael ley principle locations, 21 shared points (the alignment) in bold

The Chinese describe leys as *lung-mei*, their magnetic force personified as dragon paths that course between high mounds and mountaintops. In their philosophy these lines of force extend all over the world. The female yin force (the negative magnetic pole), represented by the white tiger, flows mainly along chains of low hills whereas the positive male yang force, symbolised by the blue dragon, follows for the most part mountainous ridges and high hills. Until recently in China every manmade construction had to be placed in the landscape in accordance with a magical geomantic system that adhered to the laws of proportion, mathematics and music. The proof of these Universal Laws that govern Creation is made evident to man in the form of beauty. Integral to this system of *feng-shui* is a corresponding belief that the various parts of the earth fall under a particular planetary influence whose powers and characteristics are passed down to the countryside via the terrestrial lines of dragon power that flow above it.

The two lines of current which spiral around the straight axis of the St Michael ley form the symbol of the serpent-entwined rod of Asclepius, the Greek god of healing. The ley marks the backbone of southern England, energized by the vital currents of earth. The myth of the dragon and its homologues—serpent, lizard, eel, worm etc.—is known the world over. The Greeks worshipped the Python. The Norse myths speak of the earth serpent, the Midgard-Worm. The Mayans saw in the night sky a huge rattlesnake slithering across the Milky Way. The Pyramid texts refer to both a subterranean and celestial serpent, while Moses taught the Jews to worship the serpent in the wilderness. The mediaeval alchemists told of the underground serpent or Oroborous under the earth that guards the Philosopher's Stone. The dragon is depicted as living on the tops of mountains and by lakes, wells and holes in the earth. It stands guard over fabulous treasure and will reveal secret knowledge to heroic figures.

The "fixing" of the earth energy at certain points is the science of Geomancy. It has been said that nowhere on the planet is such a powerful earth serpent so "nailed" down as upon the Michael and Mary ley in southern England. Once the dragon slayer fixes the serpent power in place, the omphalos, the spot where he was subdued, becomes temple, shrine, church, sacred site, alignment, circle and so on. Our forbears believed that these power places are inhabited by the spirits of the earth, the "genius loci." In East Anglia, for example, these are the Yarthlings and the Hyter Spirits.

According to legend, St Joseph of Arimathea symbolised this act of dragon power "fixing" when he planted his hawthorn staff into the ground at Glastonbury soon after the crucifixion. Tradition has it that upon the arrival of Joseph and his company these first Christians in Britain were instructed by the Druids in the secret powers of the shrines, the upkeep and purpose of the 100-square mile Glastonbury Zodiac and Tor, and its magical ley connection to Avebury and Stonehenge. Christians built chapels dedicated to St. Michael along the male serpent line on the former sites of the Celtic God, Lug. On the more shapely female line, often near water or Holy Wells, Mary Chapels were erected on former sites of Lug's consort, the Goddess.

Ancinet wisdom reveals that within every individual is the "Divine Mother" (called Kundry in Grail mythology), which is coiled like a sleeping serpent at the base of the spine. Kundalini means ball of fire and the womb of life. The raw energy of the earth and its corresponding currents in the earth's etheric fields find its human counterpart in this Kundalini power of the Mother Goddess, which in normal circumstances sleeps in the root chakra situated at the base of the spine and guards our inner Tree of Life.

White Eagle explained that the serpent, a symbol of "evil," personifies man's love of power, a mental craving that asserts itself in the lower, baser aspects of man. But at the same time, mankind's fall from grace in the far distant past also caused the development and growth of man's individual soul and mind. Therefore, in accordance with the principle of reciprocity, "evil" produced individualisation, a very necessary part of man's evolutionary growth without which there would be no stimulus or desire in man to grow to become a more complete and spiritually mature individual.

In esoteric teachings the serpent symbol is indicative of the transmutation of the creative powers of life from the lowest centre of the body—the generative centre (the hearth of the fire-power)—to the heart and head. It symbolizes the crowning of the higher triangle: the heart and the throat and the faculties that are concentrated in the head.

Indian yoga teachings refer to two subtle channels in the human body: Idas and Pingala, male and female, which coil around a central axis, the Sushumna. They share central meeting points within the 7 chakras, described in Eastern mysticism as the seats of God in the human form. The sanctuaries along the dragon's path where the two currents meet can be regarded as the "chakra" or nodal points in the subtle body of the landscape, which comprises a powerful field of geomagnetic energies. Similarly, the line's serpent powers are the geophysical equivalent of the vital energies that coil around the spine of the human body. The Michael and Mary currents have innumerable offshoots. These neural tributaries are akin to the "nadis," the nerve fibres that supply the human body with etheric prana or cosmic life-energy. The crowned or plumed serpent is the power of Kundalini, arisen and evolved from animal instinct into the Mother Goddess powers of purity and love. Scorpio, the serpent, is symbolic of the secret wisdom, the innermost wisdom of life. The Eagle is the higher aspect of the sign Scorpio. As one grows spiritually, these fire powers raise one's consciousness aloft as on the wings of an eagle.

The dragon power that flows over the global landscape is associated with fertility. It is especially active during the time of year when Nature re-animates the minerals of the earth to ensure the healthy fertilisation of crops by sun, wind and water for the continuing sustenance of life on earth. The archetypal dragon legend illustrates this ageless cycle. The dragon, born from an egg, grows quickly and devours all in its path before a heroic figure (often depicted in myth as St. Michael with lance or St. George with sword) arrives to despatch the unwelcome serpent.

In Celtic lore, the goddess Brigid is depicted as a snake that emerges from her mound on 1 February, the first day of the Celtic spring. She is the "two-faced one," one side of her face old and rugged, the other young and beautiful to personify her dual nature as crone and maiden. In Scottish tradition, Brigid is also associated with the coming of spring when she usurps the winter reign of the crone goddess Cailleach. Irish myth includes stories of the transformation of the Goddess from crone to maiden with the magical embrace of the hero, an act that symbolizes sacred marriage. An example is Morrigan, Goddess of Fallen Warriors. The Grimm Brothers relate tales in Swiss folklore that describe dragons and serpents flying out of mountain caves with the coming of spring. The role of Brigid was taken over by the Catholic St. Brigit. Her feast day is also celebrated on February 1. Rituals associated with Brigit reveal her dual aspect as the Snake Goddess.

> I smoor the hearth,
> As Mary smoors it,
> The vigilance of Brighid and Mary,
> Be upon the fire and upon the floor
> And over the whole household.
>
> Who stands on the grass outside
> Sun-bright Mary and her Son
> The mouth of God requested, the angel of God spoke:
> Angels of promise guard the hearth
> Until bright day visits the fire.
>
> —*Blessing on the Fire at Night,* a traditional Celtic poem

The battle to tame the fire-powers that reside at the base of one's etheric body is personified through the ages in such tales as St George rescuing the maiden from the dragon, and Horus (the son of the Egyptian Green Man) battling Set. Nigel Pennick defines the process of dragon taming as "the science of putting human habitats and activities into harmony with the visible and invisible world around us."[31]

St George is understood to be a representation of a pagan figure from Britain's mythic past, the Green Man. Researchers have confirmed that there are vastly more images of the Green Man sprouting nature forms from mouth, ears and nostrils in European churches and cathedrals than of Jesus. This indicates that the Green Man is a personification of a far older deity than that worshipped in the Christian rites, one which is associated with the ultimate power behind cosmic affairs and which carries out its work in harmony with Mother Nature.

In the old tales, when the last giant of his race, Geomagot ("Ge"), was slain at Plymouth the spot was marked by two turf figures, Gog and Magog, representing the giant and his foe. The practice of cutting effigies into the soil is very ancient and is demonstrated, for example, by the Cerne Abbas Giant in Dorset and various White Horse figures in the countryside, especially in southern England. Ge is the root word for George, indicating that the George figure was originally in myth a giant. The word Gorge also refers to the earth's subterranean realms, places of magic and enchantment reachable by deep fissures and chasms where one finds a mysterious world unknown to surface dwellers.

Og, the great giant of the pre-Christian era, is found in many place names, including upon the St. Michael ley: Ogborne St. George in Wiltshire (a site close to many very remarkable crop circle formations), and its neighbour Ogbourne St. Andrew, site of a neolithic mound. Both villages are situated just a few miles from the Avebury Temple complex. In Irish mythology Og becomes Ogma Sunface of the Tuatha Dé Danaan, Ireland's supernatural Tribe of the Gods. Ogma was the god of poetry, speech and eloquence and the inventor of Ogham writing, which is to be found inscribed as secret script in many megalithic stones and monuments, and said to be comprehensible only to priests and initiates.

When Edward III founded in 1348 the order of chivalry, St George of the Garter (formally called the Most Noble Order of the Garter), the king was personifying Perseus of Greek mythology who rescued the virgin, Andromeda, from a sea monster. Manly P. Hall stated that the

---

[31] Pennick, N., *The Ancient Art of Geomancy*, Thames and Hudson, 1979

Order's rituals were inspired by those of the Arthurian Cycle, which brings us to the story of Merlin in the context of the St Michael ley's extraordinary and enduring power.

Welsh mythology tells the tale of the two dragons and young Merlin. The *Mabinogion* describes an occasion when Britain was afflicted by three plagues. The first concerned the Coraniaid, a demonic people who harassed native Britons. The second was the plague of the white and red dragons. The third was caused by a giant who stole provisions from the royal stores. The king of Britain was Lludd Llaw Eraint (Lord of the Silver Hand), cognate with Nuada Airgetlám, the first king of the Tuatha Dé Danann. Lludd was the father of Gwyn ap Nudd, the Welsh king of the Tylwyth Teg (the Fair Folk) and ruler of Annwn whose palace lay beneath Glasonbury Tor.

The tale of Merlin and the dragons concerns Lludd and his brother, Llevelys, the King of Gaul. Every year on May Day eve a terrible shrieking scream was heard throughout the length and breadth of the land as the two dragons fought each other. The dreadful noise caused strong men to fall weak, women to lose their babies and the earth itself to become barren and infertile. Llevelys told his brother that to capture the dragons he must dig a pit in the exact centre of his kingdom, which Lludd determined after careful measurement lay in Oxford, a place of high importance in our journey along the St. Michael ley.

Lludd placed a cauldron of mead in the bottom of the pit and covered it with a sheet of satin. To begin with, the dragons took on the shape of terrifying animals and fought each other by the side of the pit. Then they turned into huge winged beasts and battled each other in the air. Finally exhausted, they turned into pigs, which fell to earth upon the flimsy sheet and tumbled into the cauldron. When they were drunk from the mead, Lludd wrapped the dragons in the sheet and placed them in a stone coffin. Llevelys then told Lludd to place the beasts in a pool in Dinas Emrys, a rocky woodland hillock in North Wales.

Centuries later King Vortigern, seeking a site to build a fortress chose Dinas Emrys and immediately encountered problems with its foundations. Needing a solution, Vortigern consulted wise men who said that the king needed to sacrifice a boy "not conceived by a mortal man" and sprinkle his blood in the foundations. Vortigern found such a being. His name was Myrddin (Merlin) Emrys. Merlin asked the king why he had been brought before him and received the reply that he was to be killed so that his blood mixed with the foundations would ensure the stability of the new citadel. Not intimidated by Vortigern, Merlin revealed to the king why the construction of the fortress would consequently be unsuccessful. He said that beneath Dinas Emrys was a pool in which two sleeping dragons kept waking in the tent that contained them and and then battling each other.

Merlin revealed the meaning of the mystery. He explained that the pool was the emblem of this world, and the tent that of Vortigern's kingdom. The Red Dragon represented the defenders of Britain, which would eventually rise up and repulse the White Dragon of the invading Anglo-Saxons. He told of the coming of Arthur to whom he referred as the Boar of Cornwall. Merlin told Vortigern that fate had given the ownership of the hill to himself and that the king must therefore build his royal fortress elsewhere. Vortigern followed Merlin's advice and eventually settled on Cair Guorthegirn.

Born from two opposing powers, Merlin had inherited the wisdom and knowledge of Light and Dark forces. Thus the symbolism of the dragon powers, the coming of Arthur, Guinevere and the Knights of the Round Table, and the creation of Camelot were drawn together in this tale of two dragons and Merlin's unique powers.

Geoffrey of Monmouth in his book *Historia regum Britanniae* (*History of the Kings of Britain*, 1137) says that Merlin was believed to have been the son of an incubus or demon and a human mother. This is just one of many stories concerning Merlin's bastard birth. A work of 1614, "Comte de Gabalis," states that Merlin's father was an elemental spirit of the order of sylphs who moved through the atmosphere in the form of a serpent, and that his mother was a Christian nun. The book "Merlin, Surnamed Ambrosius," published anonymously in London in 1813, says that Merlin "was conceived by the compression of a fantastical creature, without a body."

There are many stories of bastard births in the Arthurian cycle. One in the Mabinogion tells the tale of the young lad Elphin who in Arthur's time was granted a weir by his father so that he would make an easy living catching salmon. One day Elphin found a leather bag hanging from one of the weir posts. Inside was an infant of rare beauty. Elphin named the baby Taliesin, Welsh for shining or radiant brow. Little did Elphin know that the boy's mother was Ceridwen, the Goddess of the Cauldron. The boy had no father because he had been born from sorcery and enchantment. When Ceridwen gave birth she resolved to kill her son but she repented of her evil intent and placed him in a stream so that a stranger might find and care for him. When still a small boy, Taliesin was brought to the palace and sang a song for the king. Its verses are of interest in a study of Merlin's fabled beginnings and the metaphysical aspects of the Michael and Mary tradition:

"Primary chief bard am I to Elphin,
And my original country is the region of the summer stars;
Idno and Heinin called me Merddin,
At length every being will call me Taliesin.

I was with my Lord in the highest sphere,
On the fall of Lucifer into the depths of hell;
I have borne a banner before Alexander;
I know the name of the stars from north to south.

I was in Canaan when Absalon was slain.
I was in the court of Don before the birth of Gwydion.
I was in the place of the crucifixion of the merciful Son of God;
I have been three periods in the prison of Arianrod.

I have been in Asia with Noah in the ark,
I have seen the destruction of Sodom and Gomorrah.
I have been in India when Roma was built.
I am now come here to the remnant of Troia.

I have been with my Lord in the ass's manger,
I have strengthened Moses through the waters of Jordan;
I have been in the firmament with Mary Magdalene;
I have obtained the Muse from the cauldron of Ceridwen.

I shall be until the day of doom on the face of the earth;
And it is not known whether my body is fish or flesh."

The poem depicts Merlin as a timeless force who serves as both observer and participant in key historical occasions before and after Christ. He hails from the "region of the summer stars," a description mindful of the Glastonbury Zodiac's power to provide a magical gateway to worlds of enchantment.

Merlin is a wonder, neither fish nor flesh. He resembles aspects of both, an in-between creation that can ride the firmament and fly over land with equal ease. Another line in the poem—"I have been winged by the genius of the splendid crosier"—betrays Merlin's serpentlike nature, sustained and inspired by the magical waters of Ceridwen's cauldron.

Merlin is cognate with Lleu Llaw Gyffes, a boy born to Arianrod with a non-human form. Before the birth of Gwydion, Merlin was once in the Court of Don, the "Llys Dôn," the traditional Welsh name for the constellation Cassiopeia. Gwydion and Arianrod were two of the goddess Dôn's children. Arianrod's uncle Math fab Mathonwy tests his niece's virginity by asking her to step over his magician's rod. On doing this, Arianrod immediately gives birth to a young boy, Dylan ail Don, and also a blob-like entity which becomes Lleu Llaw Gyffes. Gwydion grabs the shapeless babe and places it in a chest. Before long it becomes a boy who grows at twice the normal rate; when he is four he is as big as an eight-year-old. Meanwhile, Arianrod is still smarting over her humiliation at Math's court. When Gwydion brings Lleu to court she places three successive *tyngeds* (taboos) over the boy who henceforth becomes his mother's captive on three occasions. Gwydion eventually succeeds in breaking the spells.

White Eagle described the story of Merlin and Arthur as the basis of the White Brotherhood's teachings. Merlin was the supreme magician and enchanter. Esoteric tradition tells a remarkable story of his origin and of the creation of Camelot. Subsequent to the end of Roman rule in Britain in the early fifth century AD, the White Brotherhood saw the need for a different form of spiritual energy to infiltrate this plane. It would be conveyed through inspirational people who had the ability to create and sustain dreams, who allowed individuals to imagine in a new way and impart to those on a quest an idea of what could be attained with an attitude sculpted from right thought, word and action. Hence, Camelot was created in a companion dimension to Earth to fulfil the requirement for a new and significant energy cycle.

To make it work, the Brotherhood sought an individual who was evolving in a very powerful way in the higher dimensions beyond the Earth experience. They were to be placed in a training ground, an etheric dimension out of the astral plane, closest to the physical Earth. Their role in the new cycle was to be the soul or nucleus of the new dimension and to tie it together. They would be taught how to create the vibration, the rituals and the sacraments necessary to provide the inspirational and mystical input to the new energy cycle of Camelot.

An individual came forward who had completed his reincarnational cycle in the dimension preceding the earth experience but, uniquely, had afterwards bypassed it to advance immediately to higher worlds of learning. This individual was Merlin, an extremely powerful energy from whose unique evolutionary status was created the story that he had travelled back through time via the energy of crystal to serve as the inspirational focus for Camelot.

Merlin knew upon arriving what he had to do. He began firstly to pull together those people who had converged with him into the new dimension. He focused upon finding one powerful individual who could thread the community together. He sought Arthur and trained him, teaching him all the vast knowledge he possessed, together working diligently to create the dream dimension, one with no written records so that it would catch people's imagination and be spoken of for centuries to come by those on their search for the Grail, in their quest to be an Arthur with a magical sword. Excalibur is the symbol of the cutting power of one's Higher Self and of a chalice in the form of a cross, rooted to the earth with its handles to the side and its head held high: a symbol of humanity never to be wielded in anger, judgement, frustration or fear lest it be returned to the lake whence it came.

All the while that Merlin was focused on the creation of the dream dimension of Camelot he was beset by very significant trials. Elphin's poem describes these eloquently. Because of the unique way in which Merlin had entered this plane he effectively became trapped in the energies of the Earth, which locked him in place as a restless wanderer, constantly phasing in and out of the time element of physical living, which was enormously challenging to him.

To this day, Merlin is said to wake from sleep in his glass tomb and travel ceaselessly backwards and forwards in time, appearing and creating any form he chooses until the day arrives when he is released from his earthbound imprisonment by, it is said, the power of a woman. Manly P. Hall in *The Orders of the Quest* tells of Merlin held prisoner in a house of air and mist and who finally vanished into the depths of the earth attended by nine Druid Bards, taking with him "The Thirteen Treaures of Britain."[32] Other legends say that Merlin lies in the mysterious depths of Park Wood at the very centre of the Glastonbury Zodiac.

White Eagle told his own story of the "mythical character of one King Arthur, and also to a teacher once known as Merlin." He described Merlin as an initiate of the mysteries of Egypt who was a birth-child of the fire of kundalini, born of a virgin mother and of a father supposedly of the underworld. He revealed that this story is a symbolic description of the potentialities of creation sealed within the human body. Under certain conditions these powers can be coaxed to come forward to bring about a mystical marriage, a result of the arising of the baser creative powers, seasoned with love and wisdom, to

[32] Dyrnwyn, the Sword of Rhydderch Hael, the Hamper of Gwyddno Garanhir, the Horn of Brân Galed, the Chariot of Morgan Mwynfawr, the Halter of Clydno Eiddyn, the Knife of Llawfrodedd the Horseman, the Cauldron of Dyrnwch the Giant, the Whetstone of Tudwal Tudglyd, the Coat of Padarn Beisrudd, the Crock and Dish of Rhygenydd Ysgolhaig, the Chessboard of Gwenddoleu ap Ceidio, the Mantle of Arthur in Cornwall, the Mantle of Tegau Gold-Breast, and the Stone and Ring of Eluned the Fortunate.

produce the initiate: the master of all the lower life. Gradually, Merlin unveiled certain profound truths and magical secrets to his young pupil, later known as King Arthur who formed the brethren of the Knights of the Round Table. White Eagle emphasised that although the story of Camelot is considered to be many hundreds of years old it is, in fact, as old as the world itself and intimately connected with the safeguarding and gradual dissemination of the White Brotherhood's original teachings. He interpreted the image of the twelve knights around the Round Table as the representation of the twelve signs of the Zodiac and the twelve Disciples of Christ.

The Round Table's Zodiac association is hinted at by the old saying that it could feed 4,000 people and 150 bulls. To each knight is allotted two places, one light and the other dark, so that each individual is represented as a dual being possessed of perfect balance and equilibrium. Merlin, the master sage, White Eagle explained, prophesised the future of humanity on the mystic isle of Britain and spoke of a divine power within man (a reference to the chakras), which would eventually arise and open his eyes at a time of crisis. It is said that Camelot endures (esoteric tradition refers to Camelot as "Came-a-lot" to signify its perennial nature), available to those with a healthy sense of quest adventure who seek initiation into the ancient mysteries.

After much reflection, I feel that the Camelot experience created by Merlin, aided by his deep connection with the unlimited magic of crystal, is the unseen engine that regulates the St Michael ley. In conjunction with Heinsch's "magic principle," it acts as a step-down transformer. Only then may the universal cosmic powers such as described by White Eagle and symbolised by Merlin's dragons be tamed and fixed in place by the power of one's inner Excalibur. At that moment, those who seek the Grail within may find insight and wisdom in these divine powers and forge a personal pathway to one's ideal of heaven on earth in life.

Given that there is a strong body of opinion that our planet is criss-crossed by an invisible crystalline lattice of earth energies, it is illogical to assume that the Michael and Mary currents under review in these pages begin and end in England. In fact, the work of a number of investigators has revealed the existence of other globally significant leys. One such has been dubbed the Michael/Mary-Apollo/Athena line that runs across Europe, oriented 60'11'' west of North. It shares a prime location with the English Michael and Mary ley.

In the late 1950s Jean Richer publicized the existence of a main axis of sacred sites in Greece: Athens, Delos, Camiros, Prasaias (Apollo's

Temple), Lindos on Rhodes, the Temple of Artemis at Agra, Eleusis, and Delphi where a federation of twelve tribes guarded the rights of Apollo. The line links not only Temples and sanctuaries of the god Apollo but also sites earlier dedicated to the goddess Artemis / Diana. Richer's brother, Lucien, followed up this work in 1977 in an article, "*The Saint Michael and Apollo axis*." His findings indicated that the alignment extends both southeast and northwest and connects seven monasteries from Ireland to Israel. The total length of the line is approximately 2000 km. Legend says that the line represents the sword blow inflicted by Archangel Michael on the Devil to send him packing.

To the southeast the alignment arrives at Mount Carmel in the Holy Land, 22 miles northwest of Megiddo (Armageddon). To the northwest from Delphi the line extends through Corfu (Island of Artemis, sister of Apollo), Monte Sant'Angelo (Monte Gargano) in Apulia in Italy (primary European sanctuary of the Archangel and the place of several apparitions), La Sacra di San Michele in Piedmont (Benedictine monastery at 1000m), Mont Saint-Michel of Normandy, Saint Michael's Mount in Cornwall and Skellig Michael, a small island seven miles west of the Iveragh Peninsula in County Kerry off the southeast coast of Ireland. The angle of axis is orientated SE-NW, corresponding to the zodiacal axis of Virgo-Pisces. Interestingly, the distance along the alignment between each of the three most important monasteries in Europe that venerate Saint Michael—at Piedmont, Normany and Conwall—is about 900 km.

Other crossing points along the Michael/Mary-Apollo/Athena line, include (west to east): Mayenne, Le Mans, Tours, Blois, Issoudun, Bourges, Sancoins, Nevers, Moulins, Digois, Charolles, St.Vincent des Pres, Cluny, Macon, Perouges, Lyons, Vienne, St. Beron, Bozel, San Michele (Castiglione di Garfagnana), Perugia, Dodona near Ioannina, and the Monastery of Saint Michael on the island of Symi.

There are at least three legends concerning Apollo that may refer to this line. One recalls how Abaris, a priest of Apollo, travelled on the god's golden arrow from the British Isles to Greece to visit Pythagoras (who is also said to have lived for a time on Mount Carmel). Another describes the return of Apollo from the land of the Hyperboreans (reputed to be Britain) to Delphi in a chariot drawn by swans. The third concerns what are known as the "Hyperborean Gifts." Packed in straw, these were sent from the Hyperboreans to Delos as tributes to Apollo. The nature of these mysterious gifts was not revealed.

None can tell what other alignments may be discovered around the globe in due course. For now, we shall return to Michael and Mary's journey in England. It would be tedious to list in the following chapters the hundreds of crossing points along the twin currents between Cornwall and Norfolk. On page 255 I have included a comprehensive but surely not exhaustive list. Going forward, having sketched an overview of the ley's distinguishing features, we will confine our interest to its unique waymarkers created in the far past by men and women of whom today we know little. We begin in England's beautiful West Country and its counties of Cornwall, Devon and Somerset, each rich in legendary tales of mystery and imagination.

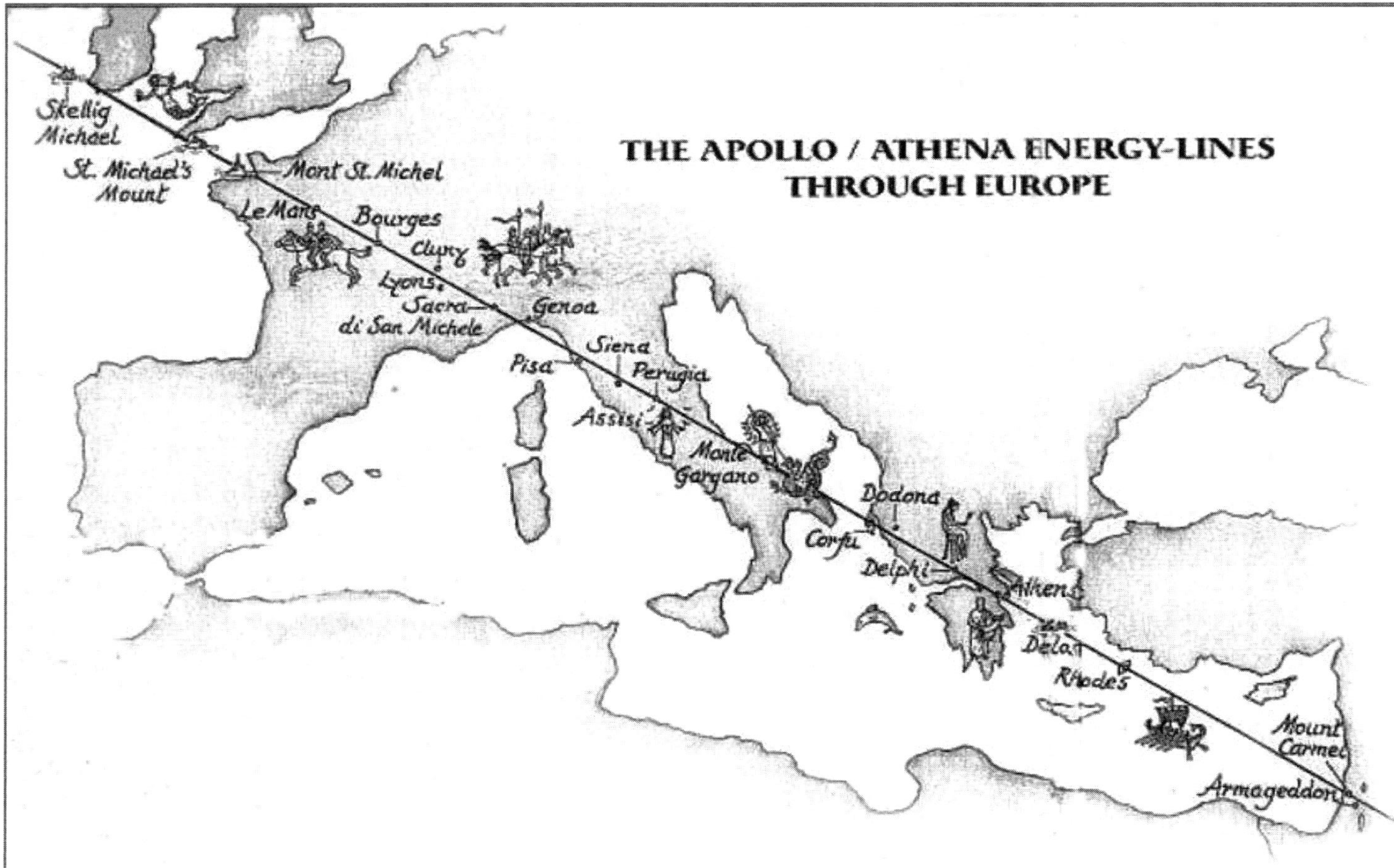

The Michael / Mary — Apollo / Athena energy line (courtesy Land and Spirit)

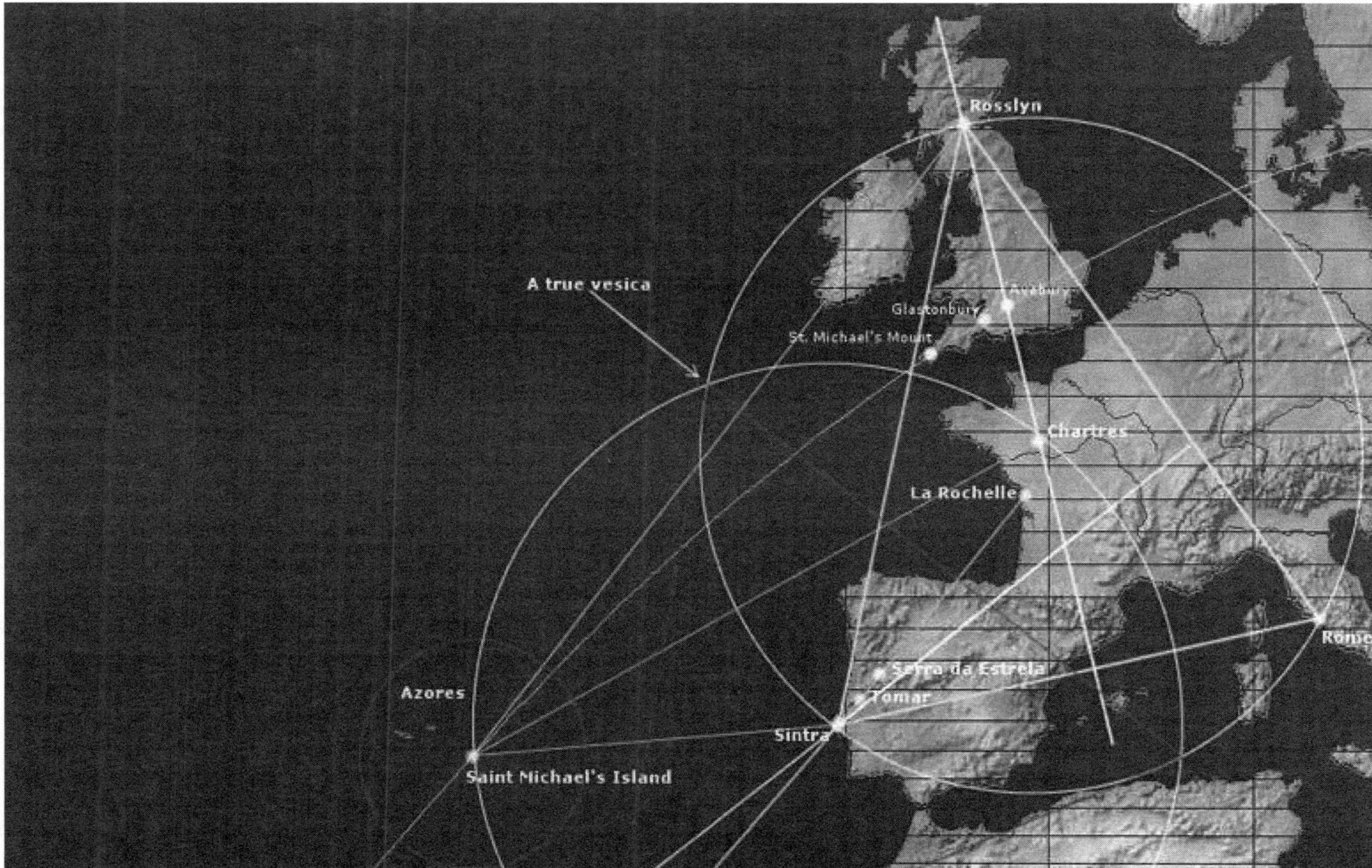

The Michael and Mary line as part of an extended global energy grid

Throughout the ages the light of the sun brothers has been centred within this mystic isle, a sacred domain, thousands and thousands years since. They travelled all over the earth but this isle was their home. They had great knowledge... of physics, of the proportions of matter. This knowledge and influence still lingers, hidden....

—Grace and Ivan Cooke, *The Light in Britain*

Chapter 3

England's West Country

"All things begin and end at Albion's ancient Druid rocky shore."

—William Blake

The West Country is a loosely defined area of southwestern England that traditionally encompasses the historic counties of Cornwall, Devon, Dorset and Somerset. It not only has a strong claim to accommodate a magical Gateway into Camelot but its counties feature substantially in a comprehensive investigation of the St Michael ley whose treasures are both visible and invisible. The ley begins its land journey across southern Britain at Carn-Lês-Boels in Cornwall (if one extends the line westwards across West Penwith from St Michael's Mount). It is the most westerly component of the West Country.

Cornwall is bordered to the north and west by the Celtic Sea, to the south by the English Channel, and is separated from Devon to the east by the River Tamar, which forms the border between them. The county forms a peninsula encompassing wild moorland and hundreds of sandy beaches, culminating at the promontory, Land's End. Cornwall's south coast, dubbed the Cornish Riviera, is home to picturesque harbour villages such as Fowey and Falmouth. Its north coast is lined with towering cliffs and seaside resorts like Newquay, which is renowned for surfing. Its most southwesterly point is Land's End and the southernmost, Lizard Point. Cornwall's administrative centre is Truro.

The county is a very popular tourist destination, visitors drawn by its sandy beaches and coves and its delicious fare, notably Cornish cream and ice cream, mouth-watering cream teas consisting of fresh scone, strawberry jam and clotted cream (always jam spread first unlike Devon's variety), and the famous 'D'-shaped Cornish pasty, the county's delicious "national" dish crimped on one side and stuffed with beef, swede, potato and onion.

Cornwall is recognized as one of the Celtic nations and was formerly a Brythonic kingdom. Its name in Cornish is Kernow. After the collapse of the Roman Empire, Cornwall (along with Devon, parts of Dorset and Somerset, and the Scilly Isles) was a part of the Brittonic kingdom of Dumnonia, ruled by chieftains of the Cornovii. Perhaps unsurprisingly, there exists a flourishing movement that is fiercely proud of its Celtic heritage and history and seeks the recognition of Cornwall as a nation apart from England.

An ancient trail runs from the far western tip of Cornwall to join the Ridgeway path at Avebury. This is a pilgrim route of great antiquity, which is currently being reinstated and dubbed the "Sunset Trail." The extension of this trail eastward follows the general course of the prehistoric Icknield Way into East Anglia.

Miller and Broadhurst[33] have suggested that Cornwall with its network of St. Michael sanctuaries has a special role to play in the dawning of a New Age. I do not doubt it. The St Michael energy, a Christianised personification of the pagan gods of Light and Dark, is very powerful. Legend tells the story of the fishermen of Mount's Bay who in 495 AD saw on a rocky ledge near the summit of a small island in the Bay the incandescent image of the Archangel Michael. Their shared vision became the start of a tradition of pilgrimage to one of the most important St Michael shrines in Britain.

Previous ages had recognized the Mount as a place of special power. Stories speak of it as the abode of a Giant called Cormoran who piled up the rocks to form the original mount. Giant's Well on the Mount commemorates the legend. Interestingly, during the rebuilding of the local church destroyed by the same earthquake in 1275 that toppled the church of St Michael on Glastonbury Tor, monks found a skeleton of a male estimated to have been eight-feet tall.

In the old Cornish language the Mount was known as Carreg Luz en Kuz, "hoar rock in the wood," hoar in Celtic often referring to standing stones or menhirs. Recent investigation has confirmed the presence of petrified stumps of various tree types in the shifting sands of Mount Bay, indicating that at one time the area was dry land before becoming reclaimed by the sea. The area was known also as a great centre of Druidic learning and worship, formerly Din Sul, "Citadel of the Sun," a description that closely tallies with White Eagle's remarks about the nature of the ancient Sun-Men's activities in England.

Two ancient rites are enacted annually in Cornwall—the wild, cavorting Padstow 'Obby 'Oss celebration and the Helston Furry Dance. The former is held in the seaside town of Padstow. The townsfolk dress in white with blue or red sashes and scarves, with

[33] ibid

posies of cowslips and bluebells tucked into their hats. The accordionists pick out the tunes and the townsfolk dance energetically around the Maypole in the square. Presently, the hobbyhorse, the Oss, appears dancing wildly. Its great whirling disc of a body is built around thick spars of oak fashioned into a boat-shaped frame covered with black oilcloth. Its conical dragon-like head mask is decorated in red and white coloured ribbons. The Oss is led by the shamanistic, cavorting figure of the Teazer waving his magic wand. Suddently, black-skirted maidens appear from under the Oss. As the ritual unfolds, the girls try to dodge the oncoming Oss as if to escape his spring fertility intentions. Finally, the spinning and whirling Oss winds down to a gradual stop as if mimicking the passing of spring and the gradual emergence of summer. The Oss dies and the onlookers intone: "Oh, where is St George, where is he-o? He's out in his longboat all on the sea-o!" Reborn, the Oss springs up and to the delight of the crowd resumes his crazy dance. All is well: the Seasons have been revivified with fresh rhythm and vigour.

Every year in Helston on 8 May (coinciding with the Feast of St. Michael) the stage is set for the enactment of an ancient rite, the Hal-an-Tow. This is Furry or Flora Day. The town's patron saint is Archangel Michael. Local legend describes the occasion when St Michael was carrying a stone to block the doorway to hell. When the devil made his attack, Michael was forced to drop the stone, hence the place-name "Helston." The stone is said to have been built into the wall of a church. Like the Oss ritual, the Hal-an-Tow is a celebration of the passing of winter and the arrival of spring. As the townsfolk gather they hear whistles and shrieks. Revellers garlanded in green with flowers and leaves, decked in the same fashion as the local cottages, emerge dancing. Among them is St George in silver dress with a Templar surcoat embroidered with the saint's red and white flag. A dragon is also dancing. St Michael, dressed in scarlet and gold, appears and joins St George who is battling the dragon. Michael helps him deliver the *coup de grâce*. But what is this? The wound is not fatal. Just like the reborn Oss the dragon lives, thus exemplifying the natural balance of cosmic order. Nature's year begins anew.

Carn-Lês-Boels, an Iron Age promontory or "cliff castle" that lies on a headland between Porthgwarra and Land's End on Nanjizal Bay is the first westerly location in England where the ley's male and female currents co-exist. In fact, according to Miller and Broadhursts' findings there are only 21 such significant nodal points along the entire length of the Michael and Mary ley.

The Michael current proceeds to St Michael's Mount, as does Mary's but not before winding through Ailsa Holy Well, Boscawen-Un and Penzance. Ailsa Holy Well, sacred to the Earth Goddess, is one of the most famous wells in Cornwall. In the past it was used by mothers to help strengthen their rickety children. It was also used for divination to determine the most auspicious occasion when a maiden and her sweetheart may be united. The stone circle at Boscawen-Un and its nearby 11-foot-tall Blind Fidler menhir was a favoured meeting place for the Druidic Bards. Penzance, located in the shelter of Mount's Bay, is the most westerly major town in Cornwall.

Continuing their dowsing work after moving on from Mount's Bay, Miller and Broadhurst traced a further half-dozen points, one of which is the Victorian chapel of Leedstown, a small village a few miles inland from the Mount. The vicar at Leedstown surprised the pair when he remarked that ecclesiastic authorities, demonstrating surprising knowledge and respect for pagan powers would often build churches on energy lines in order to keep the flow pure. The researchers found that the six points coincided with a fair degree of accuracy along a straight line drawn through St Michael's Mount at the generally accepted angle of the ley of 27° north of east. They noted that the current under investigation in this initial phase of their explorations, the Michael path, was a band of energy roughly twenty paces wide.

From the Bay, Michael makes his way without passing through places of note to the currents' next crossing point at the Iron Age hill-fort of Resugga Castle on the opposite side of the River Fal, where once were practised rituals to invoke the Earth Spirit. Mary's journey to the ancient earthwork, however, takes her through village churches at Germoe, Old Kea located in a creek of the Truro River, and St Michael Penkevil three miles southeast of Truro.

Michael and Mary then meet once more at Cornwall's former county town of Lostwithiel, the nodal point being St Bartholomew's Church with its 14th century Breton-style spire. Lostwithiel is situated in a beautiful wooded valley at the tidal reach of the River Fowey in central Cornwall. The town's name comes from two Cornish words meaning the place at the end of the woodland.

Sixteen miles to the northeast the two currents converge at an area dominated by the Hurlers and the nearby Cheesewring at Stowes Hill. The former is a group of three Bronze Age stone circles in the parish of St Cleer, half-a-mile west of Minions, a village rich in history, heritage and legend, which accommodates the highest public house in Cornwall. The granite stones have been dressed to shape and have roughly level tops. A floor of granite crystals was discovered in the middle ring. British folklore has many tales that describe how men and women were turned to stone for various wrongdoings, such as non-religious activity undertaken on a Sunday. The Hurlers' name derives from the legend that the three circles were once men turned to stone for sporting on the Sabbath.

The Cheesewring Quoit, one mile northwest of the village, is a rock outcrop of granite slabs formed by weathering. The name derives from the resemblance of the piled slabs to a "cheesewring," a press-like device once used to make cheese. Legend relates that the Cheesewring Quoit's bizarre heap of rocks was the dwelling place of a druid who possessed an inexhaustible cup of gold. Another stone close to the Cheesewring is known as the Druid's Chair. The story goes that the kindly Druid offered the cup's contents to thirsty travellers until one decided to drink the cup dry. Unable to drain it to the bottom, the traveller became enraged and rode off in such a fury that his horse fell, dashing its rider upon the rocks where the cup was buried with him. This would have remained a story of legend, except in 1818 a nearby cairn called King Arthur's Grave was opened and a gold cup, dated to 1500 BC, was found there. Another legend tells of a golden boat found in a cairn near the Cheesewring. Both the Hurlers circles and the Cheesewring tor lie on the eastern flank of Bodmin Moor.

The two currents wing onwards for another 14 miles or so before enjoying at St. Michael's Church at Brentor on Dartmoor their next assignation. We have now passed from Cornwall into Devon, a county reaching from the Bristol Channel in the north to the English Channel in the south. Its county city is Exeter. Devon derives its name from Dumnonia. During the periods of the British Iron Age, Roman Britain and the early Middle Ages, it was home to the Dumnonii Brittonic Celts. The Anglo-Saxon settlement of Britain resulted in the partial assimilation of Dumnonia into the Kingdom of Wessex during the eighth and ninth centuries AD. In 936, King Æthelstan set the western boundary with Cornwall at the River Tamar.

The north and south coasts of Devon feature cliffs and sandy shores. The county's many bays contain seaside resorts, fishing towns and ports. The coastline is known as the English Riviera. The rural inland terrain is mostly hilly and has a lower population density than many other parts of England. Dartmoor is the largest open space in southern England. Its moorland, made famous in Arthur Conan Doyle's *The Hound of the Baskervilles*, extends across a large expanse of granite bedrock. Like Cornwall, the county is also renowned for its delicious produce, not least the ever popular Devon cream tea, which, contrary to its neighbour's version, is served by spreading first the clotted cream *then* the jam, an important distinction indeed!

For centuries Dartmoor folklore and legends have encompassed tales of pixies, ghosts, witchcraft and high strangeness, all passed down through the generations via fireside stories, books and local tradition. There is no question that Dartmoor and its landscape has helped fire people's beliefs and imaginations. From the thick mists that suddenly appear and roll across the moor to the dark, bottomless mires and the craggy granite tors, each lends an air of mystery and magic, all ripe for associated legends and tales. Features such as the still treacherous Fox Tor Mire and the atmospheric Bellever Tor remind one that Conan Doyle walked for 16-18 miles a day across Dartmoor to scout the most appropriate locations for his timeless tale. Near the mire one finds a lichen-covered granite cross, which commemorates the gruesome end of Childe the Hunter, an 11th century Saxon earl and Lord of the Manor of Plymstock who became stranded by a blizzard. In an attempt to stay alive, Childe disembowelled his pony and crawled inside scrawling a message in blood to say that whoever buried his body in hallowed ground could claim his estate. He then froze to death in his pony's hollowed out cadaver. The enterprising monks of Tavistock Abbey, not ones to miss a trick, promptly recovered his body and claimed the land.

Conan Doyle's character, Sir Hugo Baskerville who abducted and murdered a woman in the mires and was then killed by a huge demonic hound, is doubtless based on Squire Richard Cabell, an unprincipled monster who lived in Brook Manor, north of Buckfastleigh, in the seventeenth century. The squire would gallop across Dartmoor accompanied by hounds the size of ponies. Local lore relates that when Cabell died the villagers buried him in Holy Trinity Church in Buckfastleigh. That very night a ghastly phantom fire-breathing pack of dogs came baying across the moor to howl at his tomb.

In Risdon's early sixteenth century "Survey of Devon," he describes Brentor as a "high rocky place on the top whereof stands a church, full bleak and weather beaten, all alone, as it were forsaken." From earliest times this site, an Iron Age fortification and settlement, has been used as a beacon serving to guide mariners into Plymouth. Local traditions tell how the foundations of the church were originally laid at the foot of the mount but the devil moved the stones to the summit. When the church was dedicated to St. Michael, the Archangel himself appeared and hurled such a tremendous mass of rock upon the devil that he never reappeared. A former inscription on the south wall of the church, referred to in the nineteenth century, read: "On this rock I will built my church, and the gates of hell shall not prevail against it."

A celebrated Bronze Age feature on Dartmoor is the stone circle near the village of Belstone known as the Nine Maidens, also called the Seventeen Brothers. The origin of "Belstone" may derive from the old Phoenician tin trade. The Phoenicians worshipped Baal, the god of life and fertility; "Belstone" represents "Baal's ton"—"Baal's settlement." Dartmoor's stone circles are said to have been made "when there were wolves on the hills, and winged serpents in the low lands."

As with the Hurlers' unfortunate menfolk, tradition has it that Nine Maidens were turned into stone and condemned to dance every noon for eternity as a punishment for dancing on the Sabbath. To this day they are said to dance at noon. It has been suggested that nine does not refer to the number but is a derivative of "none" or "noon," which was originally at 3 p.m. and the ninth hour of the day in the Roman and ecclesiastical calendars. Later, when the church service called Nones was moved to 12 p.m., the term "noon" came to mean midday.

The Nine Maidens circle functioned as a burial chamber (a cist), although the cairn has since been robbed and the cist, known locally as a kistvaen, destroyed. The circle is incomplete and sixteen stones remain. None are much higher than three feet and the diameter of the circle is approximately twenty-one feet. In a similar tale to the grisly fate of the Nine Maidens, local lore speaks of the instant petrification suffered by seventeen irreligious brothers. The ringing of the nearby church bells brings the victims to life. The Nine Maidens circle is romanticised in Philpotts' poem:

> And now at every Hunter's Moon
> That haggard cirque of stones so still
> Awakens to immortal thrill
> And seven small maidens in silver shoon
> Twixt dark of night and white of day
> Twinkle upon the sere old heath
> Like living blossoms in a wreath
> Then shrink again to granite grey.
> So blue-eyed Dian shall ever dance
> With Linnette, Bethkin, Jennifer,
> Arisa, Petronell and Nance
>
> —*the Book of Avis,* Eden Philpotts

Spinster's Rock on Dartmoor at Drewsteignton

Michael and Mary next come together 32 miles northeast in Crediton, birthplace of missionary St Boniface, born in 680 AD and baptised as Wynfrith. One of his most celebrated acts took place in the German province of Hesse, a place steeped in paganism. Boniface declared to the townsfolk that he would destroy their gods. Armed with an axe he approached a sacred tree, the giant oak of Geismar dedicated to Thor. After much effort Boniface felled the oak, its branches falling to the ground in the shape of a cross. In its descent, the falling branches crushed every other tree around except a single small fir tree, an act that may represent the origin of the Christmas tree tradition.

The two currents meet precisely in the Norman tower of Crediton's former 10th century cathedral that was dedicated to St Mary. The base of the ruined tower is now the site of Crediton parish church, more formally called the "Church of the Holy Cross and the Mother of Him who hung thereon," a poignant reference to Christ whom legend depicts as a visitor to England in the company of Joseph of Arimathea, described in mediaeval genealogies as an uncle to one of Jesus' parents.

After a thirty-five mile flight in which the two dragons each pursue their own course, they cross paths in Creech St Michael Church in Somerset, a county about which we have much to say. Somerset borders

Gloucestershire (the line of separation traditionally demarcated by the River Avon), Bristol to the north, Wiltshire to the east, Dorset to the southeast and Devon to the southwest. It is bounded to the north and west by the Severn Estuary and the Bristol Channel, its coastline facing southeast Wales. Somerset's county town is Taunton. It is a delightful rural county with a gentle climate, extensive rolling hills (chiefly the Blackdown Hills, Mendip Hills, Quantock Hills and Exmoor National Park), large flat expanses of land including the Somerset Levels, and ubiquitous apple and pear orchards.

There is evidence of human occupation from Paleolithic times and of subsequent settlement by the Celts, Romans and Anglo-Saxons. The city of Bath is famous for its Georgian architecture and is a UNESCO World Heritage Site. As might be expected, Somerset offers its own distinct culinary delights, especially its world-famous Cheddar cheese and its farmhouse cider that comes in many variations, the most potent being scrumpy. Traditionally, "scrumpy" referred to what was otherwise called "rough," a strong, harsh cider made from unselected apples. These days the term is more often used to distinguish from mass-produced brands locally made artisan ciders produced in smaller quantities and using traditional methods. The first recorded mention of cider presses as a source of income in Somerset is in a Royal Charter of 1230 granted to the Bishop of Bath, although it is known that the Romans grew apples in Britain centuries earlier.

Dragon tales feature strongly in Somerset legend. One such is the story of the Shervage Dragon or "Great Vurm," which had a girth greater than three oak trees. Its haunt was Shervage Wood on the border of the Quantock Hills. The dragon slept by day and caught and devoured its prey at night. The Vurm was not fussy. It ate livestock, ponies and the occasional human. A shepherd and two gypsies counted among its victims. Legend tells of the stranger from Stogumber village in the Brendon Hills who entered the wood to gather worts (berries). He was doing a favour for a woman from neighbouring Crowcombe so she could make her delicious bilberry pies. The Stogumber man knew nothing of the dragon legend but when he sat down to drink cider and eat bread and cheese given him by the woman he saw the log he was sitting on begin to squirm. Quickly, he swung his axe and split the log clean in two whereupon both ends began to bleed. The two halves of the dragon then ran in different directions, one towards Bilbrook and the other to Kingston St. Mary. Because the two parts could not meet up they were unable able to grow back together and the serpent died. Today in the Church of the Holy Ghost at Crowcombe visitors can admire its oak panels. One is carved with the image of a double-headed winged dragon being speared by two naked men. Another is carved with a Green Man depicted with branches heavy with berries pouring from its mouth and two club-wielding figures rising from its head.

Lying three miles east of Taunton is Creech St Michael village, its name deriving from the Celtic word crug, "hill." Parts of the parish church, located at the southern end of the village, date back to the 12th century. Next door to the church stands the former Riverside Inn, which was once a monastic building where the monks brewed their ales. The church vicar told Miller and Broadhurst that he often walked into the old part of the church through the south porch to enjoy its aroma of burning incense, a peculiar characteristic of the place, he explained, because he never used incense in his services. A groundfloor arch in the church perhaps signifies the one time presence of a crypt (local stories speak of underground tunnels). The official guide states that it is likely that the church was bult on a former site of pagan worship. Interestingly, the lines of intersection of the Michael and Mary currents take the form of a true Celtic Cross.

After a seven-mile journey one arrives at the pair's next tryst along the ley, at the spot where the altar would have been in the now ruined St Michael's Church on the summit of Burrow Mump, a hill and historic site that overlooks Southlake Moor in the village of Burrowbridge. Both words "burrow" and "mump" mean hill. The hill is 75-feet high and stands at a strategic point where the River Tone and the old course of the River Cary join the River Parrett above the low-lying Somerset Levels. Burrow Mump, a scheduled monument, is also known as St Michael's Borough or Tutteyate. It stands at a strategic location overlooking the point where the River Tone and the old course of the River Cary join the River Parrett.

Although there is some evidence of Roman visitation, the first fortification of the site was the construction of a Norman motte. It has been called King Alfred's Fort; however, there is no proof of use by Alfred the Great. A church dedicated to St Michael was built on the hill in the 15th century to replace the ruins of a former Norman castle. This church survived Henry VIII's Dissolution of the Monasteries but was partly destroyed during the English Civil War a hundred years later. The ruined church on top of the hill was built in 1793 to reclaim the site in honour of St Michael. The Mump's red soil poses a problem for archaeologists because it is not found locally and it is speculated that the hill may be an artificial construct. From the top of Burrow Mump, Glastonbury Tor can be seen on the horizon twelve miles distant. The axis of the Mump is aligned on the Tor, its extension marking the old Pilgrims' Way and forming the axis of the Tor's labyrinth. The lower western slopes of the Tor were once the location for the annual Tor Fair held on the second Monday in September and which continued for at least a fortnight. Near this site are the fragmented remains of an old megalith, the Living Rock, which has been found by dowsers to retain an active power early in the morning and late at night. Enigmatic, mysterious, enchanted, haunted, magical, charismatic, transcendant, harmonious Glastonbury is the next place of convergence for our serpentine partners' trans-Albion journey.

Glastonbury—Avalon, Yns-witrin (Isle of Glass or Crystal Isle), the Shining Isle, Gateway to the Underworld, Doorway to Fairyland, Centre of the Mysteries, New Jerusalem—has always been a place of great religious importance but it is so much more than a keystone in the earliest foundations of the Christian faith. Its metaphysical credentials reveal the ancient site to be a receptor and transmitter of cosmic energies, the focal point of Universal Creative power, the scale of which is beyond human understanding. There are few such sites on the Earth's surface and England is blessed to play host, arguably, to the most powerful of them all. Glastonbury is a relatively small Somerset town occupying a virtual island that rises from the surrounding marshy countryside, which in the distant past was an inland sea.

Burrow Mump and St Michael Church

The town lies between the Bristol Channel and the Mendips and the Poldens, two low ranges of hills. An old woman told psychic Dion Fortune in the early 1930s that she could remember water coming up to St Benignus Church when the great dykes burst their banks on Bridgwater Bay twenty miles away.

When the Ice Age glaciers receded in England roughly 12,000 years ago the re-population of the southern part of the country became possible. However, the Tor and its foothills remained wholly insulated by an inlet of sea from the Bristol Channel. These waters were dotted with tiny islands where gathered tribal settlers who navigated between the islets in canoes and coracles. Archaeologists have found evidence of these lake villages and their inter-connecting timber causeways.

Glastonbury's landscape is rich in remarkable features: a holy hill (the Tor) from where Gwynn ap Nudd rode out with his faithful hound Dormath to collect souls, holy wells, the ruins of the once greatest abbey in Europe, earthworks and stones infused with unquenched power, ley lines, a labyrinth, and, not least, the zodiac, the key to the Avalonian complex at Glastonbury to which we turn in the next chapter. Between the Tor and the town is the dome of Chalice Hill and its famous well, intimately linked in legend with the Holy Grail.

During the dowsing survey of the St Michael line, Broadhurst and Miller made a remarkable addition to our understanding of the esoteric significance of Glastonbury Tor.[34] The first line that they followed was positively charged (Michael) and it made a complicated spiral pattern on the sides of the Tor, including a long thin loop around its level summit. When they later returned to Glastonbury on the trail of the second line of opposite polarity (Mary), they found that this too made for the Tor and traced a pattern around it. The main feature of this second, feminine design was a bowl-shaped curve around the eastern flank of the hill, opposite the loop formed by the Michael current. Putting the two shapes together on a plan of the Tor produced a coherent and striking symbol, an image of sexual union. The discovery on the Tor of this symbol, created by positive and negative currents of energy, echoes the tradition that Glastonbury Tor was (and remains) a repository of the Old Knowledge and an important centre that drew truthseekers from far and wide for initiation into the ancient mysteries.

Labyrinths have traditionally been associated with the function of opening by magical means, an "open sesame," a door or gateway to other times and places. A probable date for the construction of the maze

---

[34] ibid

is the third millennium BC. As a religious structure comparable to Silbury, the maze indicates just how far religion in Neolithic times was dominated by the cult of a Great Goddess or Earth Mother. Certainly, the profile of Glastonbury hill, viewed from a certain angle, resembles a recumbent female figure with the Tor forming the left breast.

> *(Britons) are the inheritors of an ancient wisdom, a great light... Britain was once a part of Hyperborea and, later, Atlantis. Because many ancient peoples journeyed here and established mystery centres of great light and power, in Britain today is a great spiritual power which can and will wake in the future through all the people of these islands.*
>
> —Grace and Ivan Cooke, *The Light in Britain*

The Tor is also reputed to be the entrance to the land of the Fairies, specifically the abode of Gwyn ap Nudd, ruler of the Tylwyth Teg who is said to rule during the winter months. At Samhain (Hallowe'en), when the veil between the worlds is most diaphanous, Nudd emerges from the Tor to take his throne as Winter King to reign until Beltane (May Day).

Legend has it that one day St Collen, alleged converter of the Greeks to Christianity, came to "the mountain of Glastonbury" and made his hermitage in a quiet place amongst the rocks. One day he overheard two locals talking about Gwynn ap Nudd, whom they described as King of Annwn and master of the Fairies. Collen admonished them for speaking heathen words but they told him that he would have to answer for his haughty attitude. Subsequently, Gwynn ap Nudd summoned Collen three times to meet him on the Tor at midday. Eventually, Collen agreed but brought with him a flask of holy water. On his arrival, Collen saw the fairest castle he had ever seen. Around it were fair folk, musicians with all manner of instruments, horses with boys on their backs and girls of noble aspect.

A fine man bade Collen enter, saying that the king was awaiting him at the dinner table. Enthroned on a golden chair, Gwynn ap Nudd offered Collen fine food and drink which he ungraciously refused. Gwynn boasted of his courtiers' multicoloured clothing, red on one side, blue on the other. "Their dress is good of its kind," answered Collen, "but the red is that of flames, and the blue that of ice," a reference to the mediaeval belief that Hell had both ice and fire. Collen then sprinkled the holy water around him and everything disappeared, leaving the saint standing alone on top of the bleak Tor.

Many vistors to Glastonbury ask if the Tor is artificial. The answer is that it is a natural hill, shaped over time by human hands. A circle of approximately 30 miles radius would encompass the entirety of what may be seen from the top of the Tor. On a clear day it can be seen in the northwest from the Black Mountains in Wales' Brecon Beacons eastern flank and from the hill of South Cadbury to the southeast.

The Tor has around its sides a number of terraces, one above another. According to a theory put forward in an article in 1968 by Irishman Geoffrey Russell, the terraces are remnants of a maze. In 1944 Russell experienced a vision in which he saw a figure of concentric rings and believed it to be an image of the brain. Later he came across a diagram of the Cretan labyrinth, a representation of which is carved on a rock in Tintagel, and recognized it as the "brain" figure he had seen in the vision. Labyrinths then became Russell's consuming interest. In the esoteric tradition, the labyrinth is symbolic of a both an inner and an external journey. The latter could be a pilgrimage of high renown such as to Jerusalem, while the inner journey symbolises the soul's passage through life, death and rebirth.

Equipped with these transcendental insights, when Russell first saw the ringed terraces on Glastonbury Tor in 1964 it was not a big leap forward to construe them as a great three-dimensional maze, not the puzzle variety but in the sense of a long, twisting approach to a centre or a labyrinth. Russell had a survey made of the Tor and a model constructed. It was evident from his studies that the rings were seven in number which joined up to form a continuous pathway towards the top of the Tor, accurately reproducing the twists and turns of the seven-layered labyrinth which symbolized the classical Mysteries. The path seems to end before getting to the top, the spot where it suddenly disappears being marked with a large, oval-shaped stone known locally as the egg-stone.

The motif of a seven-tiered mountain has many correspondences in global cultures. Asian mythologies refer to the high dwelling place of the gods, which the Hindus called Mem. It occupied the centre of the world and was often depicted as a mountain with seven sides or levels. In Babylon the great Ziggurat or temple had seven tiers. Dante portrays Purgatory as a seven-tiered mountain. The fertility rites of Ishtar are represented in the Dance of the Seven Veils. It is argued that the labyrinth's passage round the Tor is a three-dimensional adaptation of a more complex pattern found in antiquity. It is likened to the Cretan spiral as in the legend of Ariadne and the Minotaur but its form or mirror-image has been found on a 7th century BC Etruscan vase, on a pillar at Pompeii, and on rocks at Tintagel and in Co. Wicklow in Ireland. It is known in Wales as Caerdroia: the mazes of "Troy Town."

The "Otherworldly" aspect of the Tor appears to be referenced in an allegory of the Rosicrucian philosophy. In "A Commentary on the Chymical Wedding of Christian Rosenkreutz, Anno 1459" by Margaret Bennell and Isabel Wyatt, there is a description of Rosenkreutz's voyage to the Temple of Olympus, which is located on a square island in the "sea of the etheric." Housed in a Tower on the island is a hidden laboratory where work is carried out on the regeneration of Man. Like the Tor, the Tower has a ground plan of seven interlacing circles. The "square island" conjures images of the metaphysical model of New Jerusalem, while the etheric sea is redolent of the underworld of Annwn and its magical Cauldron.

Local sources refer to a 17th century story that beneath the Tor is a tunnel leading into a large cave with two pools of natural spring water which flow to Chalice Well, also known as the Red Spring. The cave was a place of druidic initiation. The account adds that at one time there were steps from the top of the Tor which also led down into the cave. Water issues from the spring at a rate of 250,000 gallons per day and has never failed, even during drought. Iron oxide deposits give its waters a reddish hue. Like the hot springs in the nearby City of Bath's Roman baths, the water is reputed to possess healing qualities.

Wells often feature in Celtic mythology as gateways to the spirit world. In the case of Chalice Well, the overlapping of the inner and outer worlds is represented by its cover, which was designed by the church architect and archaeologist Frederick Bligh Bond and presented as a gift after the Great War in 1919. Within the design of the lid are two interlocking circles that constitute the symbol known as the Vesica Piscis. A spear or a sword bisects these two circles, a possible reference to Excalibur. Foliage in the design represents the Glastonbury Thorn.

Christian mythology suggests that Chalice Well marks the site where Joseph of Arimathea placed the chalice, which had caught drops of Christ's blood at the Crucifixion. To Christians, the red of the water represents the Cross's rusty iron nails. According to local lore, the chalybeate waters from Chalice Well have three attributes in common with human blood: the waters are red; the water coagulates in the fashion of haemoglobin; and the water is warm.

The subterranean water from the well is often warmer than the surface ground temperature. Even in winter, roses near the well bloom when other plants and flowers further away do not. Indeed, the Holy Thorn Tree, also known as the Glastonbury Thorn (*Crataegus*

Monogyna praecox), blooms in the Chalice Well garden every Christmas. The local legend says that this tree took root when Joseph of Arimathea drove his staff into the ground near the well.

Mirza Basheer-ud-Din Mahmood Ahmad in his commentary on the Quran considered the possibility that the story of the Seven Sleepers is a conflation of an earlier legend about a visit by Joseph of Arimathea to Glastonbury, with the cave being a metaphor for England. In both Christian and Islamic tradition the Seven Sleepers story describes how in around 250 AD during the persecutions by the Roman emperor Decius seven young men were accused of following Christianity. They were given some time to recant their faith but refused, choosing instead to give their worldly goods to the poor and retire to a mountain cave to pray. Decius ordered the mouth of the cave to be sealed. Once inside, the seven martyrs fell asleep. In 447, during the reign of Theodosius II, a landowner, planning to use the cave as a cattle pen, unsealed it and found the sleepers inside. They awoke, imagining that they had slept but one day. One out of their number was sent to the nearby city of Ephesus to obtain food. The Bishop of Ephesus interviewed the sleepers who told their miracle story and then died praising God.

The story of the arrival of St Joseph of Arimathea is by far the most striking of the Glastonbury legends. The tale recounts how shortly after the Crucifixion St Joseph, one of a party of twelve Christian holy men came to Britain and arrived at Glastonbury. Some versions say the date was 63 AD, others 37, the latter more likely as it was only a few years after the Crucifixion. St Joseph was accompanied by the sister of Veronica, the woman who wiped the face of Christ when He fell under the weight of the Cross on His way to Calvary. Later, the account developed into the story that Jesus had left an image of His face on the cloth. This napkin became the Vera Icon, the True Representation of Christ, from which the name Veronica derives. Joseph planted his staff upon Wearyall Hill where it took root and blossomed into the holy thorn, a species according to botanists that comes only from the Levant.

In Oliver Cromwell's day an overly pious Roundhead cut down Joseph's tree. Fortunately, monks in the Abbey gardens had taken cuttings and these were used to grow back a scion of the original thorn, a descendant that provides to this day blossoms at Christmas for the high altar of St John's.

Below the hill Joseph decided to build a church to settle his community of first Christians. He obtained from King Arviragus a grant of land consisting of 12 hides (1440 acres) and on it was founded a church dedicated to the Virgin Mary. Just as in ancient Delphi where a federal assembly of 12 tribes administered the rights of Apollo, from this time forward the Twelve Hides held a privileged status. John Michell's studies of the dimensions of Glastonbury Abbey strongly suggested to him that St Joseph of Arimathea's settlement was constructed in accordance with an ancient scheme of cosmology, which Bligh Bond had proposed was in the design of a pre-Christian temple that had formerly occupied the same site.

According to Michell[35] when Celtic missionaries chose a location to establish a Christian presence, their first task was to build an oratory at the centre of their ring of cells. Thereafter, the priests would maintain a ceaseless vigil accompanied by a perpetual chant, a sacred intonation whose magical effect was to weave an enchanting spell over the surrounding landscape. Accounts speak of a perpetual choir comprising 12 evangelising choristers singing 12-section plainchant, a custom that originated in the East and later adopted by the Druids, who themselves were an outgrowth from Britain's early Celtic settlers. This music also had an astrological aspect that was reflected physically in the landmarks and contours of the surrounding countryside. Each segment had its own symbols, music and myth to represent its unique one-twelfth part of the astrological cycle. William of Malmesbury called Glastonbury's temple area a "heavenly sanctuary on earth."[36]

Manly P. Hall[37] describes the Druids' special veneration of the nature spirits to whom they made offerings. The Druids' chief deities were Hu and Ceridwen who shared the same characteristics as Isis and Osiris and Bacchus and Ceres. In the mystery enactments, Hu, the Sun God, was ritually slain and after a number of strange ordeals and mystic ritual was restored to life. In exercising these rites, the Druids demonstrated their faith's shared characteristics with the ancient cult of Mithras, which has both a male and female aspect.

As Mithras, the god is Lord of the Sun; as Mithra, the goddess represents Nature, which is fruitful when bathed in the glory of the Sun. Like Druidism, the rites of Mithras were performed in caves. These were adorned with the zodiac constellations, Cancer and Capricorn, powerful symbols of the summer and winter solstices for souls descending into this life or passing from it on their ascent to the Gods. Cancer is the gate of descent and Capricorn ascent. Michell[38] wrote of the seven islands of special significance in the 12 hides region of

---

[35] ibid,

[36] Michell, J. and Rhone, C., *Twelve Tribe Nation*, Inner Traditions, 1991

[37] Hall, M., ibid

[38] Michell, J. *New Light on the Ancient Mystery of Glastonbury*, Thrift Books, 1990

Glastonbury: the Isle of Avalon, Beckery (also known as Little Ireland), Godney (God's Island), Martinsea or Marchey, Ferrameare, Panborough and Andrewsea or Nyland. Each was exempted from English law and neither monarch nor bishop called the tune. Beckery, now a forgotten derelict area of Glastonbury, once had a very special place among the isles for it was the dwelling place of St Brigit, who followed St Patrick to Glastonbury.

Brigit lived by an old oratory dedicated to Mary Magdalene. This place is Bride's Mound and was once the disembarking place for boats. In legend Mary Magdalene landed here after the Crucifixion. Bride or Brigit or Brighde is the Triple Goddess of Brigantia, the ancient Celtic nation that included the British Isles, Brittany and parts of Spain. She is the Brigit of poetry inspiration and healing through the reciting of poetry at sacred wells and springs. She is Goddess of the New Moon. Her symbol is a White Swan and her flower is the snowdrop.

A chapel dedicated to St. Bridget was built on Little Ireland in the fifth century. The nuns who lived here were said to celebrate Easter at the Aries full moon, no matter the day of the week. They lived in accordance with the cycles of the Moon Goddess. St Bridget's emblem as a woman milking a cow, a symbol of the nurturing Goddess, is still visible on St Michael's Tower on the Tor and around the doorway to St Mary's Chapel in the Abbey. Until quite recently, the Mound was surrounded by the tidal waters of the River Brue, which one could cross at Pomparles Bridge (the Pons Perilous in the Grail legends).

Beckery is intimately connected with Grail stories. According to John of Glastonbury it was the site of the Chapel Perilous in the Arthurian romances, which record a visit by Arthur. According to legend the king came to the Magdalene Chapel at dawn one Ash Wednesday to find the door guarded by fiery swords. Inside an aged priest was conducting mass, assisted by the Virgin Mary. She offered up her Son as a sacrifice to the world. Afterwards, Mary gifted Arthur with an equal-armed crystal cross whose image he engraved on his shield in silver and green, later becaming a treasure of the Abbey.

By virtue of the sacred isles, Glastonbury came to be seen as a virtual state that recognized no sovereign power. No trace of original buildings on the 1440-acre plot survive but the prehistoric earthwork that runs along two miles east of Glastonbury, Ponter's Ball, is believed to have marked one of the borders of the sacred enclosure.

Michell is an excellent source for particulars on St Joseph's original wattle church.[39] For hundreds of years, Glastonbury Abbey was the

---

[39] Michell, J. *The New View Over Atlantis*, Thames and Hudson, 1983

largest and richest in Britain. From the meagre information available, it can be gleaned that the original wattle church was circular, each of the 12 missionaries having their individual cell placed around it. In about 166 two missionaries sent by Pope Eleutherius, Saints Phagan and Deruvian, renewed over a nine-year period the old wattle building (referred to as the *Vetusta Ecclesia*, "Old Church"), appointing 12 of their brethren to continue the rituals of the former 12.

In 433 Patrick became the first abbot of Glastonbury, and established a monastery with 12 anchorites in residence. Patrick may have been the one responsible for enclosing the round wattle church by a rectangular wooden church. Early in the 6th century, St David visited Glastonbury and claimed the church as one of his twelve foundations, adding a building at its east end. William of Malmesbury said that some time later another church was built by Glasteing, one of the 12 brothers from the north of England. In 601 Gwrgan Varvtrwch, King of Dumnonia, gave the land of Yns-witrin to the Old Church (the Celtic Church at Glastonbury) under the auspices of Abbot Worgret. This made the whole region of Yns-witrin a monastic island.

In 633 Paulinus, Bishop of Saxon York and a companion of St Augustine encased the Old Church in wooden boards covered with lead in an effort to preserve the deteriorating sacred fabric. In 704 or 708 the Saxon King Ine of Wessex completed the stone church dedicated to Saints Peter and Paul to the east of the wooden church. Ine's charter, signed in the wooden church, affirmed the rights of Glastonbury's seven islands as a sanctuary in perpetuity.

In the tenth century St Dunstan enlarged Ine's church and added more monastic buildings. Early in the Norman period the Saxon church was destroyed and the Abbey was subsequently reconstructed on a grander scale. In 943, St Dunstan placed the monastery under Benedictine rule, linking all the old buildings into one large one. Immediately after the monastery's destruction by fire in 1184, monks under the stewardship of King Henry II's chamberlain, Ralph Fitzstephen, began the task of reconstruction.

The first task was to build a magnificent stone chapel on the site of Old Church dedicated to St Mary in order to re-establish swiftly the holy link with the Virgin and to preserve the sacred dimensions of the original wattle shrine. The title of *Vetusta Ecclesia* henceforward became the hallowed name of the new St Mary Chapel, a sacred place of worship built on the site of the original wattle church. Claims that the remains of Arthur and Guinevere were unearthed in 1190 are disputed. In 1191 the bones of three bodies, said to be those of Arthur, Guinevere and the treacherous Mordred, were discovered on the south side of the Lady Chapel at Glastonbury Abbey. The tomb was found between two columns in the Abbey cemetery. On its leaden cross was inscribed: "Hic jacet sepultus inclytus Rex Arthurus in insula Avallonia," ("Here lies the renowned King Arthur in the island of Avalon"). The remains, together with their magnificent black marble tomb, disappeared at the time of the Dissolution in the 16th century.

In Christian lore, there is a persistent belief that the original wattle chapel was built by divine hands, an account that chimes with the legend that Christ during his lifetime came to Glastonbury with Joseph who was engaged in the tin trade. A number of latter day Christian authorities hypothesise that the church at Glastonbury was founded by Jesus himself during his "hidden years" before the age of thirty. In this belief, Jesus's final religious education teachers were the Druids in Britain whose initiatory studies raised him to the status of high adept in esoteric lore and tradition.

Manly P. Hall[40] likened the blood of Christ to the ever-flowing essence in the Grail as His true doctrine, and the cup containing it to His Esoteric School, the chalice of the adepts. The search for the Grail is presented as the spiritual adventure of regeneration, the trials and challenges of the knights' initiation into the Mysteries of Christ.

In 1529 during Henry VIII's Reformation the last Abbot of Glastonbury, Richard Whiting, was dragged on a hurdle to the top of the Tor and hanged because he refused to divulge the hiding place of the Abbey's treasures. His body was dismembered and exhibited around the country. The monks were dispersed, the lead was stripped from the roof, the carved rood-screen was burned to melt the bells and the residents of Somerset used the stone from the walls as a quarry. Stories abound as to the nature of the hidden prizes.

Although the day may yet emerge when physical treasures are revealed, the true essence of Glastonbury's riches is a spiritual quality that the sincere truthseeker aspires to receive. The very air, stone and landscape of Glastonbury are infused with powerful feelings of imminent revelation concerning the fulfilment of certain prophecies. One such concerns the sixth century Book of Melchin, a lost volume of the Glastonbury library. According to contemporary chroniclers it contained the oracle of Melchin, which states that the tomb of St Joseph, together with the Grail talisman, will one day be discovered, and "Thenceforth nor water nor the dew of heaven shall fail the dwellers on that ancient isle."

---

[40] Hall, M., *Orders of the Quest*, Philosophical Research Society, 1949

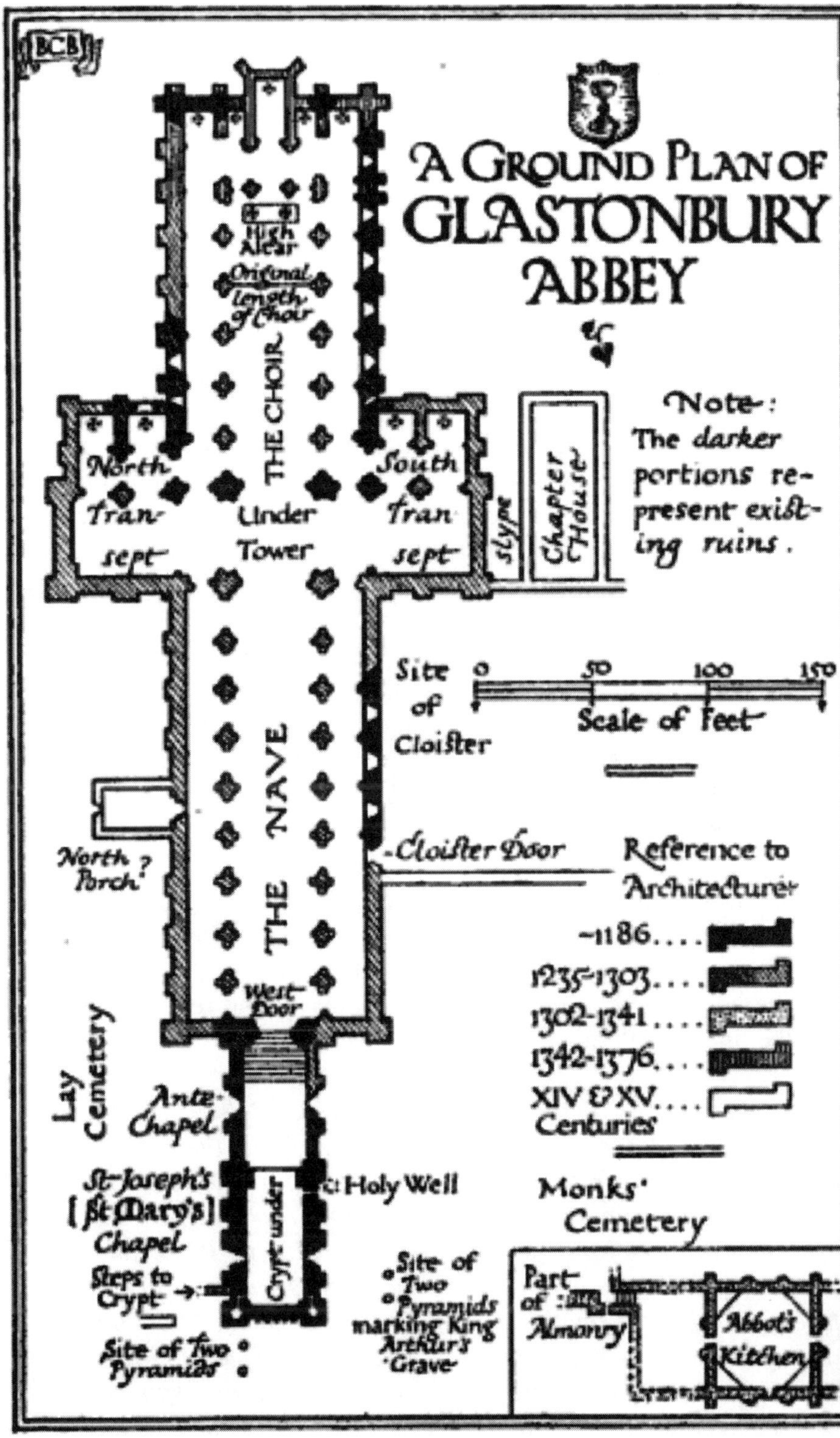

Ground plan of the Great Church built after 1184, from "Wells and Glastonury, a Historical and Topographical Account of the Cities"

The prophecy chimes with the legend of the Fisher-King, an occupant of the Glastonbury marshes whose healing, according to the Grail romances, shall make his barren kingdom flourish and restore the primeval Hyperborean Golden Age. On his deathbed, Austin Ringwode, the last of the monks expelled from the Abbey, proclaimed, "The Abbey will one day be repaired and rebuilt for the like worship which has now ceased; and then peace and plenty will for a long time abound." Powerful prophecies such as these nourish the long-held belief that Glastonbury is the English Jerusalem.

In 1907 the Church of England acquired Glastonbury Abbey and its environs. It appointed Frederick Bligh Bond as Director of Excavations to oversee a deep study of the Abbey's history and foundations. Bond, an authority on mediaeval architecture and ecclesiastical restoration, undertook his work very successfully. He uncovered the foundations of previously unknown parts of the old Abbey, including the foundation walls of the now ruined St Edgar's Chapel. No matter where Bond turned his attention, he always seemed to dig in exactly the right spot to make important discoveries. In 1918 he revealed in his book *The Gate of Remembrance* that his successes were owed to spiritualistic channelings in the form of automatic writing.

Friends of Bond had received messages purporting to be from spirit world representatives of the Company of the Watchers of Avalon, a body of former monks of Glastonbury Abbey whose names were given in the book and in a later one of Bond's, *The Company of Avalon*. The messages revealed details on the Abbey's structure and history and Bond's interpretation of these had allowed him to make his startling discoveries. In a message that echoed much of what White Eagle said through Grace Cooke about the mystical status of ancient Britain, Bond learned that Glastonbury's history as a place of special reverence dates back to the time of Atlantis:

> *The flow of spiritual forces is westward, following and impelling the forces of material things... Thus they whose habitation was in Crete, revisiting the memories and traditions of others of the same race... continued the interminable route ever westward beyond the gates of Hercules to the islands where the first fire-drawn metals be... but soon the spiritual forces which developed and sustained this immigration had deeper objects in view. They followed and transformed it by removing mundane influences and a great spiritual development arose in the places in which their instruments had*

prepared the soil. Phocis of the race of Crete trading with Poseidon [Atlantis]... *was thus brought in contact with them who worshipped the One God... thus paved the way for the building of a Temple in his settlement of Tintagella... thus first arose that measurement and design which were afterwards as accurately reproduced by that further advance which culminated in the temple of Glastonbury. And Tintagella was the ancient place of the shrine of the High God. So the temple, a reproduction accurate in every measurement, was reproduced at Glaston on this foundation.*

Bond's automatic writing scripts also emphasised the importance of reconstructing the pattern on the floor of the Old Church at Glastonbury. He understood from the communications that the floor pattern reflected the dimensions of a New Jerusalem, wherein a new Gnosis would arise incorporating the inspired synthesis of religion, philosophy, metaphysics and mystical science.

One of the remarkable episodes during Bond's tenure was the occasion when his daughter Mary, who had never received any training in draughtsmanship, suddenly began to produce automatic drawings. These were no mere unschooled doodles but sophisticated drawings of nudes, produced very rapidly and drawn in the style of da Vinci's sketchbooks. Curiously, the figures were anatomically accurate but not discernibly human. Rather, her sketches were of strange and remarkable nature–spirits and demons with striking eyes. Mary also experienced many psychic experiences in the vicinity of the Tor and wrote about these in her book, *Avernus*.

Among the many mystics drawn to Glastonbury in Bond's time were J. Foster Forbes and "psychometrist" medium Iris Campbell. Bond described one of Campbell's visions:

Beneath the abbey are remains of vast catacombs caused by natural upheavals. These are very deep down and it is through these underground channels that the magnetic currents of the world flowed. It was by this means that internal combustion was caused, known as the secret fires of the earth... Now the Glastonbury Tor is raised over an epicentre of magnetism, and that which is located there is continually churning up underneath... The contemplative order of monks drawn to this ancient site of Glaston - knowing as they did of these terrestrial-cum-celestial mysteries - made it their life's work to pray for the peace of the world. This they did by projecting their thoughts to the seething underworld.[41]

The revelation that Bond's work was guided and inspired by what was regarded as little more than demonism in the eyes of the Church caused a furore during which he was roundly condemned by archaeologists and eccliastical authorities alike. It was vital that the church should suffer no further scandal. Bond was sidelined and another architect brought in to supervise his work. Presently, when it became evident that Bond was in no way contrite about his spiritualist leanings, he was dismissed. Bond retired an embittered figure. To heap more humiliation on Bond, his excavations were grassed over, his discoveries erased from the official Abbey plans and his books removed from the Abbey bookstall.

If the authorities thought that these actions would reverse continuing episodes of anti-Christian involvement in the Abbey's affairs they were sorely mistaken. Soon, Glastonbury became a focal point for "New Age" revivalists whose ranks were not solely populated by mystics but by men of the cloth, among them Rev. Lionel Smithett Lewis who published *St Joseph of Arimathea at Glastonbury* and Rev. C.C. Dobson who penned *Did Our Lord Visit Britain as they say in Cornwall and Somerset?* From the secular perspective, Kathryn Maltwood in the 1930s alerted the world to her astonishing discovery of the Glastonbury Zodiac during her research into the Arthurian High History of the Holy Grail.

Gradually, Frederick Bligh Bond's work attracted new converts who recognized that his discoveries were years ahead of their time. In 1968, architect Keith Critchlow visited Glastonbury to check for himself Bond's claims that existing within the Abbey layout and structure is a scheme of sacred number and proportion. Critchlow concluded that Bond's findings were correct and went on to suggest that there may be a connection between the design of the original wattle settlement and the geometry of the Twelve Hides purportedly granted to St Joseph of Arimathea and his company.

Critchlow's supposition bore fruit when it turned out that the dimensions of the St Mary chapel were a microcosm of the geometry incorporated into the dimensions of the Twelve Hides. This is the not the place to go into the particulars of the Abbey's geometry (many have covered the subject very well, the most cogent and compelling, in my opinion, being John Michell in several of his works, see Bibliography)

---

[41] Forbes, J. & Campbell, I., *Giants, Myths and Megaliths*, William Chudley, 1973

but, suffice to say, the overall scheme and its archetypal cosmological framework is one that features in the foundations of temples and places of veneration throughout the ancient world. William of Malmesbury made reference to this mystical archaeology when he wrote of the mosaic design on the floor of the St Mary Chapel:

> *This church, then, is certainly the oldest I know in England, and from this circumstance deserves its name* (Vetusta Ecclesia)... *In the pavement may be seen on every side stones designedly inlaid in triangles and squares, and figured with lead, under which, if I believe some sacred enigma to be contained, I do no injustice to religion.*

William's remarks are supplemented by the content of Bligh Bond's automatic scripts, one of which stated:

> *All ye measures were marked plaine on ye slabbes in Mary's Chappel, and ye have destroyed them. So it was recorded, as they who builded and they who came after knew aforehand where they should build. But these things are overpast and of no value now... There was the Body of Christ, and round him would have been the Four Ways. Two were ybuilded and no more. In ye floor of ye Mary Chappel was ye Zodiac, that all might see and understand the mystery. In ye midst of ye Chapel he was laid; and the Cross of Hym who was our Example and Exemplar... Braineton, he didde much, for he was Geomancer to ye Abbey of old tyme.*

Miller and Broadhurst confirmed that the Mary current passes through the eastern end of St Edgars Chapel within the Abbey structure. On reaching King Arthur's Tomb, the energy divides into two, each part flowing round the tomb before recombining to run down the centre of the Great Church where it repeats its splitting manoeuvre between the third pair of columns that support the arches of the chapel of St Peter and St Paul. These are the only two occasions along the entire length of the Michael line where Miller and Broadhurst found that the Mary current behaves in this fashion. The pair felt that the splitting action in the St Peter and St Paul Chapel identifies a spot that conceals a "profound secret." Joining together once more, the two currents flow directly along the axis of St Mary's Chapel, a place of worship that has been acknowledged as the "Mother Church" of Britain. Here one should pause to reflect on another remarkable story in Mystical Christian lore.

Contemporaneous with St Joseph of Arimathea's party's arrival and activities in Glastonbury, as mentioned earlier Mary Magdalene is said to have come in France in a rudderless boat a few weeks after the Crucifixion. According to the oral tradition, once on French soil Mary Magdalene embarked on a journey along the length and breadth of Gaul to mark out and sanctify a number of power spots, the whole design when joined up geometrically taking the form of an 8-pointed star to represent Cosmic perfection. The reputed purpose of Mary Magdalene's work was to preserve in the landscape the secrets of Ishtar, the Mother Goddess, and to create sanctuaries and thresholds for those who seek "another way." Joseph of Arimathea in England; Mary Magdalene in France—two individuals intimately connected with Jesus, both establishing powerful energy structures to preserve the "Old Knowledge" and to provide waymarkers to spiritual riches.

Taking as his starting point William of Malmesbury's description of St Mary's Chapel, Bond visualised the original wattle church as a circular structure that was surrounded by twelve smaller circular cells in which dwelt Joseph and his fellow saints. Another script stated that Joseph's structure was not the first to be located on the site. A pagan temple had previously existed there and it was the dimensions of this much earlier sanctuary that Joseph and his followers took great pains to preserve in the wattle church.

John Michell's careful measurements revealed that the dimensions of the original Glastonbury saints' twelve cells relate in size to the larger round church they encircled as the moon relates to the earth.[42] The dimensions also correspond to those of the New Jerusalem as specified in Revelation, xxi. A script that came forward in connection with this remarkable fact said:

> *You know that in this designing of the Floor* (of the Old Church) *lies the future prophecy of Glastonbury, together with the inward secret of Christianity.*

The message was clear. Within the very fabric of Glastonbury lie secrets, which, once discovered and assimilated by the Grailseeker, will lead to profound mystical insights about the true relationship between an individual and God. To this day, these secrets remain to be found. In a powerful and magical way, the sublime and timeless energies of Mary and Michael facilitate the quest. And so does the Glastonbury Zodiac.

---

[42] Michell, J., *City of Revelation*, Abacus, 1973

Mary Magdalene's post-Crucifixion flight in a rudderless boat to Gaul symbolised by the Black Madonna and her ship's wheel nimbus, Church of El Salvador, Nerja, southern Spain. Photographed by the author.

Aerial view of Glastonbury Tor showing labyrinth paths

Chapter 4

The Glastonbury Zodiac

In the great mystery schools... the human body was chosen as the first study... Pictures and models of the human body were to be found in the inner temples... with every part related to some sign of the zodiac. The astrological and astronomical knowledge of the wise teachers and priests enabled the neophyte to open his understanding and his consciousness to respond to the universal powers... Through knowledge of astrological influences operating on the various parts of the body, the man obtained understanding of true healing. He recognized such influences as affecting his own life and developing that second aspect of his being, and thus opened up a world described as the 'underworld'... the 'soul world.'

—White Eagle

The term zodiac is derived from the Greek ζῳδιακός κύκλος, which means "a circle of animals" or "little animals." It is the name given by the old pagan astronomers to a band of fixed stars about sixteen degrees wide, apparently encircling the earth. Zōidion (ζῴδιον) is the diminutive of zōion (ζῷον, "anima"), an expression originating from the primitive Egyptian radicals, *zo*, life, and *on*, a being. The name reflects the prominence of animals and mythological hybrids among the twelve signs.

The Greeks, and later other peoples influenced by their culture, divided the band of the zodiac into twelve sections, each being sixteen degrees in width and thirty degrees in length. These divisions were called the Houses of the Zodiac. The sun during its annual pilgrimage passed through each of these in turn. Imaginary creatures were traced in the star groups bounded by these rectangles. Because most of them were animal or part animal in form, they later became known as the Constellations or Signs of the Zodiac.

The first six signs of the zodiac of twelve signs were regarded as benevolent, because the sun occupied them while traversing the

Northern Hemisphere. The 6,000 years during which, according to the Persians Ahura-Mazda, Zoroastrian Creator of the Universe, ruled His universe in harmony and peace, were symbolic of these six signs.

The second six were considered malevolent, because while the sun was travelling in the Southern Hemisphere it was winter with the Greeks, Egyptians and Persians. Therefore these six months were symbolic of the 6,000 years of misery and suffering caused by the evil genius of the Persians, Ahriman (the "Devil"), who sought to overthrow the power of Ahura-Mazda.

In ancient cosmology the supreme council of the gods is composed of twelve deities—six male and six female—that correspond in the sense of polarity to the positive and negative signs of the zodiac. The six gods are Jupiter, Vulcan, Apollo, Mars, Neptune, and Mercury; the six goddesses Juno, Ceres, Vesta, Minerva, Venus, and Diana.

In the Grail romances St Joseph of Arimathea's sister, Enygeus, married Bran, the Celtic Keeper of the Grail, and bore him twelve children. In the stories, Joseph went on to establish the Round Table, guarded by twelve Knights of the Holy Grail. Later, Arthur re-established in the Glastonbury region the order of Knights, symbolised by the image of the sun passing through the twelve houses of the zodiac. The "Rule of 12" and the Zodiac motif, the latter both physically and figuratively, thus become critical features in Celtic Christian cosmology.

When on a summer's day in 1925 Katherine Maltwood's inner vision captured an image of the Glastonbury Zodiac, she may have been the first person to see the secret design in the landscape for many thousands of years. Great minds gone before, such as Dr. John Dee, William Stukely and William Blake, had caught glimpses of the celestial pattern but had not been permitted a vision of the whole planisphere.

Ancient Britons were familiar with energetic earthen forms and referenced them in the language of the countryside in stories. They spoke of Dragons "of such extent that grass grew upon their backs." Some said they were "five acres" large, while others described them as so great "that riders on opposite sides could not see each other."

Maltwood, née Sapsworth, was born in Essex and brought up in her parents' large Italianate home, "Higham Lodge," in Woodford Green. Her father was a wealthy leather merchant and sometime local mayor. In 1901 she married John Maltwood, a wealthy advertising manager whose fortune enabled Katherine to devote her life to travel, collecting, sculpture and writing. Her sculpturing activities were particularly impressive. She studied at the Slade and exhibited regularly at the London Salon, the Royal Academy and at various other London galleries. In 1925 Katherine was commissioned by the British publisher Dent to draw an itinerary of the Grail Quest for its Everyman edition of the *High History of the Holy Grail*, newly translated into English by Dr. Sebastian Evans. So accurately does this mediaeval work describe the Somerset landscape that many believe it to have been written by a monk at Glastonbury Abbey. Interest in the adventures of King Arthur's Knights and the Holy Grail had been revived and made popular in the Victorian era by the Pre-Raphaelites and Alfred, Lord Tennyson.

> *The Round Table was constructed, not without great significance, upon the advice of Merlin. By its name the Round Table is meant to signify the round world and round canopy of the planets and the elements in the firmament, where are to be seen the stars and many other things.*
>
> —La Queste del Saint Graal

Maltwood was convinced that the book set out the secret location of the rumoured zodiac effigies in the Somerset countryside, the place where Grail writers had located the adventures of King Arthur. Setting up home in the Polden Hills, Maltwood dedicated herself to the task of re-discovery. Presently, she was drawn to certain configurations in the hills and waterways, which she perceived as symbolic figures.

One summer afternoon, Maltwood was standing on a low hill watching the shadows move across the plain that stretches towards Cadbury Hill. Suddenly, she recognized the profiles of a lion and a woman partly outlined by the river Cary near Somerton about four miles south of Glastonbury and interpreted these as the symbols for Leo and Virgo. Maltwood went on to identify ten other effigies within a 10-mile diameter circle. Glastonbury Tor is its northern point. Somerton and Lyte's Cary bound it to the south and to Cadbury Hill. Its centre is at Butleigh ("centre of the wheel"), three miles south of the Tor. Maltwood's named the zodiac the Temple of the Stars.

> *We have often been told that astronomy is found in a developed form among the ancient Baylonions, traceable to 3000 B.C., but not until I discovered this 'Temple of the Stars' in Somerset in 1925 A.D. and photographed it from the air, have we been able to define... the original features forming the Zodiac.*
>
> — Katherine Maltwood, *The Enchantments of Britain*

Katherine Emma Maltwood, re-discoverer of the Glastonbury Zodiac

Maltwood perceived the whole design as the original Round Table. She plotted her zodiac onto Ordnance Survey (OS) Landranger Maps together with the Celestial Equator, the Equinox as it would have appeared in 2700 BC, the stars forming the 12 zodiac constellations and the 12 astrological divisions. The heads of 11 of the effigies are turned to the west, the sunset. Some effigies such as Leo, Sagittarius and Pisces are 2-3 miles long. Each is delineated by natural features—hills, earthworks, watercourses, dykes, mounds, barrows, ditches, old roads and footpaths, streams and rivers. A notable feature of Maltwood's zodiac is that the star constellations are squeezed so that between Pisces and Aquarius there is a gap in which to fit a thirteenth constellation. Maltwood said that 10 of the 12 signs were easily discernible (although the traditional Aquarius figure is replaced by a phoenix, Libra and Cancer by a dove and a boat, and there are three fish in Pisces, the third being a whale). Significantly, if a planisphere is placed behind an OS Map and the stars and constellations are pricked through they do correspond on or near their counterparts in the zodiac pattern. Pilots have reported this good fit and aerial photos also support the layout.

The signs' correlation with tales in the *High History of the Holy Grail* suggests that the zodiac architects had a pre-cognition of the Arthur saga more than 3,000 years before the reputed time of Camelot and the Knights of the Round Table. In 1935 Maltwood published her findings in *Glastonbury's Temple of the Stars*. Her theory was that the zodiac was a combination of influences from Sumeria (from which she thought the name of Somerset may derive), Theosophy, Masonry, Egyptosophy, early Christianity and Rosicrucianism.

Mary Caine[43] has calculated that the odds against the 12 signs of the Zodiac occurring on the ground in their correct placements are 480,000,000 to 1. These mammoth odds increase if one considers that the winter signs are all to the north, the summer ones to the south and the three human figures—the Trinity comprising Sagittarius, Virgo and Gemini form an equilateral triangle across the circle. Moreover, the fact that when the planisphere is placed on the map the zodiac constellations fit over their earthly forms lengthens the immense odds even further.

Maltwood's ideas were very negatively received for many years. Frankly, they were (and are) too much of a stretch for orthodox archaeology, which says that no Middle Eastern people were in Britain during the period when Maltwood claimed the zodiac was constructed. Critics claim that anyone can select lines on a map that can be joined to make "meaningful patterns." Her technique has also been likened to the

---

[43] Roberts, A. (Ed.), *Glastonbury: Ancient Avalon, New Jerusalem*, Rider, 1978

phenomenon of *pareidolia*, whereby we look into flames, stains, wood grain and so on and see images that remind us of other things.

Maltwood's design was examined by two independent studies, one by Ian Burrow in 1975 and the other in 1983 by Tom Williamson and Liz Bellamy, using standard methods of landscape historical research. Both concluded that the evidence weighed against Maltwood's findings. They identified waymarkers on the design that were either of relatively recent historical origin (the western wing of the Aquarius phoenix was a road laid in 1782, and the Cancer boat is made up of a network of eighteenth century drainage ditches and paths) or were present day features (the eye of Capricorn was found to be a haystack).

Looking at the studies' findings objectively, they contain nothing that absolutely rules out the veracity of Maltwood's zodiac temple. Landscape features, either naturally or artificially made or re-shaped, could easily have eroded over time only to become re-defined by the actions of a later road-builder, ditch digger or farmer. Archaeologists also fail to grasp that a thorough study of the zodiac requires not just digging tools but input from astronomy, astrology, anthropology, folklore, history, esoteric tradition and help from archivists and experts in ancient languages such as Hebrew, Aramaic, Akkadian, Greek and the Celtic dialects.

More recent archaeological work has gone some way to vindicate Maltwood's theories. Professors John and Bryony Coles of Cambridge have undertaken diggings west of Glastonbury at Shapswick Heath and discovered causeway roads, consisting of a double layer of logs buried in peat.[44] Carbon dating reports a reading of 2,800 BC, a very near match to Maltwood's research findings. Moreover, an 80-year-old OS Map of Glastonbury shows menhirs in the zodiac area, which were subsequently removed. These formed an alignment with astronomical significance, marking points of critical significance and direction for the Temple of Avalon. In any case, Maltwood was not the first to make these observations. Co-founder of Theosophy, Helena P. Blavatsky, had also insisted fifty years earlier that missionaries from Egpyt fanned out worldwide to create four zodiacs, including the one at Glastonbury.

More recently, John Michell[45] described the Seven Isles of Glastonbury as places of special interest for those who formerly inhabited the area within the Twelve Hides region. Each had its own community of monks who served and maintained their chapels. The clerics' veneration was inspired by the special secret they shared. When

---

[44] *Somerset Levels Papers* (1975-1989), and *Sweet Track to Glastonbury* (1986)
[45] Michell, J., *New Light on the Ancient Mystery of Glastonbury*, Thrift Books, 1990

the seven islands are plotted on a map they reveal the pattern of the Constellation of the Great Bear. Glastonbury corresponds to the star Dubhe on which the constellation pivots. The Great Bear is long associated with Arthur, the name deriving from "Arth Fawr," meaning Great Bear. It is also associated with Arcturus (Greek for "Keeper of the Bear"), the brightest star in the Northern Hemisphere. Early English tribesfolk called the Great Bear "Arthur's Wain" or "Arthur's Wagon," the vehicle in which Arthur circles the celestial pole. Other names for the Great Bear are the Plough and Arator (the Ploughman). The fact that the Seven Isles area resembles the Great Bear suggested to John Michell that other constellations must exist in the Glastonbury landscape with the Tor representing the Pole Star, the star nearest to the imaginary line through the heavens produced by the northenward extension of the earth's axis.

Michell also considered the possibility that British priest-astronomers first perceived the Seven Isles as a microcosmic mirror image of the Great Bear when the Pole Star was located in the head of Draco at the end of the last Ice Age, approximately 12,000 years ago. Such a prominent celestial event may have been immortalised in the story of Arthur's father, King Uther (Uthyr in Welsh meaning "wonderful") Pen*dragon*.

Uther Pendragon, by Howard Pyle from *The Story of King Arthur and His Knights* (1903)

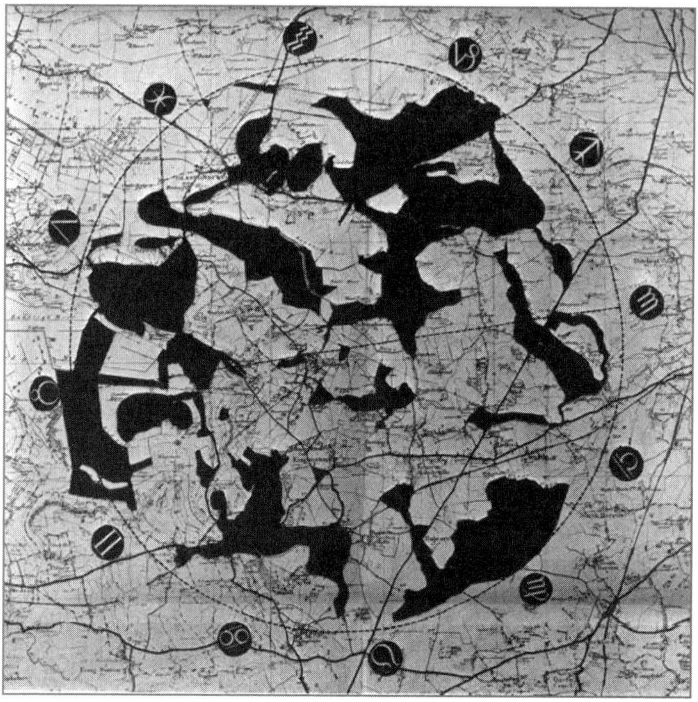

Mrs Maltwood's Zodiac Temple of the Stars, Aries at 10 o'clock position

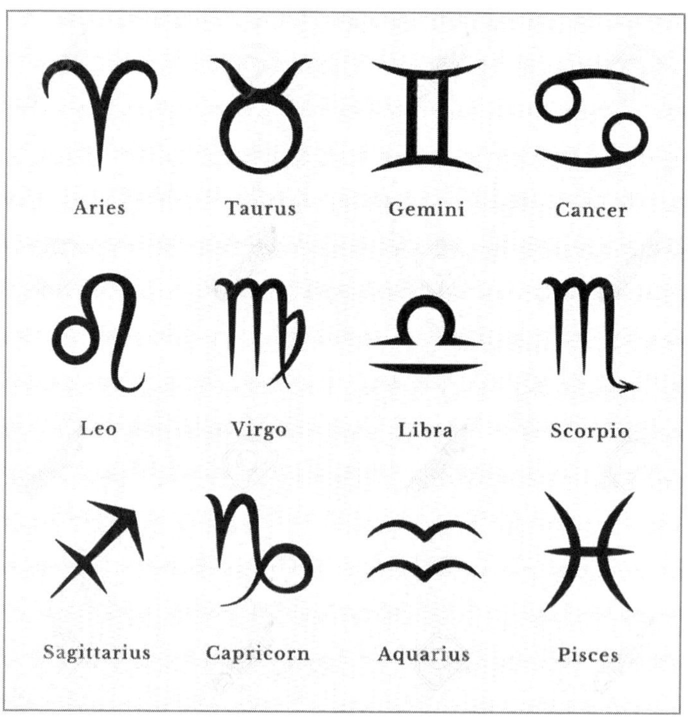

Zodiac symbols with their names

The Glastonbury Zodiac and its forms in the landscape

Aries

Since ancient times, the first sign of the heavenly zodiac is Aries. In the Somerset design the effigy is two miles long and shaped not as a ram but as a Paschal Lamb. It is located at the ten o'clock position around the zodiac circle. The shape is traced out in the landscape on a medieaval farm, together with an eagle at Lower Wick. Its head is reverted at the town of Street, just over two miles south of Glastonbury. Its back follows the contours of the Polden Hills. Walton Hill delineates Aries' body, its adjacent fields accurately marking out the form of its haunches. The stained glass at Walton church depicts two Arien stories: one of Abraham and Isaac with the ram in the thicket, and another of Christ shown as the good shepherd holding a lamb. The paschal lamb of the Jewish Passover is also carved onto the font.

Taurus

Moving widdershins around the circle we come to Taurus, an effigy touched by the folded knee of Aries. Taliesin wrote,

> *A holy sanctuary there is, on the wide lake; a city not protected with walls... The sacred ox of the patriarch is stationed before the lake.*

In Maltwood's cosmological scheme her effigy for the Bull is a depiction of the Mother Goddess, symbolising creation. Just one mile long, it is laid out over Compton, Trays Farm, Redlands and Castlebrook. Its neck is on Collard Hill, which is the site of its actual collar. Through the beech trees on his collar can be seen Glastonbury Tor. A ridge of land projecting out from the head towards Combe Hill forms the horn, which overlooks Combe Hollow. Looking south, one sees Gemini sleeping on Lollover and Dundon Hills. Ploughman's lynchets that curve around Hatch Hill make furrows in his horns. More recently, another horn has been added, marked by Hood Monument crowned by a tall stone 18th century obelisk. Its tail is at Asney (Mary Caine wonders if this refers to "Agnus Dei"). The Bull's lower jaw is at Street, his tucked-under feet at Ivybarn Hill, his chest and the back of his head traced by the old tin-track from Somerset to the Mendip Hills through Glastonbury. Its haunches are centred on Walton Hill. A former pond at Tray's Farm marks his Bull's-eye. The Pleiades fall on his collar. In an undoubted reference to the sign, Taliesin said:

> *They know not the brindled ox with his thick headband and the seven-score knobs on his collar.*

Gemini

One and half miles long, the Heavenly Twin of Dundon Hill is marked out over Castlebrook, Emblett Lane and Lollover Hill. Its head is the steep British Camp of Dundon Hill (the "fort of Don or wisdom"). It is lolling in sleep posture (Lollover Hill is in Gemini's lower body). His eyebrow by Dundon Smithy is marked by the entrance to an orchard. Lynchets trace his ribcage on Lollover Hill.

Caine later identified the Second Twin within the form of Katherine Maltwood's Griffin effigy. He is the same size as his brother and set at right angles to him. His head, facing west, is at Lugshorn to the east. Bradley Hill models his body. Maltwood found that the ship's planks on which Gemini sits measure one-thirteenth of the zodiac circle and conceal the 13th moon-month of the Druids. The recurring "13th" motif suggests that Emblett Lane may represent the Greek "embelos," meaning intercalation.

Cancer

This sign is drawn in the form of a crescent-shaped boat to the south of Gemini. The ship's planks are drawn by the dykes that drain a marsh, which winds round Gemini's hills in the Redlake Farm, Liver Moor and river Cary region. The ship is cradling a baby, which symbolises Cancer's lunar, maternal character. In C.W. King's *The Gnostics* there is an illustration of a baby in a ship. The prow is carved on the head of a griffin-like creature beneath a crescent moon (the traditional Cancer symbol).

Where the stern is positioned is an ox-head with a 4-pointed star above it, representing the Sun in Taurus. In the Glastonbury Zodiac the griffin effigy lies under the jurisdiction of Cancer and is resting at one end of the vessel carrying the Gemini child. The Taurus effigy is situated at the other end of the canal-drawn ship. Maltwood links the ship with both King Solom's ship in Mallory's *Morte d'Artur* and the Padstow hobbyhorse, the body of the latter traditionally portrayed as an upturned boat.

Leo

> *There is a formidable animal from the city of Satanas, which has made an inroad between the deep and the shallows. His mouth is as wide as the mountains of Mynnau: neither death shall vanquish him, nor hand, nor sword. There* (are) *nine hundred rocks between his two paws; there is but one eye in his head, vivid as the ice blue* - Taliesin

Situated to the right of Gemini's twin, Leo lies at Catsash Hundred, the "Field of the Lion," the only figure in the zodiac that has paws. His left front paw is weighed down by the "nine hundred rocks." The nearby villages of Catsgore and Catsham emphasise Leo's feline character. In the Celtic myths Arthur used to hunt the Cath Pulag, "Lion of the month of Lug the Sun-god." Three miles long, Britain's heraldic lion sits on the south of the zodiac. It is laid over Copley Woods, the ruined Roman villa of "Maggoty Paggoty" marked now by two stones, Christian's Cross, Charlton Adam, Lynches earthworks, the Little Dog of Littleton, Somerton, and the river Carey that draws Leo's underside. Leo's head is raised up on Hurcot, a district of Somerton. His jaws and lolling tongue are drawn by terraced lynchets on the side of Worley Hill and his muzzle is defined by Chabrick Millstream. The River Cary, rising from the Seven Lady Springs in Castle Cary, flows along Leo's ribs and foot. Its rump sits on Charlton Mackerell. Ancient trackways and footpaths delineate his back and front legs. Two pools of water known as Chalkham ponds mark his eyes.

In legend, Mithras slays the Constellation of Taurus and nourishes the Universe with its blood.

W.T. Olcott pointed out in *Star Lore of All Ages* that, astrologically, Bristol, Bath and Taunton, all within thirty miles of the effigy, are ruled by Leo. The Druids worshipped Hu, the Sun God, personified in the ancient Greek pantheon as Mithras, Lord of the Sun. In the third and final degree of initiation into the Mithraic mysteries, the hierophant was given a cape upon which were drawn or woven the signs of the zodiac and other astronomical symbols. After his initiations were over he was hailed as one who had risen from the dead, having been instructed in the secret teachings of the Persian mystics. Candidates who successfully passed the Mithraic initiations were called Lions and were marked upon their foreheads with the Egyptian cross. Mithras himself is often pictured with the head of a lion and two pairs of wings. Throughout the entire ritual were repeated references to the birth of Mithras, his sacrifice for man, his death that men might have eternal life, and, lastly, his resurrection and the saving of all humanity by his intercession before Ormuzd, the supreme source of Light.

Many later institutions exhibited Mithraic culture. In particular, the reference to the "Lion" and the "Grip of the Lion's Paw" in the Master Mason's degree have a strong Mithraic characteristic and may well have originated from this cult. A ladder of seven rungs appears in the Mithraic initiation. Scholars believe that this ladder was originally a pyramid of seven steps. May this help one to understand the original purpose behind the creation of the 7-tiered labyrinth on the Tor?

Virgo

Four miles long, Virgo is lying on her back with her head pointing west. She is outlined by Keinton Mandeville, Stickle Bridge, Yeovilton, Babcary, Wheathill, Annis Hill and the Fosse Way. The River Cary outlines her profile and front, her hands and back by roads, lanes and streams. At her feet we find Wheathill. Within her outline is the tumulus Wimble Toot. It falls where her breast ("bab") would be. Bab is also Arabic for gate, while wimble means augury. Toot or moot hills were places where the locals once gathered to receive spiritual nourishment. Toot equates with old Welsh *twt*, lookout mound, and also with teat. Moot stems from the Welsh *maeth*, nourishment. In Virgo's hands is a wheatsheaf formed by three lanes, a cone being a symbol for Isis, the Queen of Heaven, also used by the ancient Cypriots on their coinage for Venus. Cary is Ceridwen, the British Ceres, and also Keris of Cornish legend. Castle Cary's British camp guards her, a reminder that Virgo in Glastonbury is associated with old Mother Cary, Britain's sea-witch. Stickle Bridge emphasises the broomstick in her hand. Here also is Mary Magdalene's Church, a reminder that the three Marys of the New Testament personified the Triple Goddess. Beneath her head is Annis Hill, representing Black Annis, the British Ceres, Mother Goddess of the Druids' Trinity, known variously as Anu, Danu and Annwn of the Underworld. Ansford at Castle Cary also echoes the name. The Virgin's pregnant womb is at Babcary.

Libra

Libra is represented not by scales but by a dove, one and a quarter miles long, hidden within the centre of the circle over the village of Barton St David and its network of paths and streams. Flying from the head of Sagittarius, the dove is traced by the little waterfall at Baltonsborough Flights, Catsham, the River Brue, Tootle Bridge and Barton St. David's Silver Street and Gosling Street. Hurtle Pool is on his wing.

Scorpio

Two miles in length and guarding the eastern approach to Avalon is the scorpion, its tail poised above the flank of the Centaur. Caine's revised form of Maltwood's effigy is traced by Parbrook, Stone, Hornblotton, Alford, the Fosse Way and Hell Ditch. The river Brue marks its southern boundary past Lovington's old mill. Churches at Alford and Ditcheat mark its tail. West Lydford lies at its tip. Lyd means gate, the threshold to King Lud's underworld. One claw nips Arthur's head at Catsham and the other pinches his seat at Parbrook. Banked ditches by Lottisham's Lower Farm mark Scorpio's head and mandibles. Its eight legs are marked by Four Foot Farm and Bridgefoot Farm.

Sagittarius

The five-mile long image of the Centaur, symbolised in British legend as Arthur of Avalon, is marked by Catshain, Baltonsborough, Ponter's Ball, Breech Lane, Canters Green, West Pennard, the Pennard Hills, Arthur's Bridge, West Bradley and Hell Ditch. The horse is modelled by Pennard Hill ("Arddur's hilltop"), and his body lies on the plain of Baltonsborough. West Bradley on the top of his leg was formerly known in the Domesday Book as Bodelege. On his tail is Arthur's Bridge. The waterfall at Baltonsborough Flights pours its waters into the wing of the Libran dove. Baltonsborough marks his helmeted head.

The archer's leg is positioned near the Ponter's Ball linear earthwork at Havyatt in the Glastonbury parish of West Pennard. The name Havyatt was originally hagyatt, "hagy" meaning heaven or sacred place, and "yatt" gateway—the Gate to Avalon or the Summerland. (Somerset's Celtic name is "Gwlad yr Hav".) As the archer takes aim, his arm stretches almost to the centre of the zodiac at Park Wood.

Capricorn

Measuring three and a half miles, east to west, Capricorn is the northernmost figure in the zodiac. It is marked out by the Shepton Mallet-Glastonbury road, Ponter's Ball earthwork, Wick, Hearty Moor, Hartlake, Somerton, Fountains Wall, Barrow and Launcherly Hill. His shoulders emerge from the marshes around the Whitelake River. Arthur's leg descends into the horn of Capricorn. Its nose is pressed against the Tor. His back leg is the river Whitelake and runs down on to its hindquarters at Launcherly in the Pennard Hills. His feet are dipped into Hartlake; its chest wall faces onto Heart Moor. The great horn of the legendary supernatural goat said to haunt the Tor is at Ponter's Ball (some suggesting a derivation from the Etruscan "Puntes Bal": "sacrifice of Bel"), an area once known locally as the Golden Coffin. Mary Caine found a well-drawn back leg at North Wootton, thus improving on Maltwood's original design.

Aquarius

Aquarius is represented in the Glastonbury Zodiac as an Eagle or Phoenix, the precursor to the water-carrier. Measuring 1½ miles across with Glastonbury at its centre, Aquarius is delineated by Edmund Hill, Paradise Lane, Wick, South Down Hill, Edgarley, Ashwell Lane and Chalice Well. The Tor falls within the head of the bird, which is twisted round to face Chalice Hill. The hill is in its body and contains the red waters of Chalice Well, said to be the repository of the Holy Grail. The Tor's furrows mark the folds of its neck. Chalice Well is on the end of its beak. Its head is drawn by the same Shepton Mallet to Glastonbury road that defines Capricorn's back. Maltwood concluded that the Phoenix is drinking from the Druid Well, its head turned to reach for the magical healing water of the Chalice Well Blood Spring. Its west wing is drawn by two old roads to Wells that wend round Edmund Hill. The eastern wing is traced round South Down Hill, the ancient oaks of Gog and Magog by its tip, its breast by Paradise Lane.

Pisces

Approximately 5-miles across, Pisces in the Glastonbury scheme is a whale connected by a cord to two fishes. It is outlined by Wearyall Hill, Glastonbury Abbey, Fishers Hill, Pomparles Bridge over the river Brue where Arthur threw Excalibur into the water, Plunging, which marks the whale's heaving back, Wallyer's Bridge, which accommodates its jaw, Hulk Moor on the road from Somerton to Glastonbury and the Mendips that marks the tail, and Street. The jaw of the whale hangs on Glastonbury Abbey's gate. The two fishes, each less than a mile long, lie on the whale's flank. One fish, the northernmost of the pair, rests on Wearyall Hill, reputed in legend to be the burial place of the Celtic Salmon of Wisdom. The other is lower by the ram's head at Street.

In the Mabinogion tale of *Kylhuch and Olwen*, the salmon takes Kay and Bedivere upriver to rescue the Mabon (youth) from the prison of Oeth and Anoeth (Knowing and Not Knowing). The Rivers Brue and Old Rhyne outline the whale's length while Watchwell house falls on its eye and Wallyer's Bridge on its snout. Caine found a serpent's head projecting from the whale's jaws. It lies near Maltwood's serpent head in Park Wood. The stars in Draco correspond to Caine's new find. Close by the River Brue one comes across the "tree of sorrows," once a willow, now a hawthorn. Nearby is Bride's Well where Chalice Well's mysterious blue bowl was discovered in 1905 through the visions of Wellesley Tudor Pole. From here it is a short walk across the field to Bride's Mound, formerly the site of St Brigid's Chapel and part of an earlier Saxon monastery dedicated to Mary Magdalene. This hallowed place was once the traditional disembarking place for boats, and where local legend says Mary Magdalene landed on a visit to these isles.

The Girt Dog of Langport

The Glastonbury Zodiac's mysterious 13th sign is Britain's Cerberus, the guardian dog of the western Hades, the Underworld of Annwn. He also guards the sea-approach from the Severn Channel. The Girt Dog of Langport lies outside the zodiac circle to the southwest, ten miles from Glastonbury to the region of the Burow Mump, a small replica of the Tor with a processional path leading to the now ruined St Michael's church. This conical mound is the definite snout of a huge dog. It is mentioned in a old Somerset carol:

"The Girt Dog of Langport has burnt its long tail
And this is the night we go singing wassail."

Girt means great or tethered (Leazeway on the shape runs to Little Hook at its neck). The ruins of a church dedicated to St Michael's lie on its summit, as does the Glastonbury Tor. These two mounds align their lengths upon the Michael and Mary line. In the Arthurian tales the Girt Dog is referred to as the Questing Beast. Before one can enter Aries, the traditional entry point into the Zodiac, permission must be sought from the hound and to request his companionship on the journey.

Five miles long, the Dog is marked out by Michell's Burrow and Alfred's Burrow at Athelney, Earlake Moor, Head Droves, Head Rhine, Othery, the river Tone, Pathe, Leazeway Drove, Little Hook, Aller, Paradise, Wagg, Muchelney, Langport, North Curry, Curry Rivel, Curland and River Parrett. The hill at Athelney is one of a line of hills dedicated to St Michael that sit on the Michael and Mary ley.

The hound's nose is formed by Burrow Mump, an artificial mound of red clay. The ruins of St Michael's church are on its summit. Fittingly, its tail end is the hamlet of Wagg. His ear is at Earlake Moor and at Othery (Greek for ear is "otis"). His front paw is drawn by North Curry and Curry River. Other dog-reference parts are drawn on Curland and the Curload road, which leads to his nose at Alfred's Burrow. Its role as guardian of the Underworld is reflected in its placement on Helland, Hellard and Hellyard's Farm. The river Tone marks the dog's tongue.

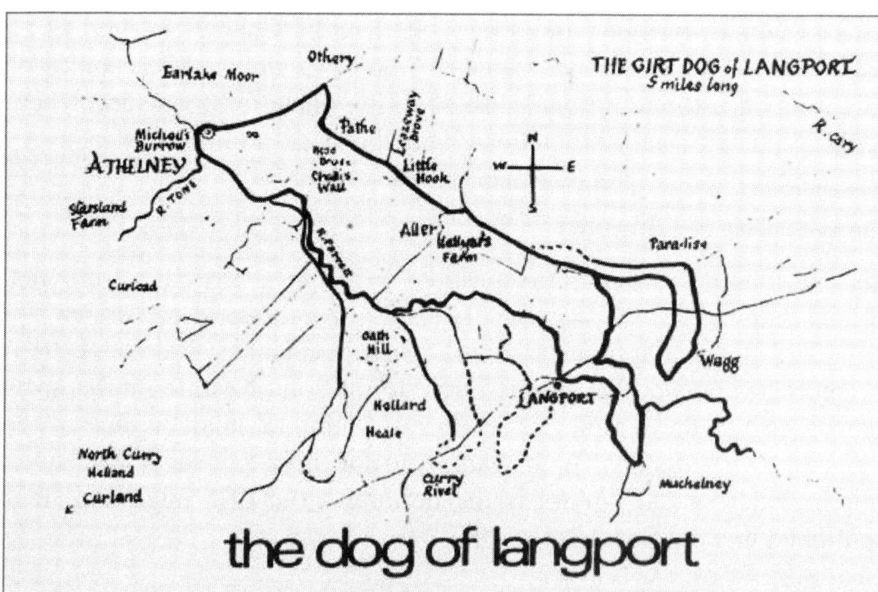

The Girt Dog of Langport has burnt his long tail
And this is the night we go singing Wassail.

Regional folklore tells the story of the Aller dragon, which terrorised locals in the villages of Curry Rivel and Aller. A church now dedicated to St Andrew was supposedly built on a patch of earth scorched by the dragon and from which grass no longer grows. The dragon of Aller was a terrifying beast. It spat both fire and venom and flew on vast leathery wings. It lived in a hillside cave and laid waste to the land. In the folk tales the dragon was finally slain by John of Aller. There are two versions of the story. In one John is a knight, in the other a lowly peasant. John covered himself in pitch and wore a mask to protect himself from the dragon's breath. After a terrible battle, John was able to thrust a long spear down the dragon's throat and slay it. In another version, John survives and finds a brood of hatchlings in the dragon's cave, which is subsequently blocked up.

The Aller Dragon Mosaic

Janet Roberts has claimed the discovery of another dog in the Glastonbury landscape. Her "Polden Hound" effigy extends for six miles across the Polden Hills. It appears to be running away from the Zodiac whose outer perimeter is a little over a mile away to the east. Its route takes it through the small village of Greinton and St Michael's church, and then on to Moorlinch, which means: "magic hillside."

As when the golden sun salutes the morn,
And, having gilt the ocean with his beams,
Gallops the zodiac in his glistering coach,
And overlooks the highest-peering hills...

—William Shakespeare, *Titus Andronicus*

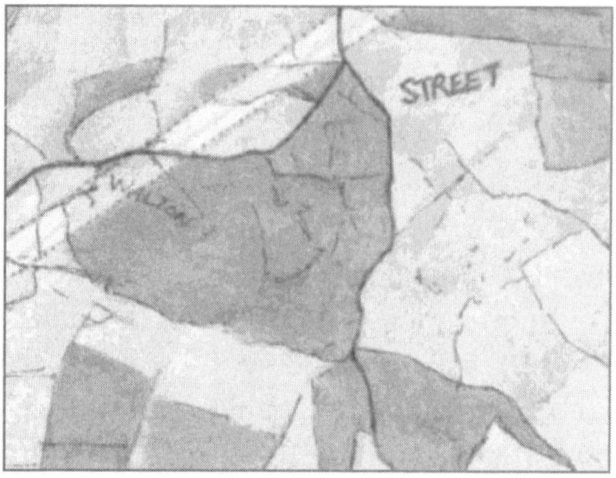

Aries, courtesy Yuri Leitch

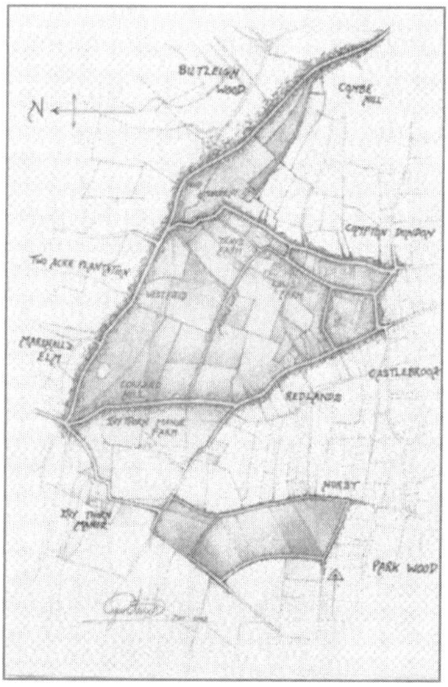

Taurus, courtesy Yuri Leitch

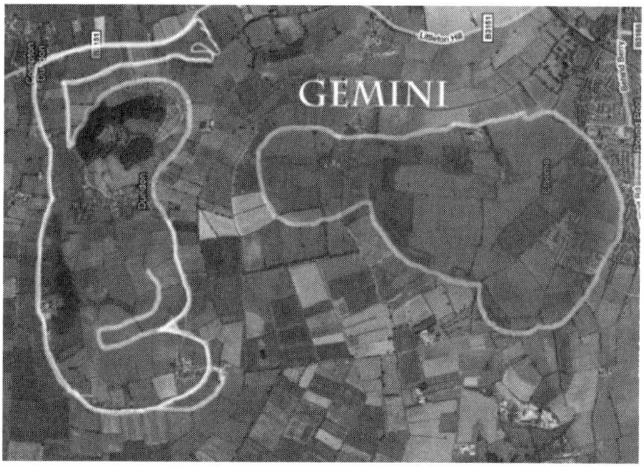

Gemini, courtesy Gail Cornwell

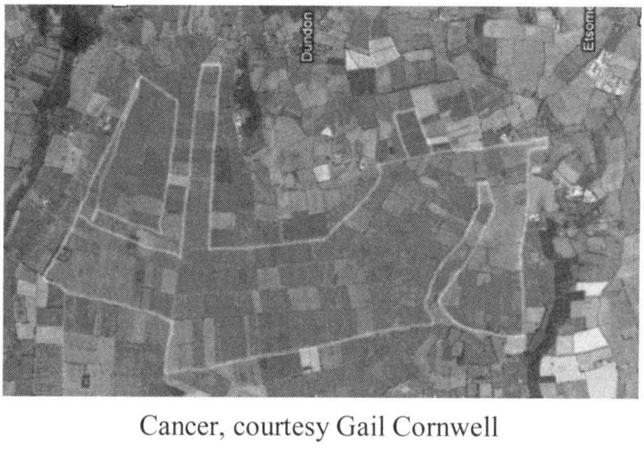

Cancer, courtesy Gail Cornwell

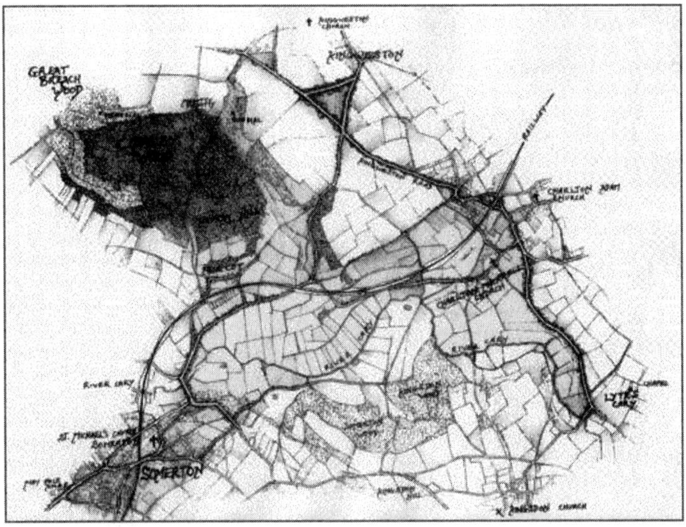

Leo, courtesy Yuri Leitch

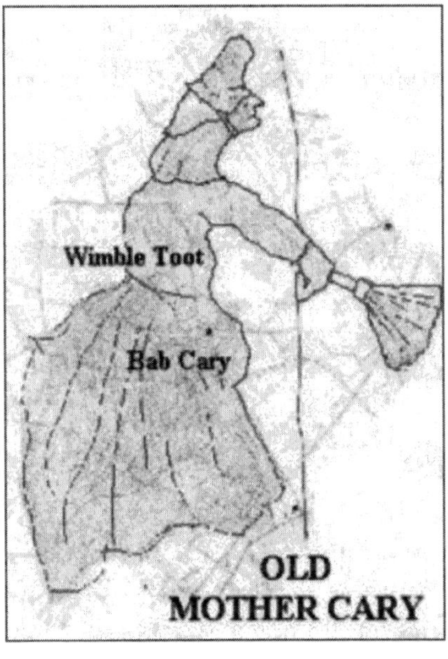

Virgo in the Glastonbury Zodiac

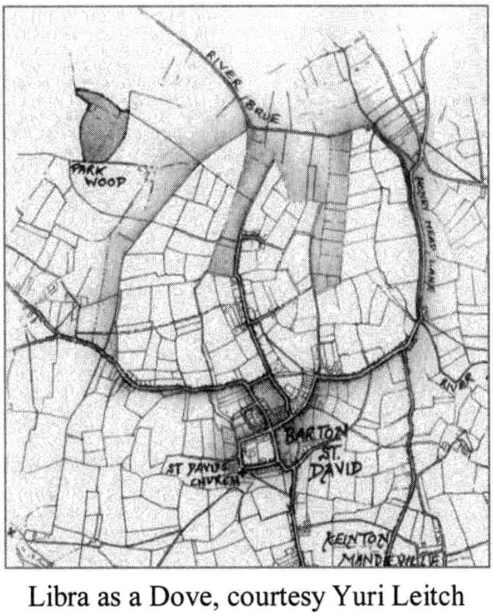

Libra as a Dove, courtesy Yuri Leitch

Scorpio, courtesy Gail Cornwell

Sagittarius, courtesy Cornwell Cornwell

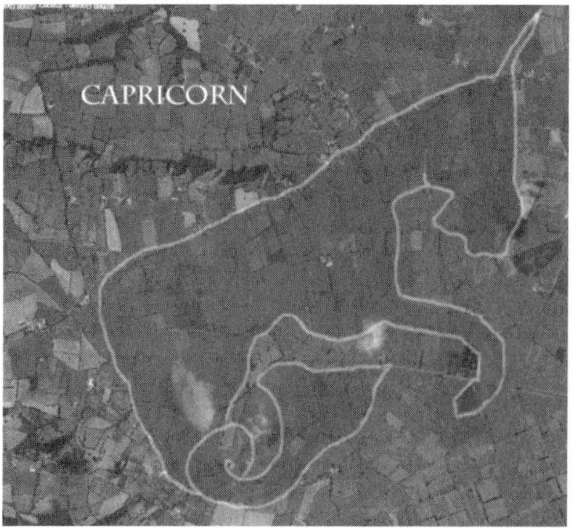

Capricorn, courtesy Gail Cornwell

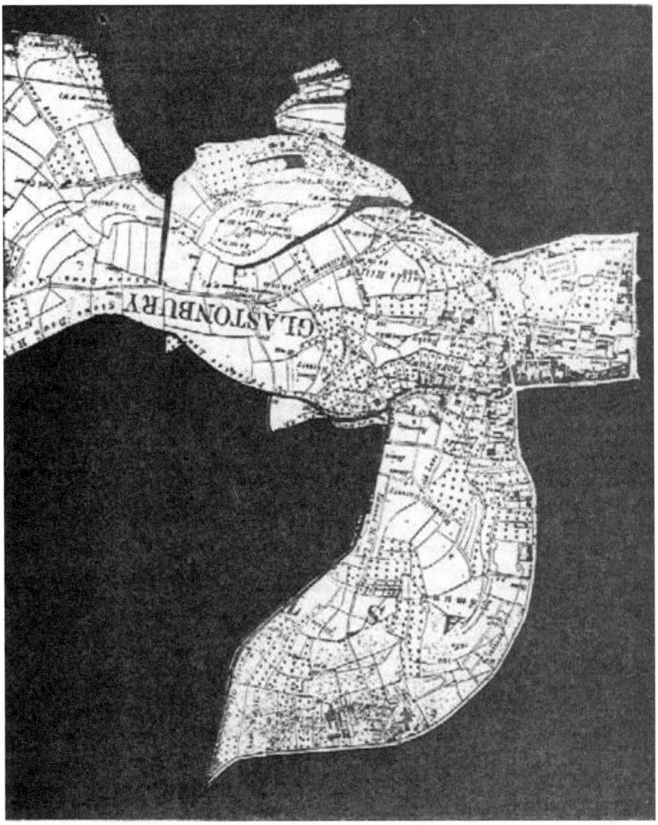

Katherine Maltwood's Phoenix effigy turning its head to drink from the Chalice Well Blood Spring, the Cup of Aquarius

Pisces, courtesy Gail Cornwell

The St Michael ley's passage across the Glastonbury Zodiac between Creech St Michael (just off the map at bottom right) and Shepton Mallett

The relationship between the Glastonbury Zodiac and the Michael and Mary currents is both geometrical and esoteric. Recall that for the most part, the ley is an abstract one-dimensional line of best fit that runs between the polar-opposite, male-female energies of Michael and Mary. Out of sight near the bottom right corner of the preceding illustration is the principle crossing point of Creech St Michael, 3-miles to the east of North Curry. The ley then proceeds northeast, firstly through Stathe and then into the Girt Dog of Langport along the upper edge of Aller Moor. One mile north at Burrow Mump is the next Michael and Mary node.

The ley then runs for six miles before clipping the prow of Cancer's crescent-shaped boat in the Walton and Ivythorn Hills. It then passes immediately into the Paschal Lamb effigy of Aries, travelling through Walton Hill, Overleigh and Street before entering Pisces a quarter-mile northeast. It javelins through South Moor and, aptly, dives out of the whale at Plunging. A half-mile further it enters the bottom right portion of Aquarius, passing through Chalice Well before immediately reaching Capricorn at the position of the goat's nose at Glastonbury Tor. It then brushes along its chest at Laurel Street before leaving the zodiac at the top of the goat's leg by Hearty Gate farm. It then passes by Pilton Church of St John the Baptist. Its Lamb and Phoenix carvings symbolise the spiritual re-birthing and transformative qualities of baptism. The ley then proceeds two miles to Shepton Mallett.

It is notable that the Michael ley passes through (or brushes past in the case of Cancer) only those five of the twelve zodiacal signs that occupy the upper left portion of the circle. The remainder bear no geometrical relationship either to the Michael ley or to its individual currents, with the sole exception of Mary who winds along the top of the Centaur's leg at West Bradley (old Bodelege) in Sagittarius.

Burrow Mump and St Michael's Church, by Saffron Blaze,
via http://www.mackenzie.co

Clearly, the fundamental relationship between the St Michael ley's male-female energy components and the Glastonbury Zodiac is determined by quality and not quantity. Consider the key locations through which the ley passes. First is Aller Moor, the serpent's lair just below the head of Cerberus. The dragon symbolises the sleeping power within humans that, once awakened with patience, learning and courage seasoned by the application of positive thought-word-action, leads to self-realisation and intimate and direct knowledge of one's inner divinity. Next are Chalice Well and the Tor, two very special places in Glastonbury, a place that has been described as the holiest on earth. Here were sacred centres where candidates once came for learning and initiation into the deepest and most profound mysteries concerning the human experience in the context of Cosmological Law.

The establishment of the Ancient Wisdom, the Old Knowledge and the Mystery Schools aeons in the past was for one purpose only: to reveal to human beings that deep within the individual resides a spark of divine Light, a perfect synthesis of male and female, knowledge of which guides them on their "Grail Quest" to become one with their inner God. Thus enlightened, the initiate is free to evolve beyond the long and arduous engagement with the curriculum of the University of the Physical and to ascend to unimaginable worlds of beauty.

To this end, the ancients created signs, symbols and patterns in the skies and landscapes to steer the truthseeker on a journey of discovery. Pyramids, stone circles, crystal caves, labyrinths, hedge mazes, manmade mounds, hills and zodiacs are a part of this global network of fingerposts that point the way to that ultimate moment of comprehension when one understands that we are so much more than we think we are.

> *It seems to me now that the purpose of astronomical features in megalithic monuments was not so much for observation as for reception, implying that astronomical influences played an important part in magic and ritual within stone circles or chambered tombs. There is good authority from classical writers for the suggestion that the overall purpose behind megalithic and later temples was alchemical, to procure the productive fusion of earth energy with the forces of the cosmos.*
>
> —John Michell, *Popular Archaeology*

My feeling is that in the context of Glastonbury's cosmological scheme, Michael and Mary's electromagnetic currents keep the zodiac charged. They pierce the circle slightly north of east. Assuming that their flow of current is west to east, the effect of their impact is to spin the circle in a clockwise direction. The resultant interaction between the Michael and Mary currents and the zodiac's unceasing spin is to produce a spiralling vortex of phenomenal energy. In accordance with the laws governing electricity, if a coil (the zodiac) is rotated by applying force in a magnetic field (the Michael and Mary influence) this results in converting rotational energy into electrical energy. What might be the purpose behind the creation of this supercharged reservoir of power in Avalon's Temple of the Stars?

One possibility has arisen as a result of efforts to identify other landscape zodiacs in Britain. Kathryn Preston has postulated[46] the existence of the "British Zodiac Circle" of 95-miles radius centered on Warwickshire's Forest of Arden. It passes through the Glastonbury Zodiac and other mooted landscape constellations at Winchester, Alton, Kingston, Ongar, Bolingbroke, Hebden Bridge and The Wirral. Reflecting on these findings, Nigel Pennick[47] suggests that the country could have been divided into geomantic provinces, each containing a zodiac. The known zodiacs—roughly 60 in Britain have been tentatively identified—fit present ecclesiastical dioceses to a remarkable degree. Pennick speculates that the zodiacs may have functioned as the equivalent of cathedrals.

This is a truly astonishing and intriguing possibility. Recall Spencer's remark that Britain once was regarded as "highly sacred, an enclosure of the gods, a land pervaded by mystery, faerie glamour and enchanted adventure." Imagine the scene, a network across Britain of mighty temples covering vast acreages of ground, each charged by unlimited terrestrial electromagnetic power of male and female polarity, equal attraction and repulsion. Each draws its share of the population to worship mighty celestial beings.

Grace Cooke described such an occasion. A great assembly had gathered in the amphitheatre below Dragon Hill in present day Oxfordshire for a grand ceremony of sun worship. Twelve high priests positioned themselves on the summit and summoned the great angels of the White Light. Among them were representatives of the Elemental nature spirits. An ever-rising spiral of golden light filled the amphitheatre, its radiation appearing as a fountain of light that cascaded brilliantly over the earth. A great being, a cosmic Christ-form White Eagle described it, appeared in the light. Then appeared another figure,

---

[46] Preston, K., *The British Zodiac Circle* – Northern Earth Mysteries Group Newsletter No. 1 (1979)

[47] Pennick, N., *The Ancient Science of Geomancy*, Thames & Hudson, 1979

a king wearing a crown of gold and robed in light, the points of his crown emitting rays of great brilliance. This was Ar-Thor, the ancient King of Hyperborea who had come to bring blessings for a ceremony convened to show people how to overcome one's material self—an act symbolised by the slaying of the dragon. After telling this story, White Eagle went on to describe Britain as the omphalos for a global renewal of divine power in which, he declared, Ar-thor, the Once and Future King, will re-emerge to do final battle with the forces of darkness.

Such occasions need the power of music. A zodiac has unique characteristics by which to create the most perfect synthesis of music and song. Based on the law of the octave, there is a direct association between colour, music and planetary bodies. This has long been known. Pythagoras and Ptolemy wrote of it and, more recently, major figures such as Rudolf Steiner and Max Heindel undertook valuable work.

Red, when regarded as the lowest colour tone in the scale of chromatics, corresponds to *do*, the first note of the solfège system of notation. Continuing the analogy, orange corresponds to *re*, yellow to *mi*, green to *fa*, blue to *sol*, indigo to *la*, and violet to *ti*. The eighth colour tone necessary to complete the scale is the higher octave of red. When the colours are related to the twelve signs of the zodiac, they are arranged as the spokes of a wheel. To Aries is assigned pure red; to Taurus, red-orange; to Gemini, pure orange; to Cancer, orange-yellow; to Leo, pure yellow; to Virgo, yellow-green; to Libra, pure green; to Scorpio, green-blue; to Sagittarius, pure blue; to Capricorn, blue-violet; to Aquarius, pure violet; and to Pisces, violet-red.

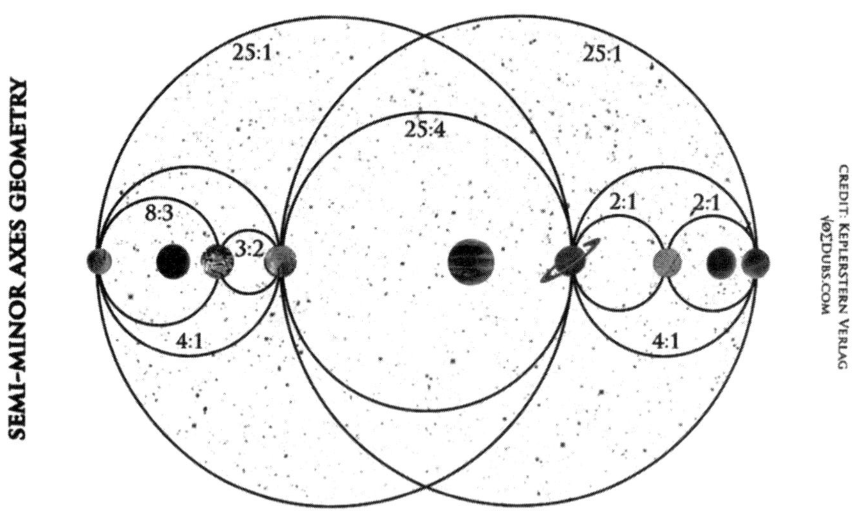

Mercury, Venus, Earth, Mars, Jupiter, Saturn, Uranus, Neptune and Pluto with principle musical ratios: 2:1 Octave, 3:2 Perfect Fifths, 4:1= octaves, courtesy Joe Dubs

In his Republic, Plato wrote of the basic structure of the ideal city of Magnesia. In this Utopian society it was important that its citzens worship their native gods. Plato emphasised that in the furtherance of this celebration there should be no fewer than 365 festivals in Magnesia in the course of the year. This unbroken festival in honour of local deities should be enhanced by continual singing, whose harmonies borrowed from the Heavenly Choir of divine music, which had been created, taught Pythagoras, by the motions of the heavenly bodies. The tradition of the Perpetual Choirs of Britain echoes these teachings.

John Michell[48] referred to the Welsh Triads in which the sites of three of the Perpetual Choirs are listed as Glastonbury, the Choir of Ambrosius or Stonehenge, and Llantwit Major in Glamorgan. At each of these choirs, 2,400 saints maintained a ceaseless chant, 100 for each hour of the day and night. Stonehenge and Llantwit Major are both 38.9 miles from Glastonbury. Two straight lines drawn on a map from Glastonbury to the other two choirs form an angle of 144°, an important cosmological characteristic of the New Jerusalem scheme of proportion.

The complete scheme consisted of ten Perpetual Choirs, enormous open-air cathedrals of worship arranged in the shape of a decagon. Its centre is at Whiteleafed Oak in the Malvern Hills where the three counties of Herefordshire, Worcestershire and Gloucestershire meet. Whiteleafed Oak was formerly the site of a grove held sacred by the Druids. Even up the 19th century local people held it in awe. It is said to be the oldest geological formation in Britain. The circle of choirs contains 7,983,360 acres. Compare with Revelation's dimensions for the New Jerusalem circle of 79,833,600 square feet. Thought provoking synchronicity!

Given the known relationship between the heavenly zodiac, colour and music, it is impossible to imagine that Glastonbury's Temple of the Stars is unrelated to the purpose and workings of its once magnificent Perpetual Choir. While the zodiac circle appears to be in a state of ceaseless spin by virtue of its interaction with Michael and Mary, it is possible that Britain's wider ley system may also be keeping Glastonbury's 9 sister choir centres in constant etheric excitation. The analogy that springs to mind is that of an intergalactic "Spielbergian" Mothership revolving in stationary orbit high above the earth in choreographic step with its encircling satellites. Together they are making cosmic music, an indescribably beautiful choral symphony that not only fills the heavens but also floods the earth with healing harmonies. I have little difficulty in attributing the crafts' earthly

[48] Michell, J., *The Dimensions of Paradise*, Inner Traditions, 2008

counterparts, the Mother Choir of Glastonbury and its nine magnificent partners, with the same healing powers.

Just because we can no longer see nor hear 2,400 saints singing their hearts out across the British countryside does not mean that at the etheric level the ten choirs are not still very much at work. If when we walk the countryside and succeed in unburdening ourselves of our daily cares for a while we may, at a deep but not unattainable level of perception, hear the gods in concert. In synergy with the limitless powers of Michael and Mary, sacred Glastonbury and its zodiac landscape provides the environment in which the principle conductor of the Perpetual Choirs (Merlin? Arthur? Guinevere?) coaxes the most sublime performances from the invisible choristers.

We now leave Glastonbury and follow Michael and Mary into Wiltshire, a region no less sacred than Somerset. It is home to the magnificent stone temples at Avebury and Stonehenge and the highest proportion of crop circles seen anywhere in the world.

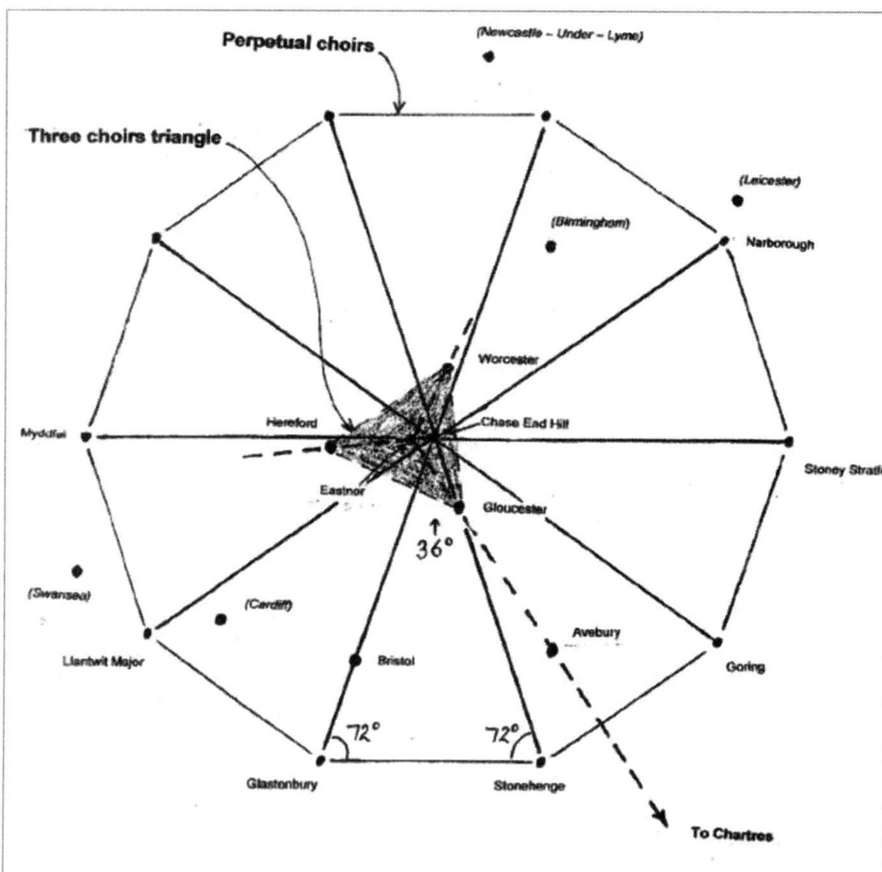

Roy Snelling's diagram of the Perpetual Choirs Decagon and its interior Three Choirs Triangle, reproduced with permission

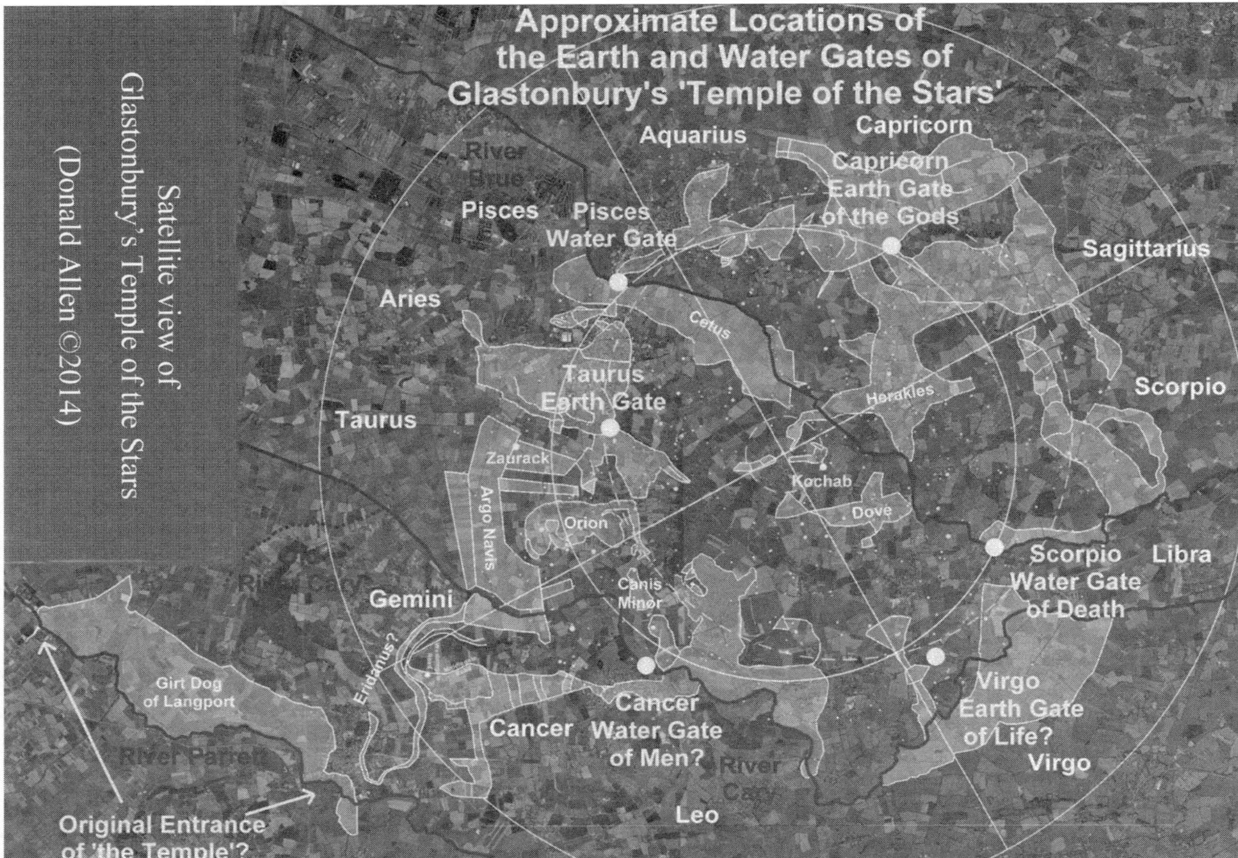

Satellite view of
Glastonbury's Temple of the Stars

(Donald Allen ©2014)

"Anatomy of the Human Body as Governed by the Twelve Constellations," extract from the *Virginia Almanack* pasted into George Washington's diary

Pagans believed that the zodiac formed the body of the Grand Man of the Universe divided into 12 major parts under the control of the respective celestial powers that dwell in the zodiacal constellations. Believing that the entire universal system was epitomized in man's body—the Microcosm (the Little World), pagans evolved the figure of the "Man of the Signs" by allotting a sign of the zodiac to each of the 12 major parts of the human body.

Chapter 5

Wiltshire

Thus, this stupendous fabric, which for some thousands of years has braved the continual assaults of the weather, and by the nature of it, when left to itself, like the pyramids of Egypt, would have lasted as long as the globe, has fallen a sacrifice to the wretched ignorance and avarice of a little village, unluckily placed with it.

—William Stukeley

After Michael and Mary leave the zodiac behind and complete their journeys through Somerset, the former via Doulting Church with its dragon carvings and the large stone slab of The Devil's Bed and Bolster, the latter through East Pennard and the Small Down Knoll earthwork, they cross the River Frome into Wiltshire.

The landlocked county of Wiltshire occupies an area of 1,346 square miles and borders the counties of Dorset, Somerset, Hampshire, Gloucestershire, Oxfordshire and Berkshire. The county is characterised by its high downland and wide valleys. It is notable for its pre-Roman archaeology. The Mesolithic, Neolithic and Bronze Age people that occupied southern Britain built settlements on the hills and downland that cover Wiltshire. Stonehenge and Avebury are the most famous Neolithic sites in Britain.

In the 6th and 7th centuries Wiltshire lay at the western edge of Saxon Britain, as Cranborne Chase and the Somerset Levels prevented any further advance to the west. In 878 AD the Danes invaded the county. Following the Norman Conquest, large areas of the country came into the possession of the crown and the church.

The local nickname for Wiltshire natives is "Moonrakers." This originated from a story of smugglers who managed to foil the local Excise men by hiding their alcohol, possibly French brandy in barrels in a village pond. When apprehended by the excise men they raked the surface to create ripples by which to conceal the submerged contraband. Acting like simpletons, when questioned they claimed that they were trying to rake inshore a large round cheese visible in the pond, which to the bemused officials was obviously a reflection of the full moon. The excise men fell for the ruse, taking the locals to be gormless idiots and left them alone. Many villages claim the tale for their own village pond but the story is most commonly linked with The Crammer in Devizes.

After eleven miles Michael and Mary cross paths at a small spring half-filled with timber at Bowerhill, a seemingly insignificant encounter but noteworthy because it is the only nodal spring along the entire length of the St Michael ley. A 7-mile flight finds the pair re-embracing at Roundway Down Iron Age hill-fort, also known as Oliver's Castle because Cromwell fought at the Battle of Roundway Down in 1643. The surrounding hillside is sculpted. Inside is an impressively large central enclosure with a rare surving example of a prehistoric dewpond. Below the hill is a hand-terraced large earthen platform and below that a copse containing a holy well. Miller and Broadhurst discovered that the currents converge across the centre of the platform before running on into the enclosure, making Oliver's Castle a special location in the overall Michael and Mary ground plan.

The currents pick up speed and make a beeline for a very special place in Britain's cosmological landscape. Seven miles later, in the blink of an eye, they arrive in the Wiltshire parish village of Avebury nestled in the Marlborough Downs. The village is 80 miles west of London and 10 miles south of Swindon.

Oliver's Castle near Devizes in Wiltshire

Arial view of Avebury henge

Within the chalk landscape of Avebury's Stone Age complex are remnants of two stone avenues, Britain's biggest henge enclosure, England's largest prehistoric tomb and Silbury Hill, Europe's tallest artificial mount only recently re-discovered to be an image of the Mother Goddess. Avebury is host to the largest stone circle in the world, originally made up of 600 sarsen megaliths taken from the nearby Lockeridge Valley. Michael Dames[49] has argued that the entire Avebury complex was designed to be read as a sequence of visual images of Neolithic man's female deity.

The importance of Avebury as a central temple in Stone Age times is evident by its sheer size and from its dominant position in the ancient trackway network. A quick check on a map shows that Avebury is virtually at the centre of southern England. One may approach it from the east from the market town of Marlborough and along the northern bank of the River Kennet. After five miles one sees a line of dome-shaped mounds along the Ridgeway, a route described as Britain's oldest road. The section, clearly identified as an ancient trackway, extends from Wiltshire along the chalk ridge of the Berkshire Downs to the River Thames at the Goring Gap, part of the Icknield Way, which ran from Salisbury Plain to East Anglia. Straight ahead is the massive structure of Silbury Hill. Before reaching it, one takes a right-hand turn to Avebury village a mile further on. Soon, the stones reveal their mighty presence, first in the henges and then in two rows across the field to the left. This is West Kennet Avenue, which leads to the southern edge of the Temple.

Avebury Henge covers a circular levelled area of some 30 acres with a diameter of 1440 feet. Built within a landscape which nature designed as an Elysium, a place of great power and beauty fit for the spirits of the blessed departed, it had always been a place of assembly for the early tribes. They held an important yearly festival on Windmill Hill above the Avebury temple. Its core landscape and cluster of prehistoric stones and earthworks encompasses the Neolithic camp at Windmill Hill to the north, Overton Hill and The Sanctuary to the east, East and West Kennet long barrows and Silbury Hill, the biggest manmade mound in Europe, in the south, and Beckhampton to the west. Paul Devereux[50] has described Windmill Hill as the "grandmother" of Avebury henge, for Neolithic man had commenced using it by or before 3700 BC. On the lower southwesterly slope of Windmill Hill is Horslip Long Barrow, now seen only as a rise in a field.

---

[49] Dames, M., *The Avebury Cycle*, Thames and Hudson, London, 1977 and 1996

[50] Devereux, P., *Symbolic Landscapes*, Gothic Image Publications, 1992

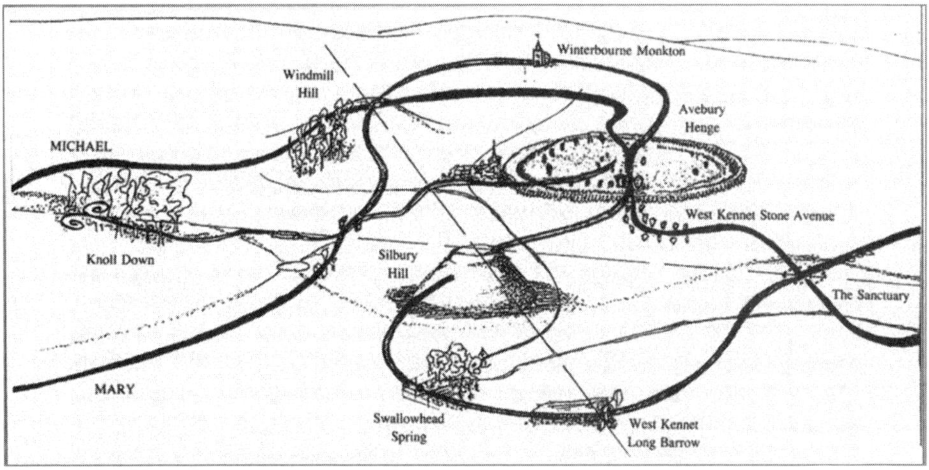

The paths of Michael and Mary in Avebury, courtesy Miller and Broadhurst

Miller and Broadhurst dowsed Michael's path through Wansdyke and Bishop's Canning, down a lane by the White Horse chalk figure at Cherhill, along a track to Windmill Hill and its immense earthworks, and through East Farm and Rutlands Farm to Avebury Henge, entering from the west by the Swindon road. It passes through the centre of the henge and the two cove stones within the northern inner circle, which are amongst the largest and finest stones of the whole monument.

The "male" and "female" cove stones in Avebury's northern inner circle

At the north side was once a third stone which completed the cove and faced the existing slender "male" stone. This fell in 1713 and was destroyed. Michael then passes within a few feet of Avebury United Reformed Church built from smashed megaliths in 1670. It proceeds to the Obelisk's concrete marker, the exact point marking a node, and flows onwards through the southern entrance via the most magnificent stones of the outer circle, including the massive Devil's Chair stone. This place also marks the spot where the exact countryside alignment of the St Michael ley crosses the circle, as well as the point at which the West Kennet stone avenue joins the henge. Michael then runs along the West Kennet avenue, its stones marking with great precision the dimensions and flow of the current. Miller and Broadhurst had now been following the St Michael line energies for 150 miles during a 12-month period.

In the 1930s Alexander Keiller, heir to his family's famous marmalade business, used his wealth to acquire a total of 950 acres of land in Avebury for preservation. He went on to conduct excavations and re-erect stones on the Avebury site. Keiller's team was able to re-position 27 sarsens that had been buried, and also to locate another 37 prehistoric stone holes, which were subsequently marked by concrete plinths. He also obtained as much of the Kennet Avenue as possible. It is to Keiller's credit that during his restoration programme the West Kennet avenue stones were re-erected to within just a few inches from the edge of the Michael current.

Michael then winds his way up the summit of Overton Hill on the crest of the ancient Ridgeway track before meeting, to the dowsers' puzzlement, with another, feminine energy in the head of the serpent at the Sanctuary. Miller and Broadhurst had made their first aquaintance with Mary! Situated beside the A4 road on Overton Hill, the Sanctuary is the site of a stone circle that once formed the terminal point of the West Kennet Avenue. Large enough to contain the outer ring of stones at Stonehenge, its earliest parts are dated to around 3000 BC, which is about the same period that the cove in the northern inner circle of the henge was erected. Now destroyed and only consisting of small concrete markers where the various elements once stood, the Sanctuary is believed to have played an important part in the function of the henge. When Aubrey saw it he recorded it as a double ring of stones.

Although Stukeley also recorded quite a number of stones on his drawing he was to witness much of its destruction during the period of his visits. The destruction was so complete that the site was to become lost and forgotten until Mrs. Maud Cunnington was able to locate it once more in 1930 prior to her excavation work. Because of his belief that the henge and its avenues represent a gigantic serpent shaped by the druids, William Stukeley often referred to the Sanctuary as the hakpen (serpent's head). As a result, he also spoke of Overton Hill as Hakpen Hill.

The Sanctuary was built over a complex fissure system radiating from the centre like dartboard wires. Fissure systems are geological fault lines, some of which are only 4-6 inches wide. They run within the Michael and Mary currents as they flow into the southern entrance of Avebury's henge. On 11 September 1275 the churches on Glastonbury Tor and on St Michael's Mount toppled, simultaneously causing a minor earthquake suggesting they are linked by a geological fault line.

Miller and Broadhurst set about tracking this new, female current in the Avebury Temple environs. From the Sanctuary Mary flows firstly southwest, then swings north towards Avebury, courses through West Kennet long barrow, follows the bank of the River Kennet and passes through Swallowhead spring. (The Kennet's former name was the Cunnit, indicating the water's feminine nature and Avebury's ancient associations with the Mother Goddess and fertility rites.)

Mary then passes along the western side of Silbury Hill. Remarkably, Europe's largest manmade mound has never eroded because the people who shifted 35 million basketloads of chalk understood soil mechanics. Their achievement has been likened in complexity to a modern space program.

Approximate orientation of the St Michael ley through Avebury Henge between Oliver's Castle southeast and Ogbourne St George Parish Church northwest

Mary next crosses over the River Kennet and a small bridge at the foot of Walden Hill. She flows past two massive entrance stones that mark the end of West Kennet Avenue and joins the Michael current at the node point in the henge between the two stones. The two currents, solar and lunar, run together to the next node point at the Obelisk. Shortly, they part company with Michael going off to the northeast. Meanwhile Mary travels on to the hamlet of Winterbourne Monkton, passing through its old church dedicated to St Mary. She then winds her way up to a massive tumulus on Windmill Hill to meet once again with Michael. Mary then crosses Horslip Bridge, passes between the Long Stones at Avebury Trusloe and runs past the tumulus by Beckhampton Road to the Wagon and Horses pub. By now, Miller and Broadhurst knew that there was nothing else for it but to return to Cornwall and trace this new feminine energy in its entirety.

One enters Avebury through a gap in the henge's enormous embankment and trench. Placed all around are huge stones weathered over millennia into fantastic shapes. Dotted here and there are low concrete pillars that mark the sites of missing stones, many of which were used to build the village's dwellings. The site consists of three stone circles, two of them contained by the third. They stood side-by-side, 340 feet in diameter, with other stone structures in their centres. The northern ring consisted of two concentric circles, the inner of 12 stones and the outer of 27. The two other stones at the site were part of a trio of gigantic size, which formed a cove at its centre. The southern circle contained other stones including its central feature, the tall obelisk, which is no longer standing. These circles are surrounded by a ring, formerly of about 100 stones, geometrically arranged in a series of arcs. It stands within the circular earthwork, through which there are four entrances: roughly north, south, east and west.

The chronology of Avebury's construction is unclear. It was not designed as a single monument but is the result of various projects that were undertaken at different times during late prehistory. Archaeologist Aubrey Burl[51] suggests dates of 3000 BC for the central cove, 2900 BC for the inner stone circle, 2600 BC for the outer circle and henge, and around 2400 BC for the avenues. Radiocarbon dating and analysis of pollen in buried soils have shown that the environment of lowland Britain changed around 4250–4000 BC due to changes in farming techniques. Pollen is poorly preserved in the chalky soils found around Avebury, so the best evidence for the state of local environment at any

[51] Burl, A., *Prehistoric Avebury*, Yale University Press, 2002

time in the past comes from the study of snail shells. Different species of snail live in specific habitats, so the presence of a certain species indicates what the area was like at a particular point in time. The available evidence suggests that in the early Neolithic period Avebury and the surrounding hills were covered in dense oak woodland. Gradually, the woodland around Avebury and the nearby monuments receded, replaced by grassland.

Avebury was only one among a group of monumental sites that were established in this region during the Neolithic. Such large-scale constructions indicate to archaeologists that a stable agrarian economy had developed in Britain by around 3500 BC. Other notable ceremonial henge types include Stonehenge, 17 miles south-southeast of Avebury, Dorchester henge in Oxfordshire, and nearby Maiden Castle in Dorset.

During the early mediaeval period there were signs of human settlement at Avebury, with a *grubenhaus*, a type of timber hut with a sunken floor being constructed just outside the monument's west bank in the 6th century. Only a few farmers appeared to have inhabited the area at the time, and they left the Avebury monument largely untouched. In the 7th and 8th centuries, the Anglo-Saxon peoples began gradually converting to Christianity and during the 10th century a church was built just west of the monument.

In 939, the earliest known written record of the monument was made in the form of a charter of King Athelstan, which defined the boundaries of Overton, a parish adjacent to Avebury. In the following century, invading Viking armies from Denmark came into conflict with Anglo-Saxon groups in the area around Avebury, and it may be that they destroyed Avebury village, for the local prehistoric monument of Silbury Hill was fortified and used as a defensive position, apparently by a local Anglo-Saxon population attempting to protect itself from Viking aggression. In the twelfth century a Benedictine Priory was built where Avebury Manor now stands.

By the late mediaeval period, England had been entirely converted to Christianity, and Avebury, an evidently non-Christian monument, began to be associated with the Devil. The largest stone at the southern entrance became known as the Devil's Chair, the three stones that once formed the Beckhampton Cove became the Devil's Quoits and the stones inside the North Circle, the Devil's Brand-Irons. At some point in the early 14th century, villagers, inspired by religious zeal, began to demolish the monument by pulling down the large standing stones and burying them in ready-dug pits at the side. Burl suggests that it might have been at the prompting of the local Christian priest, the likely contenders being either Thomas Mayn (who served in the village from 1298 to 1319), or John de Hoby (served 1319 to 1324). During the toppling of the stones, one of them (which was 3 metres tall and weighed 13 tons), collapsed on top of one of the men pulling it down, fracturing his pelvis and breaking his neck, crushing him to death. His corpse was trapped in the hole that had been dug for the falling stone, and so the locals were unable to remove the body and offer him a Christian burial in a churchyard, as would have been customary at the time. When archaeologists excavated his body in 1938, they found that he had been carrying a leather pouch in which were found three silver coins dated to around 1320–25, as well as a pair of iron scissors and a lancet. From these latter two items, the archaeologists surmised that he had probably been a travelling barber-surgeon who journeyed between market towns offering his services, and that he just happened to be at Avebury when the stone-felling was in progress; a tragic case of wrong place, wrong time.

It appears that the death of the barber-surgeon prevented the locals from pulling down further stones, perhaps fearing that it had been retribution for their toppling them in the first place and enacted by a vengeful spirit or even the Devil himself. The event appears to have left a significant influence on the minds of the local villagers for records show that in the 18th and 19th centuries there were still legends being told in the community about a man crushed by a falling stone. Soon after the toppling of many of the stones, the Black Death hit the village in 1349, almost halving the population. Those who survived focused on their agricultural duties to grow food and stay alive.

By the beginning of the Victorian period in 1837, the majority of Neolithic standing stones at Avebury had gone, having been either buried by pious locals in the 14th century or smashed up for building materials. Meanwhile, the population of Avebury village was rapidly increasing, leading to further housing being built inside the henge. In an attempt to prevent further construction on the site, the wealthy politician and archaeologist Sir John Lubbock, who later came to be known as Lord Avebury, purchased much of the available land in the monument, and encouraged other buyers to build their houses outside rather than within the henge, in an attempt to preserve it.

It was in the first half of the sixteenth century that Avebury was first recognized as an antiquity that warranted investigation. Around 1541, John Leland, the librarian and chaplain to King Henry VIII, travelled through Wiltshire and made note of the existence of Avebury and its neighbouring prehistoric monuments. Despite this, Avebury remained relatively unknown to anyone but locals and when the antiquarian William Camden published in 1586 his Latin language guide to British antiquities, *Britannia*, he made no mention of it. He rectified this for his English language version in 1610 but only with a fleeting reference to the monument at "Abury," believing it to have been "an old camp." Further antiquarian investigation was prevented by the outbreak of the English Civil War (1642–51), which was waged between the Parliamentarians and Royalists with one of the battles taking place five miles away from Avebury at Roundway Down.

After the war a new edition of the *Britannia* was published in 1695, which described the monument at "Aubury" in more detail. The antiquarian and writer John Aubrey, who privately made many notes about Avebury and other prehistoric monuments, had written this entry. Aubrey had first encountered the site whilst out hunting with friends in 1648 and, in his own words, had been "wonderfully surprised at the sight of those vast stones of which I had never heard before… (Avebury) doth as much exceed Stonehenge in grandeur, as a Cathedral doth an ordinary Parish Church." He attributed the stones to the Druids.

Hearing of Avebury and taking an interest in it, King Charles II commanded Aubrey to come to him and describe the site, which he did in July 1663. The two subsequently travelled to visit it together. His interest piqued, the king commanded Aubrey to dig underneath the stones in search of any human burials. Aubrey never undertook the king's order but in September 1663 began making a more systematic study of the site, producing a plan that has proved invaluable for later archaeologists, for it contained reference to many standing stones that would soon after be destroyed by locals. This was achieved in a method that involved lighting a fire to heat the sarsen, then pouring cold water on it to create weaknesses in the rock, and finally smashing at these weak points with a sledgehammer. At around the same time as Aubrey was undertaking his detailed studies, natural philosopher Walter Charleton, who believed that the Danes built Stonehenge, was also producing his groundplans of the henge.

With the arrival at the site in 1719 of antiquarian and Freemason, William Stukeley, serious study of the Avebury complex well and truly got under way. Stukeley was a Lincolnshire man and had come across a reference to Avebury in Aubrey's records. Stukeley was appalled to witness the wanton destruction of sarsens by local people such as farmers "Stone-Killer" Tom Robinson who wrecked 10 stones in the Henge in 1700 and John Fowler who burned 5 in the south circle. Two other farmers, Green and Griffiths, were responsible for much of the damage at The Sanctuary, its form only being rediscovered in 1930 during Alexander Keiller's restoration efforts. These destructive actions were encouraged and influenced by the rise of anti-pagan Puritanism in the village. Massive stones that had been a part of the monument for thousands of years were smashed up for use as building material. People built their homes from the "frustrums" (fragments) of broken sarsens. Some stones were used to build a meetinghouse within yards of the Obelisk.

When the obelisk was felled it lay close to a group of relatively small, buried stones, which, now restored, are known as the D-feature. Stukeley remarked that "this stupendous fabric, which for some thousands of years, had brav'd the continual assaults of weather, and by the nature of it, when left to itself, like the pyramids of Egypt, would have lasted as long as the globe, hath fallen a sacrifice to the wretched ignorance and avarice of a little village unluckily plac'd within it."

Stukeley visited the village and its monument six times up to 1724, sometimes staying for two or three weeks at the Catherine Wheel Inn, its own construction material incorporating twenty cartloads of stone from a megalith broken up by farmer Stretch. During his visits Stukeley made meticulous measurements and drawings of the site, considering it to be a "British Temple." Like John Dee more than one hundred years earlier and Katherine Maltwood two hundred years later, Stukeley sensed that there was something of a sacred quality hidden in the landscape. He glimpsed the recurrent forms of the serpent and the winged circle, which he interpreted as symbols of and a monument to the Old Religion, the one and eternal true faith. Stukeley recognized also the image of the serpent passing through the circle as a familiar symbol of alchemical fusion.

He saw that from the great circle there extended two avenues of stones, 50 feet wide and each a mile and a half long. One reaches out southeast and terminates in another stone circle of 130 feet diameter, known as The Sanctuary, on top of Overton Hill. The other, a sinuous double curve towards the southwest, no longer exists having been destroyed shortly after Stukeley made his drawings. He recognized these avenues as forming the Solar Serpent: The Sanctuary circle representing the head, and the Kennet and Beckhampton avenues forming the body, which passed through the Avebury circle—the Sun Symbol. Stukeley believed that this figure proved that the Druid priesthood had anticipated the doctrines of Christianity, for the circle is the symbol of the Godhead, and the Serpent represents the Son proceeding from the Father. In his view, the Druids had laid out a sacred pattern to invoke the blessings of Providence. Avebury church font is carved with images depicting two bishops holding a book in one hand and a crozier in the other with which they are spearing writhing dragons. Behind the roodscreen is an ancient carving of the Green Man. Avebury seemed to Stukeley to depict a great serpent fertilising an egg.

Stukeley's work, *Abury, a temple of the British druids, with some others, described* (1743), set out his research findings undertaken twenty years earlier (1719-23). He concluded that the purpose of Avebury was to serve as a "Serpent Temple" to worship the opposing cosmic forces of the sun and the moon, and the powers of fertility of the earth. He further posited that a network of such temples, "Dracontia," existed across Britain. He wrote:

> *The ancients indeed did make huge temples of immense pillars in colonnades, like a small forest; or vast conclaves of cupolas to represent the heavens; they made gigantick colosses to figure out their gods; but to our British Druids was reserv'd the honour of a more extensive idea, and of executing it. They have made plains, hills, valleys, springs and rivers contribute to form a temple of three-miles in length.*
>
> *They have stamp'd a whole country with the impress of this sacred character, and that of the most permanent nature. The golden temple of Solomon is vanish'd [and] the temple of Diana at Ephesus perish'd and obliterated, whilst Abury, I dare say, older than any of them, within a very few years ago... was intire.*

Reverend Thomas Twining published in 1723 his *Avebury in Wiltshire, the Remains of a Roman Work*. Whereas Stukeley claimed that Avebury and related prehistoric monuments were the creations of the druids, Twining believed they had been constructed by the Romans.

Bob Forrest has remarked that someone looking along the Michael and Mary corridor towards Avebury from the southwest would note that the sunrise alignment at the location currently occurs on 7 May and 5 August and at Bury St Edmunds on 2 May and 10 August. The sunsets occur on 3 February and 9 November. These dates correspond very close to the ancient fire festivals whose dates have been calculated with accuracy by astro-archaeological means: Spring (Beltane), Sun at 15 deg Taurus, 5-8 May; Summer (Llughnasad, Lammas), Sun at 15 deg Leo, 2-7 August; Autumn (Samhain), Sun at 15 deg Scorpio, 5-7 November; and Winter (Imbolc), Sun at 15 deg Aquarius, 2-7 February.

The Components of the Avebury Temple

The Great Outer Circle

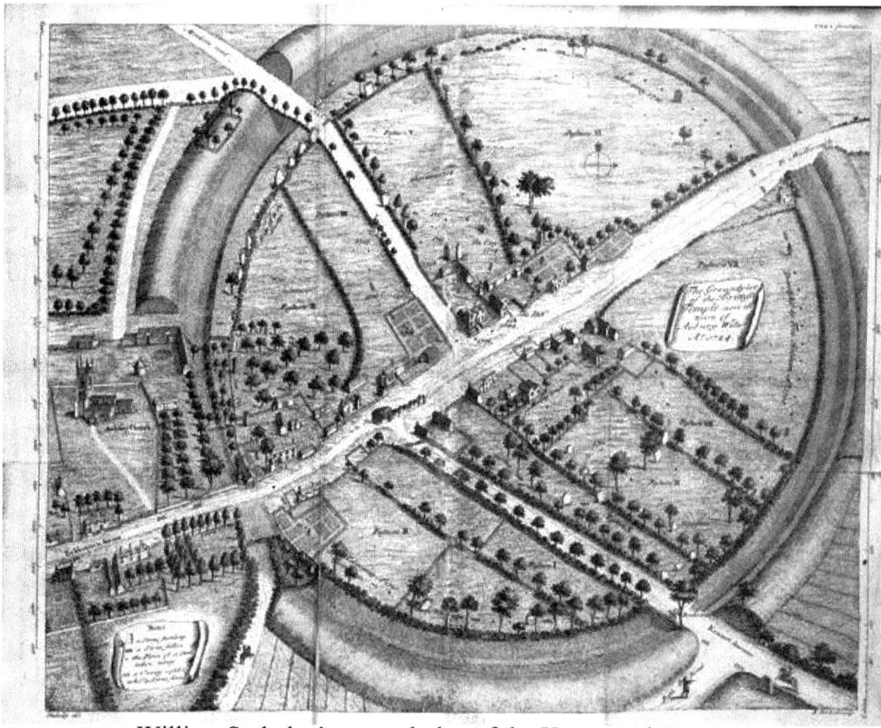

William Stukeley's ground plan of the Henge and Avenues

The henge consists of a large circular bank with an internal ditch that was dug out with red deer antler picks, a colossal feat. The stones of the great circle stand on the inner lip of the ditch. The henge is not perfectly circular and measures 380 yards in diameter and over 1,090 yards in circumference. Within the henge is Britain's largest stone circle (and one of Europe's largest), with a diameter of 1,305 feet.

AVEBURY HENGE STONES					
	Diameter	No. of stones Orig.	No. of stones Now	Av. Dist. apart	Height
Great Outer Circle, containing:	1305 ft	98?	30	36 ft	9 ft-18 ft
1. North Circle with:	322 ft	27?	4	36 ft	9 ft-13½ ft
Inner North Circle	65 ft	12		30 ft	9 ft-13½ ft
The Cove	22 ft	3	2	6 ft	15½ ft
2. South Circle	340 ft	29?	5	36 ft	9 ft-13½ ft
D-feature	80 ft	13	6	12 ft	4 ft
Obelisk		1			21 ft

Radiocarbon findings indicate a construction date of around 2870–2200 BC. It is thought that there were originally 98 sarsen standing stones, some weighing in excess of 40 tons, others as heavy as 60 tons. Only 30 stones remain standing in the outer circle.

The sarsens are of Eocene sandstone brought from the surrounding chalk downs where they lie on the surface. Approximately 4000 tons of stone were moved to construct the henge, a staggering achievement. The stones varied in height from 9-13½ feet, evidenced at the north and south entrances. The two large stones at the southern entrance had an unusually smooth surface, likely due to having stone axes polished on them. Respective groundplans made by Aubrey and Charleton discovered in 1988 by the late Professor Peter Ucko, show portal stones at the henge entrances (3 in Aubrey's plan, 4 in Charleton's).

The ditch was originally around 33 feet deep, now 15 feet after the build up of silt over the centuries. Its bank rose to a height of 20 feet. Burl calculates that 97,000 cubic yards of chalk were removed from the ditch, which is more than half a mile in length. This is roughly the same volume as the seven pyramids erected by the Pharaohs of the 5th Dynasty, yet another mind-boggling Avebury statistic.

It is estimated that it would have taken 250 people more than 20 years to have completed the bank and ditch. In 1934, 12 workmen under the supervision of a experienced foreman took 5 days to re-erect a relatively small 8-ton stone in one of the two avenues of standing stones on the approach to the great circle.

The complex continues to yield surprises. In 2017, a geophysical survey by archaeologists from the Universities of Leicester and Southampton revealed "an apparently unique square megalithic monument within the Avebury circles" which may be one of the earliest structures on this site. No significant archaeological excavation work has yet been undertaken in the henge's northeast quadrant

The Inner Circles

Nearer the middle of the monument are two additional separate stone circles. The northern inner ring is 322 feet in diameter; only two of its four stones remain upright. A cove of three stones stood in the middle, its entrance facing northeast.

Based on experiments undertaken in Orkney, the archaeologists Joshua Pollard and Mark Gillings[52] believe that any sounds produced inside Avebury's Inner Circles would have created an echo as sound

[52] Gillings, M. and Pollard, J., *Avebury*, Bloomsbury Publishing, London, 2004

waves ricocheted off the standing stones. The southern inner ring was 340 feet in diameter before its destruction in the 18th century. The remaining sections of its arc now lie beneath the village buildings. A single large 18 feet monolith, the Obelisk, stood in the centre together with an alignment of smaller stones.

The Avenue

The West Kennet Avenue of paired stones leads from the southeastern entrance of the henge. Traces of a second, the Beckhampton Avenue, lead out from the western entrance. Within the Avenue a standing stone in a hedge is visible a few hundred yards to the east, the sole survivor of Falkner's Ring, which was a circle of 12 sarsen stones. The avenue was defined by 100 pairs of stones, set at intervals of 80 feet. In 1722 there were 72 stones intact; in 1934 only 4, 9 having fallen.

A feature of Kennet Avenue is that looking towards Avebury the stones alternate between thinner straight ones and wide angular shapes. During 1723-24 a local farmer removed the avenue stones and used them in his buildings at Beckhampton. The site was only rediscovered during aerial photography in 1930. It lies on the southern promontory of Hackpen Hill.

The West Kennet long barrow is one of the largest chambered Neolithic tombs and was created by the Wessex people around 3500 BC. The wedge-shaped barrow is 340 feet long, 75 feet wide with a line of impressive façade stones at the eastern. The largest stone stands 12 feet tall. On either side of the central aisle are two pairs of burial chambers to house the bones of the deceased.

The West Kennet Avenue, courtesy Diliff - Own work, CC BY-SA 3.0
https://commons.wikimedia.org/w/index.php?curid=33014611

Beckhampton Avenue, the tail end of the serpent, no longer exists. It was destroyed in the 18th century and lack of evidence threw doubt on Stukeley's claim that its stones once existed. However, when excavators removed the topsoil to reveal stone holes in the underlying chalk Stukeley was proved right. A mile outside the main circle of the henge on the line of the vanished tail of Stukeley's Serpent Temple, stand the Longstones, known locally as "Adam," 16 feet high, weighing 62 tons, and "Eve," 10 feet high. Massive, squat Eve is believed to have been a stone that formed part of Beckhampton Avenue, while Adam, with three other stones now vanished, formed a four-sided cove similar in structure to that in the north circle of the henge. Thankfully, Stukeley made a drawing of it.

When Adam fell over in 1911 the re-erection team found it extremely difficult to put it back in place, even with the benefit of powerful lifting gear. In the team's initial efforts, steel ropes tested to 50 tons breaking strain snapped without the stone budging. It appears on Stukeley's drawing that this cove was intact not very long prior to his visit but during it was being destroyed by Richard Fowler "of the Hare & Hounds Inn" who was a serial stone wrecker. An element of this cove of which Stukeley was probably unaware was found during an excavation in 2000. It was a vast stonehole where a massive but now destroyed blocking stone had once existed. Recent excavations in the area around the Longstones also found evidence of a sizeable enclosure. This has been dated at about 2900 - 2700 BC, which is the same period as the first phase of the ditch and bank that surrounds the henge.

Part of the henge's outer ditch—CC BY-SA 3.0,
https://commons.wikimedia.org/w/index.php?curid=73498

Silbury Hill

In the time of its construction, the Avebury area lacked one vital ingredient: a mighty summit upon which to draw down the powers of the cosmos. The Tors at Burrowbridge and Glastonbury had their pyramidal high points; Avebury had to be similarly equipped. The builders set to work, the result being the magnificent Silbury Hill. White Eagle confirmed Watkins and Heinsch's instinctive assessments that these and other tors in the Dartmoor served as altars upon which magical ceremonies were enacted.

Silbury lies a half-mile south of Avebury village while a half-mile to the east and west sit the respective hamlets of West Kennet and Beckhampton. The mound is built on the end of a spur reaching northeast from Thorn Hill; part of the spur can still be seen just beyond the ditch. It sits on the valley floor of the River Kennet at a point where the capacity of the stream is increased by contributions from a small tributary, together with water from a spring where the stream dramatically changes its course. The River Kennet itself ultimately rises at Broad Hinton, 5 miles to the north of the site and takes in a number of small winterbourne tributaries as it flows south through Winterbourne Bassett, Berwick Bassett, Winterbourne Monkton and Avebury. (A winterbourne is a stream, typically on chalk or limestone, which flows only after wet weather.) At Silbury the Kennet gathers momentum as it is joined by a small brook that rises in the Beckhampton-Devizes valley, flooding the monumental ditch every winter. To the south of Silbury Hill, the Swallowhead spring is located at the mouth of a narrow steep-sided but now dry coombe.

The origin of the place-name remains uncertain. Aubrey recorded that country folk call the mound Zelbury Hill, in commemoration of a local tradition that King Sil or Zel was buried there on horseback. The mound was then constructed over his resting place and "raysed while a posset of milke was seething." Aubrey himself, however, preferred other explanations and compared the name to Silchester, believing it to be linked to that of the Roman town. Whereas Silchester was "Sili's castrum… Silbury might be his monument or mausoleum." Writing 80 years later in 1743, Stukeley, by contrast, believed the name to be Saxon in origin and interpreted it as "the great or marvellous hill." Others have suggested that the name derives from Solis-bury, the mound of the Sun.

Aubrey depicted "Selbury or Silbury hill" as a truncated conical mound with a circular ditch set around its circumference. In his drawings a pathway is shown ascending the mound in a remarkably similar position to that of the path today. On the south side two causeways run from the roadside footpath to the mound, with only a short section of ditch between them. The base of the hill is seemingly circular, 548 feet in diameter. Its conical mound is 130 feet high, 548 feet in diameter and covers 5½ acres. The summit is flat-topped and 98 feet in diameter. Silbury is not a simple mound of earth but was made permanent by an inner structure of chalk blocks weighing around one million tons. Its internal makeup is complex and consists of a circular, six-stepped pyramid made of chalk cubes. It is calculated that it took 18 million man-hours to build, equivalent to 500 men working for 15 years (Atkinson 1974) to deposit and shape 12,500,000 cubic feet of earth!

The original ground surface on which Silbury was built is chalk bedrock overlaid with flinty clay. The soil would be expected to be up to a foot thick. Instead, the chalk beneath the mound was covered with just a few millimetres of smooth, grey, silty clay and was virtually free of stones. This indicates preparation of the site involving the stripping away of the topsoil and the compressing of the subsoil, a mammoth undertaking that would have taken many years.

In 1776 the Duke of Northumberland and Edward Drax engaged miners from the Mendip hills to sink a vertical shaft. Letters written by Drax describe a 40-foot "perpendicular cavity," 6-inches wide. As wood fragments have been found in the hill's interior, it has been suggested that the cavity held an oak tree or "totem pole." Drax also found a considerable number of deer antlers. A subsequent dig was carried out in 1849 by Dean Merewether who tunneled horizontally for 300 feet to beyond the centre of the hill. Neither his nor Northumberland's excavation found any artefacts.

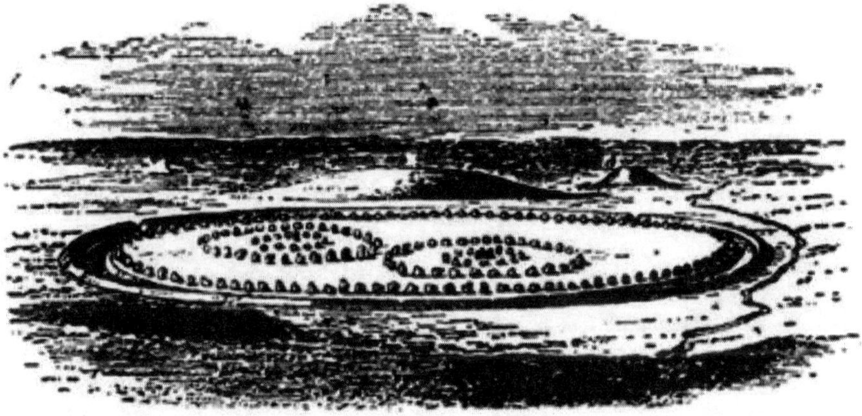

The postulated original layout of Avebury, published in a late 19th-century edition of the Swedish encyclopaedia Nordisk familjebok. Original illustration by John Martin, based on an illustration by John Britton

Silbury Hill viewed from the River Kennet

River Kennet flowing through the grounds of Littlecote House near Hungerford, the former residence of King Henry VIII's third wife, Jane Seymour. Nearby is the Roman Villa mosaic depicting the story of Orpheus. Photographed by the author.

Merewether's dig inspired Wiltshire poet Emmeline Fisher (1825-1864) to write "The Poem in the Urn":

Bones of our wild forefathers, O forgive,
If now we pierce the chambers of your rest,
And open your dark pillows to the eye
Of the irreverent Day! Hark, as we move,
Runs no stern whisper through the narrow vault?
Flickers no shape across our torch-light pale,
With backward beckoning arm? No, all is still.
O that it were not! O that sound or sign,
Vision, or legend, or the eagle glance
Of science, could call back thy history lost,
Green Pyramid of the plains, from far-ebbed Time!
O that the winds which kiss thy flowery turf
Could utter how they first beheld thee rise;
When in his toil the zealous Savage paused,
Drew deep his chest, pushed back his yellow hair,
And scanned the growing hill with reverent gaze, –
Or haply, how they gave their fitful pipe
To join the chant prolonged o'er warriors cold. –
Or how the Druid's mystic robe they swelled;
Or from thy blackened brow on wailing wing
The solemn sacrificial ashes bore,
To strew them where now smiles the yellow corn,
Or where the peasant treads the Churchward path.

In 1970 a dig was carried out under the supervision of renowned Stonehenge archaeologist, Professor Richard J.C. Atkinson. Attracted by the prospect of finding ancient British treasure, the BBC financed and publicized the undertaking for a television documentary. Atkinson ascertained that the hill had been constructed in three phases. In the first, a ring of 120-foot diameter was staked out on a small hillock along the winterbourne stream that runs at the base of the western flank of Waden Hill. Threads of woven grasss were placed radiating from the centre of the ring. Within it a gravel core was prepared with a revetting kerb of stakes and sarsen boulders. Alternate layers of chalk rubble and earth were placed on top of this and subsequently filled, at first with a low mound of clay and gravel and then turf and soil to a height of about 15 feet. This was then sealed by layers of gravel and soil taken from the valley floor forming a core mound of about 120 feet diameter and 23 feet in height. Next, the mound was enclosed within an area 350 feet across surrounded by a larger ditch that was never fully completed. Then a second mound was constructed over the first using chalk blocks. It was built in sloping step fashion and held together with an intricate arrangement of interconnecting walls. When finished, the hill took the form of a glistening white seven-stepped structure. The first ditch was filled in and a much larger one dug. Earth was then piled on top of the terraces, and the entire structure buried and grassed over to create the massive mound seen today. Remarkably, the structural engineering techniques used created a dynamic tension in the chalk, which ensured that the artificial hill's form did not collapse or slump.

The initial structures at the base of the hill were perfectly circular. Surveying reveals that the centres of the flat top and the cone that defines the hill lie within a metre of one another. These three phases have been likened to the method whereby one would create a battery, suggestive of a deliberate attempt by Silbury Hill's Neolithic builders to create a giant natural power storage facility. The mound is tiered. If, like Glastonbury Tor, the tier is actually a spiral it is arranged clockwise from the top downwards. To walk it, one would descend anticlockwise. None of the excavations undertaken have revealed the hill's purpose; they have merely weakened its structure. After heavy rains in May 2002, a collapse of the 1776 excavation shaft caused a hole to form in the top of the hill. English Heritage undertook a seismic survey of the hill to identify the damage caused by earlier excavations and to determine the hill's stability. Repairs were undertaken but the site remained closed to the public. As part of this remedial work, English Heritage excavated two further small trenches at the summit and made the discovery of an antler fragment, the first from a secure archaeological context at the site. In March 2007, English Heritage announced that a Roman village the size of 24 football pitches had been found at the foot of Silbury Hill. It contained regularly laid out streets and houses. Work by English heritage to radiocarbon date the construction of the mound suggests a 95% probability of the following:

Lower organic mound constructed 2460-2375 BC

Upper organic mound constructed 2460-2370 BC

Bank and Ditches constructed 2435-2330 BC

Final Mound constructed 2450-2375 BC (52% probability) or 2355-2295 BC (43% probability)

GPS analysis of the mound in 2001 indicates that it is *not* in fact circular and that its form may be dictated by a series of radial spines, between which are straight construction lines that resemble a spider's web. Some of these "spines" can be isolated and identified at points where the contours collectively project and disrupt the general curvature. Accordingly, the number of straight sides is not absolutely clear (much of the surface is masked by weathering) but, remarkably, the mound appears to be a nine-sided structure—a nonagon.

Few prehistoric artefacts have been found on Silbury Hill. At its core there is only clay, flints, turf, moss, topsoil, gravel, freshwater shells, oak, hazel, sarsen stones, ox bones and antlers. Roman and mediaeval items have been found at the site since the nineteenth century and it seems that the hill was re-occupied by later settlers.

Silbury Hill is an archaeological enigma, its original purpose unknown so the topic is ripe for all manner of speculation. In the past the hill has been considered to be the burial mound of a royal person, a constituent part of the Avebury temple, a temple to Mercury, a mound for assemblies and law making, a platform for astronomical observations or for druidical sacrifice or beacons. It has been thought to be dedicated to the sun, to represent the earth or to be the motte of a castle. It has also been identified as Cludair Cyvrangon, the heaping up of the pile of assemblies of Welsh legend. It has even been suggested that Silbury may represent the axis mundi: the centre or navel of the world. Another local legend says that priests of Avebury stopped the Devil from dropping a bag of soil on the citizens of Marlborough and instead persuaded him to deposit his load in the Avenbury countryside, thus bringing Silbury Hill into being.

Silbury Hill – by Greg O'Beirne

Michael Dames has suggested that the hill is a symbolic effigy of the ancient Mother Goddess and therefore associated with fertility rituals that marked the course of the year. The festival of Lugnasadh (or Lammas) in August, when it is thought Silbury was founded, celebrates the first fruits of the harvest. Another explanation argues that Silbury Hill was deployed as a solar observatory by means of the shadows cast by the mound on the levelled plain to the north, towards Avebury.

John Michell connected Silbury's function with dragon paths, saying:[53]

> *In view of the fact that in China mounds like that at Silbury were erected upon lung-mei, the paths of the dragon, there is good reason to suspect that Silbury itself was sited by pre-Celtic Druids on a dragon line with the assistance of a geomancer's compass. It may also be inferred that the Chinese lung-mei stretch over the entire globe. Many centres of English dragon legend stand at the junction of well-marked leys, one notable long-distance example being the St Michael's line that runs from the Avebury circle to the extreme west of Cornwall.*

The Mary current courses through the hill as do numerous other ley lines. As Guy Underwood noted, Silbury is built directly over the region's power centre, a vast skein of energy filaments. Stonehenge is similarly sited. Silbury is located over a blind spring which has several underground streams flowing from it, some of which surface as springs.

Following the 2007-8 works, archaeologists posed the question of whether Silbury Hill was the only such mound built by the people of the time or if there might be other comparable mounds that have not been recognized as prehistoric. A strong candidate is Marlborough Mound, also known as Merlin's Mount and "Silbury's little sister," in the grounds of Marlborough College, 5 miles east of Silbury Hill, downstream on the same River Kennet. The mound is 59 feet high, less than half the height of Silbury, and has a diameter of 270 feet.

There are archaeological and documentary indications that Marlborough Mound had been used for mediaeval fortifications, and it had been assumed it was built as a Norman motte. However, a team of archaeologists led by Jim Leary in 2011 arranged for core samples from two 10cm diameter boreholes to be analysed. Charcoal found immediately below the mound showed it had been built in or around the period following 2500 BC, making Merlin's Mount, to the astonishment of the archaeology community, a close contemporary of Silbury.

---

[53] Michell, J., *The View over Atlantis*, Sago Press, 1969

In folklore, the mound is reputed to the place where Merlin lies in ageless sleep after his brush with a powerful sorceress. The Normans built a royal residence on its summit, which became home to King John. In this period, John created an important statute that stipulated that no person could invade one's property without a warrant, thus establishing one of the bedrock foundations of civil liberties.

The mystical essence of the Avebury landscape

White Eagle[54] explained that monuments and circles were set up as a representation of the stone worshippers' ideal of God. Circles were commonly constructed because they symbolised the idea of the encircling and protective power of God, and also the notion of God as the source of all life. This source being light, the ancients recognized that physically the source of light was the sun. They also understood from the teachings of wise men among their communities who were developed mentally and spiritually that there was a correspondence between the power of the sun in their lives and the influence of heavenly bodies.

In ancient times stone was considered to be a representation of the bones in the human body. Astrology teaches that Saturn influences this skeletal structure. By worshipping the stones, Neolithic communities indicated that they were largely under the influence of Saturn. From this early custom of stone-worship eventually sprang the worship of the spirit of fire, which later developed into Sun-worship. Ancient peoples discovered that fire could be sparked by friction of stone with stone, which led them to believe that fire or life existed both in stone and in man. The fire that could be produced by striking stones together was also produced within the inner man by some kind of friction brought about in the human body. They believed that life was a fire and that fire was life. They also discovered that there was something within them—a psychic sense or a spiritual awareness—that was affected and influenced by the heavenly bodies, which enabled them to receive communications from deceased companions and teachings from higher dimensions of existence.

Avebury itself was associated with the moon and with obeisance to the moon goddess who was enthroned upon Silbury Hill. The mother-rituals enacted in this favoured part of southern England had their origins in Mu, the Motherland. White Eagle explained that long before

---

[54] *White Eagle on Divine Mother: the Feminine & the Mysteries*, White Eagle Publishing Trust, 2004

the young earth had fully solidified, the Sun-priests travelled here on rays from the higher spheres, all rays converging on the Isle of Britain. Avebury and Stonehenge mark the locations where the cosmic rays meet. The fairies and elemental nature-spirits of the etheric worlds united with the Sun-priests to perform inconceivable acts of power. The rituals concentrated upon the movement of the cells and the building up of form to bring about the physical manifestation of life born in the etheric world.

Later, the wise men of Atlantis, knowing of a coming cataclysm, were directed by the higher powers to make a journey. Some came to Britain, then an island outpost in Atlantis's western region. Here the wise men, the forerunners of the British Druids, established centres of power and learning, building Avebury and Stonehenge as physical portals into the inner worlds and temples of magic. Merlin reputedly said that he built Stonehenge so that it may be his "observatory of the seventy doors and windows," an etheric gateway from which the initiate may travel unhindered by the physical laws of time and space.

Stonehenge is neither situated on the St Michael ley nor traversed by either of its male and female currents. Nevertheless, Stonehenge's relative proximity to the Avebury Temple (17 miles separating the two sacred centres) places it firmly into the hinterland and influence of the trans-England serpent power. White Eagle revealed[55] that the stones of Stonehenge were firstly created on the etheric level and brought into physical existence by the rituals conducted in the sacred landscape, all the stone temples in Britain being created in this manner.

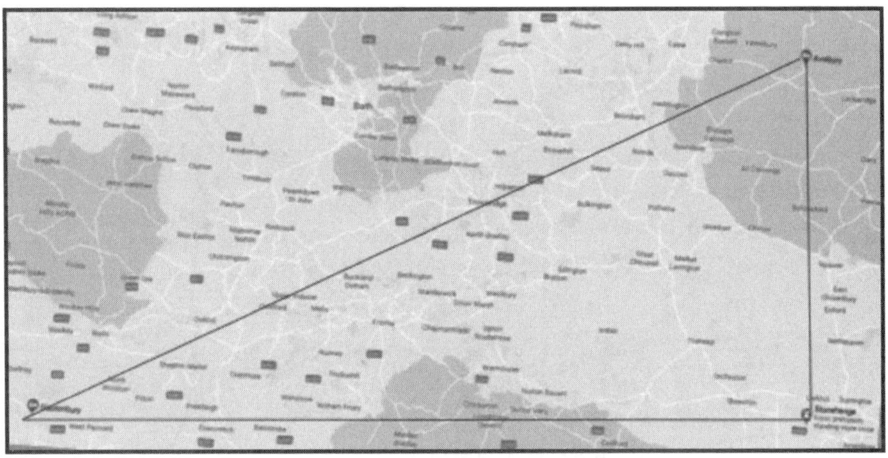

Map showing the 90° geometry between
Glastonbury Tor to the west, Avebury north, and Stonehenge east

[55] Cooke, G. & Cooke, I., *The Light in Britain*, The White Eagle Publishing Trust, 1971

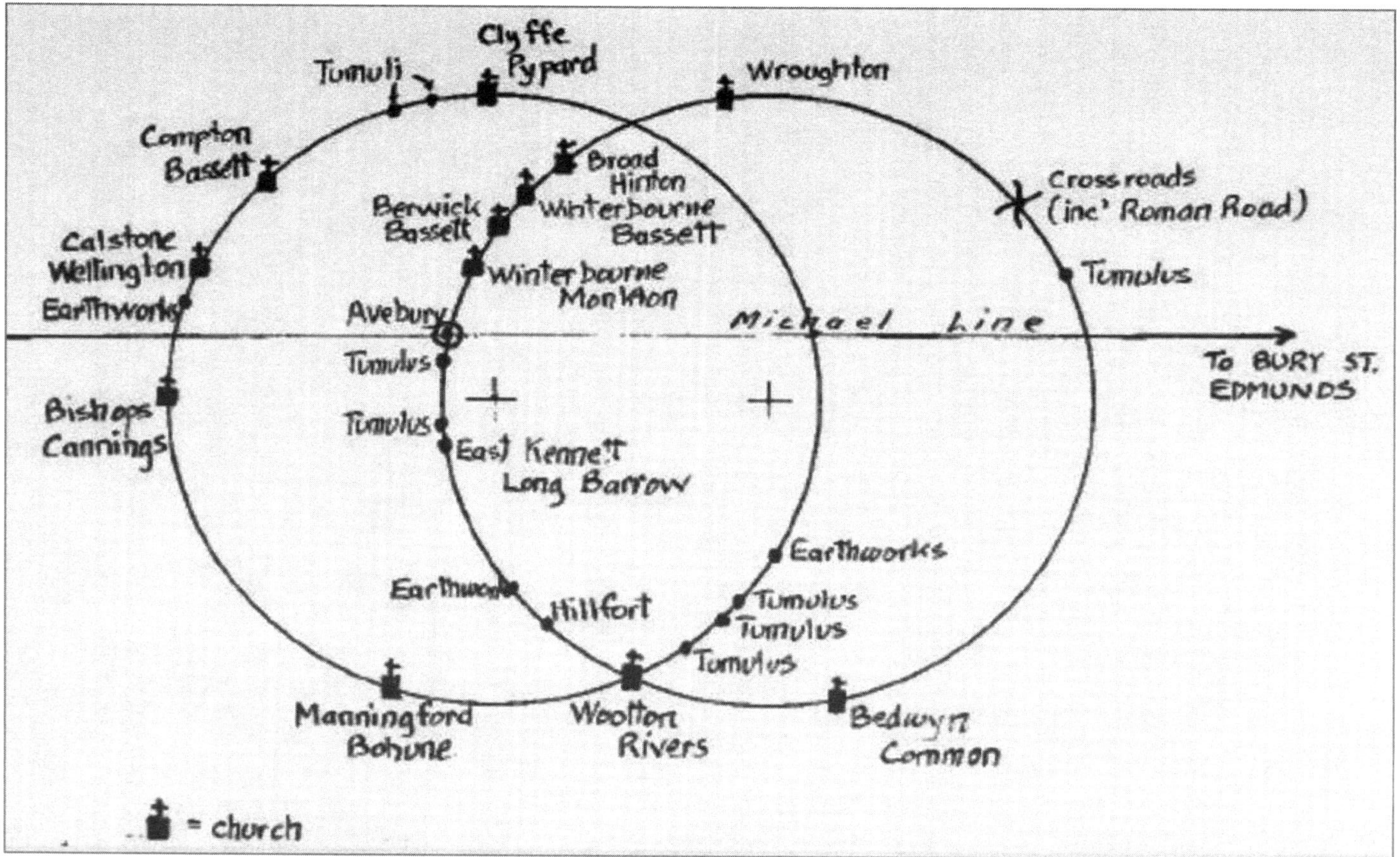

Roy Snelling's diagram of the Vesica Piscis alignments and Michael Line at Avebury, reproduced with permission

Before the present day circle was built there was an earlier "Stonehenge," which consisted of an extremely ancient temple in which rituals were practised. The land subsequently disappeared in one of the vast earthquakes in the period of the Flood and the temple's stones were toppled and dispersed for a long time beneath the waters. Eventually, the waters receded and the Druids re-assembled the stones on astronomical lines into a new temple for the joint study of the heavens as well as for Sun-worship. White Eagle spoke of vast caves that lie far beneath Stonehenge and which are connected to the megaliths by an underground passage. These caves were used as halls of initiation.

Culturally, Stonehenge is on a par with Delphi and Eleusis as a centre of esoteric power. Indeed, Geoffrey of Monmouth described Merlin as the "prophet of Demeter," the goddess of corn to whom the Mysteries of Eleusis were dedicated. In an apparent reference to the Avebury-Stonehenge complex, Apollo's high-priest Abaris worked from a "circular sun temple" located in the green island of Hyperborea in the North Sea, regularly returning to visit Apollo in his fiery chariot.

Records pertaining to the Sumerian and Egyptian civilisations complement White Eagle's descriptions of Silbury Hill's mystic purpose. Its architecture strongly resembles that of 4th millennium BC Sumerian ziggurat structures, constructed so as to generate a harmonious coupling of the forces of heaven and earth on their peaks. Moreover, Silbury Hill was built in approximately the same period that Imhotep, the "divine architect," built the 6-stepped limestone pyramid of Zoser at Sakkara near Memphis in Lower Egypt. Ancient records describe Zoser, High Priest at Heliopolis, Chancellor of the Empire, and the inventor of heiroglyphics, astronomy and medicine, as the "Leonardo da Vinci" of his age. He was a prophet of Thoth (the Greek Hermes and the Roman Mercuria), one of the original gods of Egypt: the "neteru," meaning Watchers. Egyptians described their original homeland as "ta neter," the land of the Watchers.

After travelling along the Red Sea and then rounding the Arab Peninsula, one reaches a country called of old "Shumer," "the country of the Watchers" and the seat of the Sumerian civilisation. Its capital was Ninevah. The oldest known chronicle from Sumer, listing its kings from the 3rd millennium BC, begins, "When the heavenly kingdom came to Earth before the flood…" Their tradition states that the gods descended from heaven and created man, charging the under-gods, the Anunnaki, to build the Garden of Eden and to "fathom the Earth's paths from Heaven," seemingly a reference to a sacred geomantic task. The chronicle says that the existing hominids on Earth were fertilised with the godly semen of the Anunnaki to form the "lulu" (the mixed)—Adama. The chronicle states that mankind was created around 280,000 years ago in what is now Zimbabwe. We return to the mysterious Watchers in the next chapter, which looks at the unfeasibly high number of crop formations in the St Michael ley counties.

In the meantime, we turn to the 2001 GPS analysis of Silbury Hill, which indicates that the mound is nonagonal. Nine-sided ceremonial structures were just as uncommon in antiquity as they are now, a present-day exception being the Temples of the Baha'i Faith.

In esoteric mythography there appears to have existed just one ancient civilisation that placed great importance in nonagonal architecture. In the western metaphysical tradition stories are told of a community that migrated to the Andes region after the fall of Atlantis, taking with them their deep and powerful knowledge of crystals. Once in their new home the community set to work fashioning nine life-size skulls of pure quartz, a task of such delicate craftsmanship and complexity that it took successive generations of families centuries to complete. When the magical skulls had been sculpted they were placed on columns around a nonagon star in a small amphitheatre. In tremendously powerful ceremonies the community's leaders used the crystal skulls to draw down cosmic energy to assist the earth in its post-cataclysm healing process. Thousands of years later the community, believing that its work was completed, concealed the crystal skulls and dispersed far and wide. Some have been found; others remain hidden.

The British Sun-priests' ceremonial practices described by White Eagle appear strikingly similar to those performed by the mountain-top skull community, including deployment of a magical nonagon power in the high Andes and, we now understand, at Silbury Hill. We have learned that men of wisdom came to Britain many thousands of years ago, drawn by a unique force in its landscape that echoes the powers of the cosmos and the invisible gods of creation. Might remnants of the dispersed South American community have been among them, guided by the Sun-gods of the heaven worlds to what is now southern England to resume their mystical practices in the fabled land of Hyperborea? May even their supreme mastery and application of crystal power have been wielded afresh to create the Michael and Mary serpent energies?

(Interestingly, mediaevalist Otto Rahn [1904-1939], whose search for the Grail in France at Himmler's request is the subject of an earlier work[56] was described by *Bild* newspaper in 2011 as having possessed a

[56] Graddon, N., *Otto Rahn and the Quest for the Grail*, AUP, Kempton, Illinois, 2008

crystal skull. In "*Kristallschädel von SS-Führer Heinrich Himmler entdeckt?*" Bild reports on a newly discovered list, which states: "*35 valuable art treasures that should be transported on the orders of... Adolf Hitler and Heinrich Himmler... can be found on the... four-page paper, including... 263-2 FRSS collection Rahn, no. 25592, leather, Crystal Skull, colonies, South America.*'" *Bild's* source was Luc Bürgin, editor of *Mysteries* magazine, who found hidden in an old wooden box in a Bavarian attic the list and the crystal skull: 12-kilos in weight, 17.5cm high and 21cm deep. This was the so-called 13th skull of the Mayans. Legend foretold that all 13 together would on 21 December 2012 create a new age of light to prevent the Apocalypse.

Together with his alchemist friend Gaston de Mengel, Rahn studied earth energies. In 1937, when Rahn sought the Golden Fleece, de Mengel wrote Rahn: "*The axis, which is northeast of Paris, works very well... but the axis is neither near Berlin nor Helsinki. I was able to calculate the origin of the forces from the average of the axis. It is in Murm approx. 35 degrees eastern length and 68 degrees northern breadth in the vicinity of Lowosereo, Russia, I have also located the place of the big black centre... within the big triangle... formed by Kobdo, Urumtschi and Bakul, near Sin-kinag in western Mongolia.*"

At my request Bruce Cathie analysed the co-ordinates and conveyed his remarkable conclusions: "*It appears that the SS did have some knowledge of the grid and harmonic maths. The latitude and longitude... has connections with the harmonic 288 (twice the speed of light) and also the answer to one of the unified equations. They were getting close to the truth. Much is being kept hidden.*"

Pravda reported in 2002 the findings of scientists at Bashkir State University of a stone slab etched with a 3-D relief map of the Ufa region, situated in the Republic of Bashkortostan between the Volga River and the Urals. The scientists concluded that the map proves the existence of an extremely ancient civilisation. Tests indicated that precision tools machined the map and that it shows a view that could only have been plotted by aerial survey. It highlights precise details of massive civil engineering undertakings, including irrigation and dams that would have required the removal of more than a "quadrillion" cubic metres of earth. The scientists believe that the map is only a fragment of a much larger one that showed the planet's entire surface.

One can readily imagine that these extraordinary technologies, brought to Britain by the Sun-priests of Atlantis and safeguarded by the Druids, were used to astounding effect at Avebury, Silbury, Stonehenge and at other great Sun-centres of celebration, evocation and initiation.)

From Avebury, Michael and Mary continue their flight unabated, converging next on a 20-foot high conical earthwork in a field near the Roman Road and the village of Ogbourne St George. Miller and Broadhurst first thought that the mound had considerable age to it but learned that a local man had built it during the Second World War for reasons unknown. The currents then part, Michael travelling through Ogbourne St George Church while Mary crosses the River Og. Two miles away the couple re-unite in the churchyard at Ogbourne St Andrew, the exact node coinciding with a prehistoric mound within the same raised circular bank that contains the church.

Mary then takes her own path across the Marlborough Downs and enters Merlin's Mount, Michael's path taking it through Marlborough College Chapel fifty yards away. Leaving Marlborough, the currents flow along the banks of the Kennet to St George's Church at Preshute, Manton, former home of annual Michaelmas Fairs, and the beautiful valley at Lockeridge Dene with its random bed of sarsens. They then speed on to reach the point ten miles east-northeast where the counties of Wiltshire, Berkshire and Oxfordshire meet.

Oxfordshire is "Alice's" county, in that it was along the stretch of the River Thames known locally as the Isis that Lewis Carroll, on a "Golden Afternoon," first told his tale of *Alice's Adventures Underground*. There is a special thread that connects Alice with the St Michael ley and we will examine it shortly.

Firstly, before we plunge down the rabbit hole we shall first seek to understand why the counties along the Michael line, Wiltshire especially, regularly accommodate such a huge number of crop formations compared not only with the rest of England but with the entire world.

The Barber Stone in Avebury Henge

Merlin's Mount, Marlborough Collge, photographed by the author

Chapter 6

The Gods in the Fields

There have been many more crop formations in the St Michael ley counties over the past 25 years, Wiltshire especially, than simple laws of proportion would otherwise allow. Database sources accessed[57] report around 2,800 formations worldwide in the 1994-2019 period of which just 760 were outside Britain. Putting aside any other contributory factors, if one was to assume a simple equal distribution of crop formations throughout the earth's landmass then England's share of the whole should have been just 2 circles, although its actual number was 860 (to the nearest 10). (England's landmass of 50,350 square miles is 0.09% of the earth's landmass of 57,505,694 square miles.)

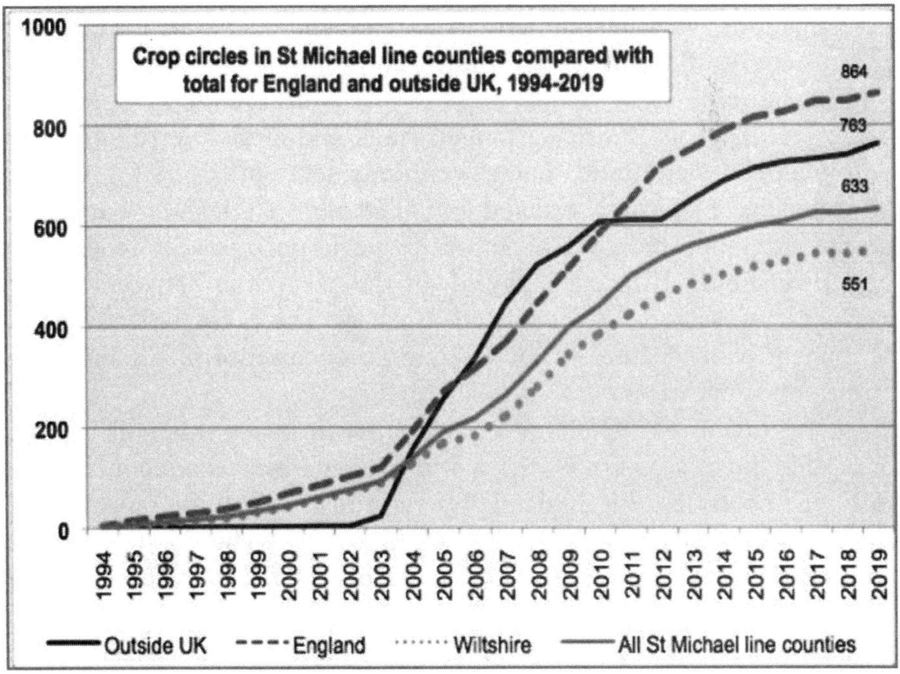

Crop circle data for England and rest of the world 1994-2019

[57] ukcropcircles.co.uk, cropcirclesonline.com and cropcircleconnector.com

As shown in the chart, the results for Wiltshire raise the word "impressive" to a new level of meaning. Its landmass of 1,346 square miles is a miniscule 0.0023% that of the earth's. In statistical terms, it should actually report just 0.07 of a circle yet the county that hosts the Avebury Temple, Silbury Hill and Stonehenge reported 550 formations in the period, punching more than 8,000 times above its weight by share of global landmass. When one factors in "Alice's" Oxfordshire's 41 circles, the joint result for Wiltshire and Oxfordshire was still 5,200 times the two counties' combined theoretical share by area.

Very evidently, there is something going on in the southern English countryside, more specifically in the dominant St Michael ley counties, which is influencing the placement of formations by the circle makers. By circle makers, I do not mean hoaxers but the as yet unknown agency whose work continues to astound, delight and baffle in equal measure. One obvious contributory factor to the region's embarrassment of circle delights is the presence of Michael and Mary, the solar and lunar serpent energies that snake through the English countryside and which appear to grow in power as they weave through the Avebury complex.

Miller and Broadhurst found that all 51 crop circles, which had been recorded at Avebury and Silbury Hill up to and during their investigations, were positioned "exactly on the course of the 'female' [Mary] energy flow." In 1988 they were amazed to discover that one morning after a light in the night-sky was seen shining down over Silbury Hill, geometrically arranged rings and circles were embedded within a nearby cornfield. These were only some of the 58 crop circles of quincunx (a circle bordered by 4 smaller circles) or quadruplet design that appeared over a period of weeks in this year in the field opposite Silbury Hill, each placed on the Mary line between Silbury and nearby sacred Swallowhead Spring. Their placement near a prominent water feature is not an unusual occurrence in the history of circle appearances.

It is known that 93.8% of crop circles are made on chalk. This is characteristic of crop circles the world over and has been recorded in 54 different countries. In England, by far most formations appear over shallowly buried parts of a giant chalk aquifer. The country has the world's deepest such aquifer (the white cliffs of Dover are a view of one side of it), which also has some of the world's greatest seasonal fluctuations of water levels of up to 100 feet. Rain falls on Wiltshire's chalk downs and percolates through the porous material and through fissures to the underlying impervious clay. It runs along the clay until it emerges on the surface as a spring. This springline is often in the sandy soils that adjoin the chalk. What may be the interactive elements between the underground waters and the mechanisms that create the circles?

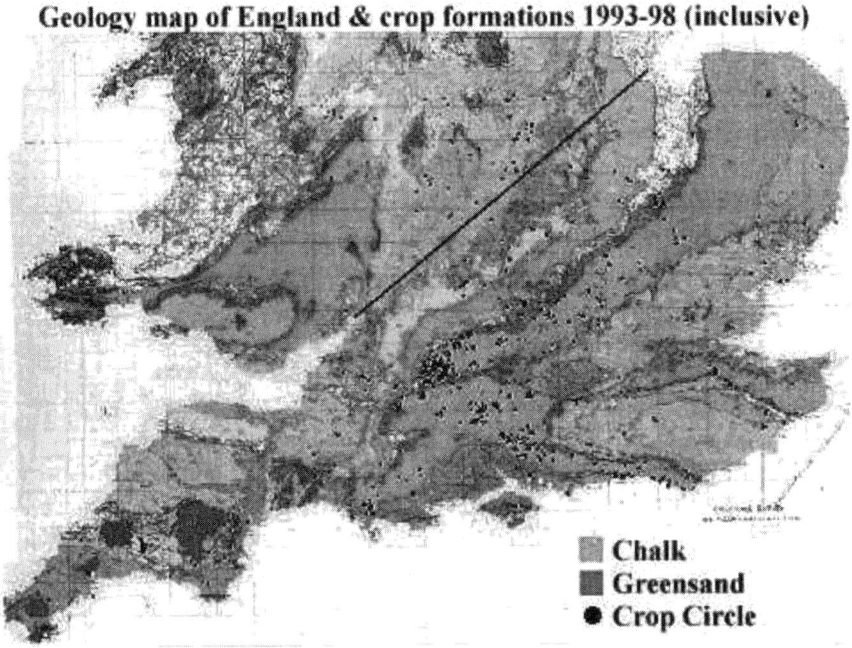

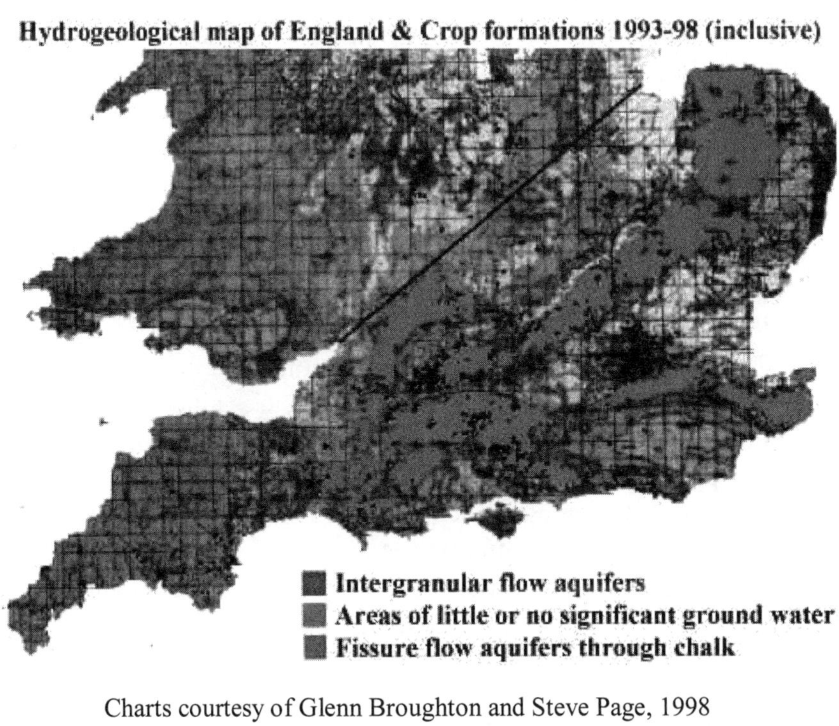

Charts courtesy of Glenn Broughton and Steve Page, 1998

Nearly all British crop circles appear over aquifers and / or over chalk and greensand (an olive-green sandstone), and are often aligned with ancient sacred sites and ley lines as detected by dowsing. One scientific school of thought is that circles are formed by the action of plasma in the ionosphere, a process that requires the presence of an aquifer. The force spirals to earth in the form of a vortical plasma and hits the ground at exceedingly high voltage for just a nanosecond to avoid burning the crop.

There are certain features of southern England's giant aquifer that may attract plasma from the ionosphere. Water percolating through any kind of porous rock creates electric charge, an action caused by "adsorption" in which electrons are stripped of water droplets as they move through rock pores. The process leaves a net negative electric charge behind on the rock and a net positive charge on the water that drains through it. A corresponding factor is that water flows through restrictive channels such as fissures in a spiralling action (like disappearing bath water) and so vortexial energy becomes involved.

Another theory suggests that there is a strong connection between underground water reserves and earth energies, such as the Michael and Mary currents. Callum Coats[58] has pointed out that "pure water will not transmit an electric current... the greater the content of dissolved and suspended matter in the water the greater its capacity to carry an electric current." The waters in England's aquifers are laden with minerals, a geological circumstance that makes them highly conductive conduits for the energy currents that flow through the earth. Furthermore, their very high chalk content is alkaline and saturated with water. There is also acidic clay which contains a lot of flint (silicon or quartz) that underlies the chalk and also a thin layer on the top ridges of the chalk Downs. The result is an alkaline solution sandwiched on either side by an acidic layer. This attracts and is then activated and charged by the earth energy currents. Researchers Glenn Broughton and Steve Page[59] have likened the phenomenon to a massive energised whiteboard upon which the circlemakers are able to apply their construction "programmes" and thereby facilitate the presentation of their messages to the surface world.

French medical scientist Jacques Beneveniste made a remarkable discovery while testing homeopathic remedies for the alleviation of allergy symptoms. In one experiment he placed a small container of a toxin on a copper coil, which was connected to another coil on top of

---

[58] Coats, C., *Living Energies*, Gateway, 1996

[59] http://www.journeyswithsoul.com/articles.php?id=19, accessed 13/01/2020

which was a container of water. After passing an electric current through the coils he discovered that the water, which had never been in physical contact with the toxin, had the same effect on laboratory rats as the toxin itself. This illustrates that an energetic blueprint can be "fixed" in water by the application of an electric current.

As Wiltshire's chalk downs provide the water supply for much of southern England, Broughton and Page have suggested, remarkably, that a third of the population of the nation has literally been drinking the messages in the fields. And, considering that all underground water is connected to springs, streams, rivers, the seas and oceans, this opens the mind-boggling possibility that everyone in the world has been imbibing the circles' homeopathic communications!

One other way, of course, for plasma or similar electrical charge to materialize for the purposes of interaction with a below-the-ground water source is for an intelligent force to create it. As we will see in the following pages, there have been many reports of strange lights and energy beams at play over sites that hours later were to accommodate crop circles of staggering design, beauty and mathematical flare.

John Michell's investigations[60] indicated that the earliest record of crop circles came from UFO investigators in the 1960s. Areas of crushed grass or corn associated with UFO appearances were observed in Australia, Britain and elesewhere. At the time these were called "UFO nests."

Michell[61] supported alchemist Patrick Harpur's opinion that the "god' behind the circles is Hermes, the messenger of the gods, the Soul of the World, the guardian of mysteries, and the inventor of the first symbols in the birth of writing. He is the notorious trickster associated with the wandering, nocturnal spirit of the earth whose mysterious flickering lights were known in old England as "Hermes lights." Looking at the messages and symbology in the fields has been described as like seeing something once known but now quite forgotten. Michell and Harpur believed that Hermes seems to be once more speaking to us in person, an act that they describe as uniquely and immensely important for humankind, which is providing a new revelation that we must take pains to recognize, interpret and act upon.

Moving forward ten years to the mid-1970s, the phenomenon ramped up when light aircraft first observed circular formations of beautiful symmetry in the cereal crops of southern England. At first there were a relatively small number of circles but over time the

---

[60] *Crop Circles: Harbingers of World Change*, ed. Bartholomew A., Gateway, 1991

[61] Michell, J., *The Face and the Message*, Gothic Image Publications, 2002

numbers grew rapidly. By 1990 several hundred had been reported but in that year the formations evolved beyond the simple circle design into highly complex patterns in the form of "pictograms" or "agriglyphs." These newer, more sophisticated designs not only appeared in Wiltshire, Hampshire and Oxfordshire but in other parts of Britain and also overseas. Most appeared in wheat, barley and oil-seed rape but also reported in rye, oats, flax, maize, sugar cane, peas, potatoes, sunflowers, grass, fruit orchards, rice paddies, snow and even ice. In diameter they can vary from a metre (the "grapeshot" variety) to an average 50 metres. Very large formations can cover up to 10,000 square metres. The overall structure can be highly complex, many presenting beautiful layering and weaving effects.

Pioneer investigator Colin Andrews defines a crop circle as a circular shape usually found in cereal crops in which the vegetation is bent over at right angles and spiraled into an often complex pattern. The forces involved in creating crop formations can physically alter the tissue of the flattened (and, sometimes, the internal upright) plants in several ways. However, in cases where no human agency is involved there is never any lasting damage to the plants, despite their being bent up to 90 degrees. They usually continue growing as if the plant tissue, especially in the nodes, softened significantly at the moment of flattening.

A small number of scientists, notably physicist Eltjo Haselhoff[62] and the late biophysicist William Levengood,[63] found differences between the crops inside the circles and outside them, citing this as evidence that they are not manmade. Levengood also discovered that flattened plants frequently have enlarged nodes (the little "knuckles' that form along the stems of cereal plants) and sometimes have "expulsion cavities" in the same areas, where, it seems, moisture has exploded outwards. Remarkably, some investigators have concluded that the energy that creates the formations informs each stem in the design as to exactly where and how it must lie in the overall pattern.

Seed germination trials have shown that when a formation occurs in an immature crop, the seedlings usually do not develop or their growth is severely reduced. However, if a formation occurs in a more mature crop of plants, the seeds grow at up to five times the normal rate. Some formations seem to make use of tractor tramlines as guidelines, while

---

[62] Haselhoff, E., *The Deepening Complexity of Crop Circles: Scientific Research & Urban Legends*, Frog Ltd, 2001

[63] Levengood, W., (1994). "Anatomical anomalies in crop formation plants." *Physiologia Plantarum*. 92 (2): 356–63.

others do not.

60% of circles appear on rainy nights yet farmers and researchers often observe that there is no mud on flattened crop, which would otherwise have been the case had humans been at work using mechanical implements. Moreover, readily crushable balls of chalk are sometimes found intact beneath the flattened plants. In addition, when a formation occurs on soil containing small, sharp rocks such as flint the stems rest on top of the rocks without leaving crease marks, showing that no weight has been applied.

Unusual powdery deposits are sometimes found on the plants and soil inside crop circles. These include magnetite (magnetic iron ore), possibly deriving from meteoric dust, which is constantly drifting down to the earth's surface. The concentration in circles is up to 600 times higher than the normal value, indicating the presence of strong magnetic fields around crop circles. In a small percentage of formations, in both simple and complex designs there is clear visual evidence in the newly planted field of the previous season's crop circle. The new plants in the area where the previous formation was located may be shorter or taller than the surrounding crop or slightly different in colour. This effect usually lasts no more than two years after the appearance of the original circle.

To the chagrin of arch-sceptics who insist that crop circles are the product of night-hour hoaxers, many formations appear in broad daylight. Several eyewitness reports confound the manmade theory. Over the years, some 70 people have said they witnessed the formation of a crop circle. Most eyewitnesses speak of a very powerful but localized force like a wind hitting the field and spinning the crop down extremely rapidly, within about 10 to 20 seconds, usually in the early morning or early evening.

In 1931 a boy and a farmer in Essex in the east of England witnessed a crop circle form in a matter of seconds. The farmer attributed it to the "Devil's twist," a form of whirlwind blamed for similar manifestations in the area since at least 1830. In July 1934, a woman was gazing over a field of corn when she heard a sound like cracking flames and saw a whirlwind in the centre of the field, spinning stalks, seeds and dust up into the air for about 100 feet. Afterwards, she found a perfect circle of flattened corn, hot to the touch, the plant stalks being interlaced and plaited. One evening in July 1981, Ray Barnes while out walking his dog witnessed a "wave" or "line" moving through the heads of a cereal crop in a field in Westbury in Wiltshire. After travelling across the field in an arc, the line descended to the ground and radially described a 75-foot circle in a clockwise direction in a single sweep in about four seconds, which was accompanied by a hissing noise. He said that the crop went down as neatly as if scythed by a giant flan cutter. In the summer of 1983 another Wiltshire man, Melvyn Bell, was riding a horse on the northern edge of Salisbury Plain when he noticed frenzied activity in a wheat field 60 yards in front of him. He then saw a 30-foot circle being flattened before his eyes. He heard no noise during its formation but saw dust, dirt and light debris spiralling into the air. He later described the cause of the circle as a "stationary whirlwind." In June 1989 a witness saw a big orange ball of light about 30-40 feet in diameter descend into a wheat field in England. The bottom flattened as it touched the crop and the ground, and disappeared a few seconds later after a single bounce. The next morning a ringed circle was found at the same spot.

Gary and Vivienne Tomlinson witnessed a circle forming at Hambledon in Surrey in May 1990. They were walking by a wheat field one evening when a whirlwind appeared. It resembled a shimmering mist and made a tremendous noise. A strong gust of wind then pushed them from the side and above. They both felt tingly all over and their hair stood on end. All at once, the wind picked them up bodily off the path and dropped them into the field. Within a couple of seconds, a two-metre-diameter circle formed around them. It rapidly grew outwards from the centre in an anti-clockwise spiral. The whirlwind then split into two, one part zigzagged over the top of the wheat while the other formed a second circle. They described it as looking like a transparent glowing tube stretching endlessly into the sky. Miniature whirlwinds—small, glistening vortices about four inches apart—had meanwhile appeared in the circle in which they were standing. They whirled around the crop in small bunches towards the perimeter, gently laying the wheat down and enlarging the circle. The whole episode lasted about seven minutes. The couple felt lethargic and nauseous for a week afterwards, and Vivienne suffered perforated eardrums.

One late sunny afternoon on 26 July 1990, photographer Stephen Alexander observed the making of a formation in a wheat field beneath Milk Hill at Pewsey, the highest part of Wiltshire. The Alton Barnes White Horse is located nearby. Pewsey Vale, a beautiful part of Wiltshire, is studded with celebrated crop formation sites, among them Alton Priors, Alton Barnes, Stanton St Bernard, All Cannings and Tan Hill. Legend has it that that the body of Guinevere and her entourage travelled over Tan Hill at night *en route* to her entombment at Glastonbury where her husband was buried. Alexander filmed the event. He saw a small white light source, approximately 8"-10" in diameter, travelling around the heads of wheat at a speed of 4-7 mph. It moved erratically, sometimes shifting, other times flickering as if reflecting sunlight before slowing down and blinking out of sight. It then reappeared, motionless, before repeating the same process. Within thirty seconds it had completed the entire formation. Local farmer Leon Besant saw it as he was driving his tractor in the adjacent field. He described it as a "silver glinting light… the size of a beach ball… that was flying in the corn, on top of the corn." He compared it to tinfoil blazing in the sun. Japanese video experts analysed Alexander's footage and concluded that the object was a pure source of light, which between flashes went out of existence. It is known as the Stanton St. Bernard formation below Milk Hill and Clifford's Hill. Experts calculated that the light source was moving at around 40 feet per second.

Another amazing example of a major formation made by invisible hands occurred in 1996 opposite Stonehenge on another July day. This design raised exponentially the mathematical symbolism and complexity of crop formations. Remarkably, it arrived in daylight opposite a busy tourist spot surrounded by roads teeming with traffic. The design became known as "The Julia Set" because it resembled the mathematical fractal called by that name. The formation comprised 196 perfectly graded circles that spiralled out from the centre and extended to a diameter of over 1000 feet. It was first spotted from an aircraft at 6:15 p.m.

Forty-five minutes earlier, the pilot had crossed over the field with a passenger (a medical doctor taking pictures) at 5:30 p.m. and both reported that there was no formation in the field at that time. The security guards at Stonehenge, who claimed that the formation was not in the field earlier in the day, corroborated this. The pilot landed his plane at the nearest airfield, the passenger disembarked, and the pilot refueled for another flight. The pilot took off again and crossed the field at 6:15 p.m. when he saw the Julia Set formation in the field. Fifteen minutes later his previous medical doctor passenger drove past Stonehenge to see onlookers' cars pulled off the side of the busy road. The airspace around Stonehenge is secure airspace due to the proximity of the top-secret air base at Boscombe Down. This means that all flights are monitored and reports made.

According to researcher Lucy Pringle, a woman came forward to say that a taxi driver and passenger were with the parked vehicles and the occupants could not believe what they were witnessing. They stood for 20 minutes witnessing this large design form under a swirling cloud of mist. The witness said:

> "There was an apparition, an isolated mist over it [the formation] and as the circle was getting bigger the mist was rising above the circle. As the mist rose it got bigger and the corn circle got bigger. There was a mist about 2-3 feet off the ground and it was sort of spinning around, and on the ground a circular shape was appearing, which seemed to get bigger and bigger as simultaneously the mist gets bigger and bigger and swirled faster. It was gradual and you are standing there and you are thinking what is going on and everyone is discussing it and more and more traffic is building up and everything and you just think that all the time you don't really realise what is happening and then you think then that's it and the thing is getting bigger and you are thinking of the beginning and end. But you don't realise what you are looking at. I didn't understand what was happening."[64]

Joining geometrically the centres of corresponding circles with three lines generates a series of equilateral triangles that spiral, rotate and expand from the centre outwards with incredible precision. A US surveying company stated that to mark out the Triple Julia Set to this degree of accuracy by manual means would take three to five days, adding two days for calculation time and another three if the construction were working at night, a possible ten days in total. And yet there are still those that cling to the facile belief that geometrically and mathematically complex formations, such as the Julia Set, are made by humans equipped with boards, ropes and a jaunty attitude.

Fractals are fascinating because they seem to show that one can have an infinite number of levels, scales or iterations within a limited structure. In other words, anything that is finite and fractal contains the infinite within itself. Mathematicians are finding that it is theoretically possible to calculate an infinite number of iterations by zooming continuously and indefinitely within a finite space. A study of fractals suggests that the universe is composed of an infinite number of parts, which equally have an infinite number of parts—an incomprehensible infinity of infinites within an infinite. To witness such a mind-wrenching concept requires the presence of a fractal phenomenon. A small number of people were privileged to witness the birth of such on that summer's day in mystic Wiltshire.

Many accounts of balls or discs of of light have been observed over

[64] http://www.freerepublic.com/focus/chat/2364207/posts

fields in which crop formations are subsequently found. Often, these are observed flying over circles already made, sometimes weaving back and forth as if inspecting the formation. In one videotape shot in daytime, a hawk dives down towards a ball of light, only to veer away at the last moment when it realizes that it is not edible. Military jets and helicopters have been seen trying to intercept balls of light, which then proceed to toy with their chasers, sometimes blinking out and reappearing behind the craft that is giving chase. There are also several dozen accounts of a trilling sound being heard prior to crop circles forming. In July 1989 a BBC crew recorded a trilling sound with a frequency of 5.2 kHz in a crop circle. Other noises heard inside them include buzzing, humming, hissing and high-pitched whistling.

There are numerous reports of electronic and mechanical equipment malfunctions in crop circles. Cameras frequently fail to work and even when they do the results may be overexposed, streaked, smeared or entirely black. Video equipment can be especially vulnerable and often suffers from severe interference. Battery draining is quite common; even fresh power packs can die. Mobile phones often fail to make a connection within a formation but sometimes regain it once taken outside the formation. At Warminster in Wiltshire, a tractor's electrical system failed the moment it crossed a circle's perimeter but sprang back to life as it was towed out. In another incident, a tractor was seized by "static discharges which shone like sparks over the body of the vehicle." The next day, a circle appeared at the same spot in the field. Farmers have also reported the deflating of perfectly sound, heavy-duty tyres inside circles. After the appearance of the "Beltane Wheel" formation at Silbury Hill in May 1998, the BBC was conducting a radio interview inside the glyph but the tape speeded up so much that it stopped. When the interview was continued 50 yards outside the formation, the equipment worked normally again. The experiment was then repeated inside the formation but the technical problems returned. Later in the day a crew from ITV Bristol Television arrived and suffered similar problems.

Magnetic compasses frequently behave erratically both inside crop formations and in aircraft flying directly over them. Witnesses report television, mobile phone, smoke alarm and security device interference or malfunctions during nights when a crop circle forms nearby. The night before the appearance of the 1991 tetrahedron in the Wiltshire village of Barbury Castle, residents in nearby Broughton experienced a power blackout. Others reported seeing overhead balls of coloured light along with a low rumbling noise where the formation later manifested.

Watches and clocks might run faster or slower in crop circles. Some see this as evidence that time has literally slowed or quickened, and have linked crop circles to warps in time and space. Certain photographic distortions have been attributed to the same causes.

The effects of crop circles on humans vary widely. Many people inside crop formations experience heightened awareness and feelings of elation, peace and wellbeing. The converse is also reported. Some experience nausea, headaches, dizziness, disorientation, abnormal menopausal bleeding, lack of mental clarity, and excessive fatigue (although both positive and negative effects have also been experienced in manmade formations).

Animals may exhibit strange behaviour near circles. Dogs may refuse to enter while others become nervous or uncontrollable and some become sick afterwards. Before the emergence of a new formation, dogs have been known to bark incessantly in the early hours. In one case a sheepdog tried to bite a hole through a thick wooden door. Sheep sometimes try to move as far away as possible from a field where a crop formation later appears. Horses may refuse to cross a circle's perimeter or become nervous in their vicinity. Deer have been seen to avoid them. Birds, too, tend to stay away from genuine crop circles, even though the downed plants offer easy access to seeds. Flocks of geese have been observed to break formation directly over formations.

Just who *are* the circle makers? Over the years, crop formations have been attributed to a variety of causes: drunks armed with string and planks, wild young farmers, disillusioned art students, out-of-work journalists, over-application of fertilizer, mobile phone interference, squabbling birds, geometrically-minded cows, mating animals, hedgehogs and, as already noted, various light and sound phenomena.

Hoaxers

Many circles have been manmade; some fakers have identified themselves, others have chosen to remain silent. One infamous pair of charlatans were pensioners Doug Bower and Dave Chorley, the "Men Who Conned the World," according to Britain's *Today* newspaper of 9 September 1991. This was the year when Bower and Chorley claimed it was they that had started the phenomenon "for a laugh" in 1978 with the use of simple tools consisting of a plank of wood, rope, and a baseball cap fitted with a loop of wire to help them walk in a straight line. Inspired by Australian crop circle accounts from 1966, Bower and Chorley claimed to be responsible for more than 200 of the 1200 or so crop circles reported during 1978–1991. Not without some skill, Doug and Dave on one occasion constructed a circle in front of journalists after which expert Pat Delgado, unaware of the set-up, was invited to examine the design and, to his subsequent embarrassment, declared it to be authentic.

In what has been described as a watershed moment in the history of crop circle making, in 1991 Bill Drummond and Jim Cauty of the acid-house band KLF (Kopyright Liberation Front) faked a formation in Wiltshire. Investigator Colin Andrews phoned in to BBC Breakfast News to report that his team had just witnessed the overnight creation of a crop circle in Bratton Castle on Salisbury Plain. The interviewer asked: "Are you quite sure you couldn't have been the victim of some elaborate hoax last night?" Andrews replied: "No, not indeed. We have high quality equipment here and we have indeed secured a major event… we do have something of great, great significance… Yes, we have everything on film and we do have, as I say, a formed object over a field… We are doing nothing more now until we have helicopters over the top, to film in detail what we have, before anyone enters the field." It was red faces all round when it was pointed out that Andrews and his companions had ignored certain blue items inside the circle, which turned out to be a board game called Zodiac Spells, placed beneath crossed sticks in the centre of each of the six circles. Andrews had to admit that this circle was a hoax but sought to turn embarrassment into insight when he stated disingenuously: "As soon as I saw the edges of the first circle, I could tell at once it was an obvious hoax… This affair has improved our credibility, as we were able to detect a hoax within seconds… our equipment can tell within seconds whether a ring is a hoax or not… It even detected the heat of the bodies of the perpetrators!"

Puzzlingly, investigator George Wingfield received information from high-level contacts within the military that a special army unit under direct orders of the Ministry of Defence had made the Bratton Castle formation in order to get "circle fever" under control and to deflect attention from Government failure to offer any kind of convincing public response to the phenomenon.

Manmade formations invariably leave substantial clues as to their artificial origin. Cereal stalks are trampled and broken and footprints are evident. Most tellingly, the rules of geometry so precisely observed in genuine circles are not followed because even if the fakers had the skill to produce, for example, highly complex fractal formations such as the Julia or Mandelbrot Sets, to do so requires a large team and perhaps days of work. Some of the most complex circles reported of unknown origin have been produced in minutes, accompanied only by blinking lights over the field.

Weather effects

Circles have been attributed both to cyclonic whirlwinds and to electrically charged whirlwinds, the so-called plasma vortices. While Levengood and Talbott[65] argue that crop formations are created in this manner, Haselhoff[66] draws attention to serious errors in his fellow scientists' methods, proposing instead that formations are created by a point-like or spherical source of radiation rather than a plasma vortex. His studies indicate that a circle's energy source is consistent with heat being induced by a small electromagnetic charge that originates a few metres above the field.

Gaia

The Gaia hypothesis, also known as Gaia theory, proposes that all organisms and their inorganic surroundings on Earth are closely integrated to form a single and self-regulating complex system, maintaining the conditions for life on the planet. The hypothesis was formulated by the chemist James Lovelock and co-developed by the microbiologist Lynn Margulis in the 1970s. Initially received with hostility by the scientific community, it is now studied in the disciplines of geophysiology and Earth system science, and some of its principles have been adopted in fields like biogeochemistry and systems ecology.

In the 1990s the Gaia hypothesis theory was revived as an explanation for the increase of crop circles, both in numbers and complexity, and was thus interpreted as an SOS call by our planet.

Native Americans believe that crop circles are delivering messages that Mother Nature is in serious difficulties, a view that corresponds with Lovelock's Gaia hypothesis in which human activity has created a tumour that is affecting the Earth's ability to effect the self-preserving, self-regulating adjustments necessary to maintain optimal conditions for life.

Cambridge physicist Rupert Sheldrake supports the theory, suggesting that the Earth's organic systems are regulated not only by physical laws but also by "morphogenetic fields," an invisible "form-producing" consciousness inherent in nature. In this model, the Earth

---

[65] W.C. Levengood; Nancy P. Talbott (1999). *Dispersion of energies in worldwide crop formations*, Physiologia Plantarum. 105 (4): 615–24

[66] E.H. Haselhoff, *Dispersion of energies in worldwide crop formations*, Physiologia Plantarum, vol. 111, 2001, pp. 123-4; Haselhoff, 2001, pp. 71-81.

appropriates the symbols in the fields from human thoughtforms deriving from our collective unconscious or "egregore." This being the case, the crop designs are necessarily formulated from *within* the earth itself.

Sky trumpets

Strange sounds in the sky, called by some "sky trumpets," "sky quakes" or "acoustic gravity waves" have been reported from around the world in recent years. People have been puzzled by what they describe as low frequency hums, trumpets, or horns, which seem to emanate from the top of the sky or from under the earth. Most of these sounds have never been heard before now, which makes the phenomenon unnerving. These noises have a groaning quality overlaid with a metallic, vibrating sound similar to that of musical instruments. In some instances, the sounds seem to include unintelligible voices.

Theories abound about these strange sounds and their origin. Some point to natural phenomena, perhaps the result of solar plasma interacting with the earth's magnetic field, sounds produced by the movement of tectonic plates, or a shift in the earth's North magnetic pole. Others point to a human cause, perhaps deriving from industrial or military sources such as the US Government's HAARP or Project Blue Beam programmes, the latter constituting an extremist conspiracy theory in which NASA is attempting to implement a technologically-simulated Second Coming to usher in a New Age religion with the Antichrist at its head! While, inevitably, some attach a spiritual significance to the sky trumpets and hear them either positively as a divine message that we are living in the last days and so must prepare for heavenly transition, or negatively as sounds generated by Satan's forces to frighten and confuse people.

Laser technology

With the rise of surveillance technology used by governments and the military, some believe that crop circles are made by hidden agencies using space satellite laser or other exotic devices to conduct training, environmental control or simply to study how people's reactions.

UFOs, fairies, daimones and the spirits of the dead

Some are convinced that UFOs are responsible for the circles. It is a fact that 20% of all circles are preceded by a UFO event. Warminster, a premier UFO hotspot, occupies the centre of the Glastonbury-Avebury-Stonehenge triangle. Its surrounding hills indicate its pole position in the cosmological landscape with names like Heaven's Gate, Jacob's Ladder, Star Hill, Cradle Hill and Lord's Hill. In *The Warminister Mystery*,[67] Arthur Shuttlewood described Warminster as a "window to a different dimension." The particularly busy UFO wave of 1964 is regarded as a trigger to the oncoming southern England crop circle phenomenon. Once circles began to appear in abundance their association with UFO sightings continued as frequently as ever

At around 11:00 p.m. on 13 July 1988, Mary Freeman, a young Marlborough resident, was returning home from Avebury. It was a dark and cloudy new moon night. By Silbury Hill she saw an intense golden-white glow through the clouds, brighter than the moon. A narrow bead of white light then projected from it, falling at an angle of around 65° on to the area in front of Silbury Hill. She was both frightened and gripped by the scene. "...There was something ethereal about it," she later said. Thirty-six hours later, farmer Roger Hues discovered the first of five Celtic Crosses that were to appear in the region of Silbury Hill that summer, this first appearing exactly where Freeman had seen the light beam.

Michael Hesemann[68] points to the similarities between Freeman's experience and an archetypal UFO encounter such as experienced by German parachutist and circle investigator, Willy Gehlen. One night in September 1976 in a Warminster field, Gehlen was woken by a buzzing sound and saw a tall figure. Mistaking it for the farmer, he apologised for parking his car by the field. He then saw a red pulsing light rise up from the field and fly away.

Winchester resident Mrs Joyce Bowles claims she met ETs on 4 occasions in 1976-77, and that she was once taken aboard a UFO that landed on a field at Chilcomb near Winchester. An occupant said, "This is our field..." His companion showed her a map with "all kinds of lines." In the middle was a circle surrounded by rings. A few months later, formations showed up in this field. Hesemann suggests that this process is the travellers' adopting a strategy of gradually habituating us to their presence to show that we are not alone.

Prior to the appearance in 1991 of the "mother of all pictograms" at Barbury Castle, circle hunters Brian Grist, Gary Hardwick and his girlfriend Alison saw at Beckhampton three strange lights cross the sky, followed by many white lights and objects pulsing green, red and white, sometimes disappearing towards the north, other times to the south. Finally, an enormous dark object passed noiselessly overhead. Some of

---

[67] Shuttlewood, A., *The Warminstser Mystery*, Tandem, 1976
[68] Hesemann, M., *The Cosmic Connection*, Gateway, 1995

the pulsing UFOs seemed to fly towards the three observers on several occasions. The scene reminded Grist of scenes from Speilberg's "Close Encounters of the Third Kind." "I couldn't believe what was happening there," he said. Two weeks later, a UFO was sighted when a circle surrounded by a ring of 10 satellites appeared in a field at Hopton-on-Sea, the most easternly point of the St Michael ley. A large red light surrounded by a Saturn-like ring, as large as the full moon, descended on the site of the formation. When it touched the ground it suddenly went. In their choice of design, may the circlemakers have been saying something important about Britain's 10 Perpetual Choirs?

When Hesemann discussed these events with John Michell, the latter said, "There isn't just a connection with the UFO phenomenon; both are expressions of the same phenomenon. The mysterious lights in the sky, the peculiar noises and the strange effects and things which people experience in connection with crop circles indicate this."

In July 2009, Andy Russell[69] received a call from a contact within Wiltshire Police. The off-duty officer had been driving past Silbury Hill early Monday morning (the 6th) when he saw three figures standing in a formation. The formation coud not be seen from the road but the officer knew from prior conversations with colleagues that there was one in the field. He felt strongly that the trio were standing inside it. When later questioned how he "knew," he said that, "you know what day of the week it is, but no-one has told you, you haven't seen a calendar, you just know."

At first he thought they were forensic officers as they were dressed in white coveralls. He stopped his car and approached the field. The figures were all over 6 feet and had blond hair. They seemed to be inspecting the crop. When he got to the edge of the field he heard what he believed to be a sound not dissimilar to static electricity. This crackling noise seemed to be running through the field and the crop was moving gently, close to where the noise was moving. He felt the hair on his arms and back of his neck raise up. He shouted to the figures, which at first ignored him. When he tried to enter the field they looked up and began running.

He said, "They ran faster than any man I have ever seen. I'm no slouch but they were moving so fast. I looked away for a second and when I looked back they were gone. I then got scared. The noise was still around, but I got an uneasy feeling and headed for the car. For the rest of the day I had a pounding headache I couldn't shift."

---

[69] http://thetruthhides.wordpress.com/

After the experience the officer suffered what he called poltergeist experiences. Several electrical items began to malfunction and there were strange knocks at the front door. When the officer answered the door there would be no one there. He had the strongest feeling that he had brought something home with him. Several days after the experience he felt a presence within his home. Sometimes, when walking out to the kitchen, he saw in his mind's eye a brief flash of a towering black figure, around 8-feet tall, standing before him. He felt also that there were pieces of the experience coming to mind that he was not at first aware of. He came to believe that the beings were identical, both in a clone-like manner and in shared intelligence and behaviour resembling a hive-like mentality. He also felt that he should not have seen what he had seen and that this was communicated to him.

In terms of symbological interpretation, Carl Jung suggested[70] that phenomena such as UFOs (and, by extension, latter day crop circles) may be regarded as examples of what he termed a "visionary rumour," typified by the visions seen during WWI by soldiers at Mons and the Catholic faithful at Fátima. The first requisite for a visionary rumour is the experiencing by the many of an unusual emotion, experienced as intensification into a vision and a delusion of the senses that springs from a stronger excitation and, therefore, arises from a deeper source. Jung argued that psychological projections such as these must have a psychic cause because striking phenomena such as UFOs cannot possibly have no importance in the grander scheme of human consciousness and, therefore, represent a psychological situation common and meaningful to all mankind.

Clearly, crop circles have become a more recent component of the mass-visual phenomena that Jung described. He argued that these only occur when in society there is a split between its collective conscious attitudes and the unconscious contents opposed to it. Precisely because the collective unconscious does not know about them and is thus confronted with a situation from which seemingly there is no way out, these strange contents cannot be integrated directly but instead express themselves in our minds indirectly through inexplicable opinions, beliefs, illusions and visions. On such occasions the unconscious has to resort to drastic measures in order to make its contents perceived. It does this most vividly by projection, by extrapolating its contents into an object (a UFO or crop circle, for example), which then mirrors what had been previously hidden in the unconscious. In these circumstances,

---

[70] Jung, C.J., *Flying Saucers: A Modern Myth of Things Seen in the Skies*, ARK edition, London, 1977

we find eyewitnesses who sincerely claim to have seen with "their own eyes" the "signs in the heavens." These wondrous things seen and experienced become a living myth.

Importantly, these signs have meaning, which is important for society. Often, we stand back and scratch our heads while we ponder the meaning concealed in the latest crop formation but now and again we hear of claims that solutions are being found. The late Anthony Dodds, for example, British police officer and UFO investigator, was a supporter of the crop circle-UFO theory. He told German researcher Michael Hesemann that he understood from his contacts in the intelligence community that government cryptologists worldwide had succeeded in decoding some of the pictograms, seemingly formed so that scientists could discover how to read them, and that NASA and some leading universities were also interested.

Jung also regarded these phenomena as symptoms of psychic changes that invariably appear at the beginning of a Platonic month of approximately 2,160 years. (One Platonic month is one-twelfth of a Great Year, defined by scientific astronomy as the period of one complete cycle of the equinoxes around the ecliptic, 25,772 years being the currently accepted number.) Jung visualised these periods as changes in the constellation of psychic dominants, archetypes or "gods," which bring about long-lasting transformations of the collective psyche. The advent of Christianity marked the transition from Aries to Pisces to this present period at the threshold of the constellation of Aquarius. Jung theorised that UFOs and similar phenomena are vital aspects of these transitional signs.

Fairy folk are high on the list of suspected candidates behind the creation of crop circles. In a previous work I argued, however, that UFOlk and fairy folk share a common origin.[71] In support of my theory I quoted many authorities of the same mind, among them the late Gordon Creighton who in an article for *The Flying Saucer Review* said:

> *"...beings from flying saucers are much more probably creatures who share this earth with us; regarding whom science has not a single word to say; but about whom our own written and oral traditions, in all our civilisations, speak volumes."*

Creighton's astute remark pre-supposes the belief that our plane of existence does not solely consist of the physical globe on which we live but that Earth has sister dimensions that surround and interlace it much

[71] Graddon, N., *The Landing Lights of Magonia: UFOs, Aliens and the Fairy Kingdom,* AUP, 2018

like the invisible energy field, the aura, that clothes the human body. According to esoteric tradition, some dimensions of the earth have coarser vibrations than the physical plane, while others are higher in vibrational quality. It was the latter that White Eagle to referred in his discourses concerning the White Brotherhood, the ancient Brethren of the Sun who inhabit a "heaven world" composed of finer ethers located just within our own "solid" world and which interpenetrates all physical life. Just because we cannot ordinarily perceive these neighbouring worlds does not mean that they are not home to lifeforms who also call the total earth dimension their home. In *The Landing Lights of Magonia* I argued that these companion planes are home to energy forms that humans, according to the prevailing memes and traditions of one's time, variously label aliens and fairies among other descriptors.

Folklore from all corners of the globe reveals that humankind has always recognized that it shares the earth with supernatural beings. Up to the time of the nineteenth century Industrial Revolution our traditions referred to them as fairy folk, elusive beings inextricably associated with the natural world. Consequently, unusual forms if glimpsed or experienced in former times were readily associated with nature and invariably described and stories told of them in terms of the earth's basic elemental makeup.

The *Magonia* work described how prior to the advent of large-scale industrialisation, individuals were more attuned to the rhythms of nature's cycles and seasons. Thereafter, as land was increasingly given over to factories and industrial processes, affinity for the countryside and its secrets gradually became a sense of deep mourning for the loss of a sacred fellowship with nature. This emotional upheaval presented many challenges, a process about which Jung reflected at length. He understood that the fears engendered by rapid social change encouraged humankind to look to the skies for guidance because the depleted natural scene had become so much harder to "read," hence the appearance of signs in the skies. What once would have been described as an encounter with fairy folk became more of a technological experience that revealed itself to observers as a flying disk, unusual lights in the sky or a strange circle in a wheat field. I suggested that by removing the social, cultural and traditional factors that characterise otherworldly experiences one is free to describe meeting a fairy or UFOnaut as an encounter with a non-human entity (NHE), though *not* necessarily non-human in appearance and manner.

In making this argument, one must distinguish between an authentic naturally borne biological lifeform and an artificial entity made by such.

In most cases of "alien" contact, observation and scientific analysis has determined that NHEs fall into the latter category. Briefing papers concerning UFOs that crashed in New Mexico in 1947 reveal a consensus among scientists that the "alien" ships were short-range reconnaissance craft piloted by advanced robotic constructs. Professor Robert Sarbacher, one time scientific consultant to the R&D Board at the U.S. Defense Department, told nuclear physicist Stanton Friedman that he and his colleagues were convinced that the Roswell UFO crews, the archetypal "greys," were biological robots. He later said that the "aliens were constructed like certain insects, wherein because of the low mass the inertial forces involved in operating the craft's instruments would be quite low."

The late physicist, Professor David Bohm (1917-1992) coined the term Implicate Order (akin to Jung's substrate), an infinite sea of space and energy out of which matter could be unfolded (the process of "explicating") and enfolded ("implicating"). In Bohm's cosmology the Implicate is the ground from which reality truly emerges and, thus, the source of the physical world, the Explicate Order, which includes all the abstractions that humans normally perceive. Gradually, and unusually for a scientist, Bohm sensed that the Implicate Order is both a physical and metaphysical construction created by an inconceivably vast Intelligence that contains within itself all things, which it enfolds or unfolds so they emerge into the physical experience we perceive as real.

Bohm considered a human being to be an "intrinsic feature of the universe, which would be incomplete in some fundamental sense" if the person did not exist. He believes that individuals participate in the whole and, consequently, give it meaning. Bohm went so far as to suggest that consciousness is actually a subtle form of matter that is at work in the organisation of the Implicate and Explicate Orders.

Cambridge biophysicist Professor Rupert Sheldrake developed this idea in his visualisation of an interacting universe whose tiniest element—he gives the example of a hologram but a crop circle will equally suffice—contains the information of the entire universe. In this model there is no process of "chance," only a blueprint of evolution, which is transmitted throughout the entire universe. Progressing these cutting edge scientific opinions, there are those who believe that the two-dimensional designs we see in the fields are an unfoldment from their true multi-dimensional forms.

Present day emergence theory describes the phenomenon of "quasicrystals," irregular but not random patterns, which are created by projecting a crystal from a higher dimension to a lower one. Imagine projecting a 3-dimensional image onto a 2-dimensional plane at a certain angle. By analyzing the 2-D projection, it is possible with the correct mathematical toolkit to recover the "mother" object in 3-D (perhaps the circle makers' aim?). Such thinking reflected Anthony Dodds' informed understanding that government cryptologists were beginning to decode some of the pictograms because the circles' inherent maths and geometry had been deliberately seeded so that scientists may discover how to read them and, most importantly, act on them. Emergence theory then goes further, positing that the 3-D mother object is, in turn, a projection from a higher dimension of a 4-D quasicrystal (an aspect of Bohn's Implicate Order), which is itself a projection from an 8-D crystal (akin to Bohn's "plenum," a special energy existing at the very depths of the ground of all existence).

The master geometry that governs the entire process of emergence is ruled by the Golden Mean, the Phi constant to which we return in the next chapter. Emergence theory also demonstrates that the building block of our 3-D universe is a tetrahedron at the Planck size level (one to the minus 35th of a metre). Planck tetrahedra join together in a process of ever increasing "kissing numbers" to create what we perceive as reality. The tetrahedra can choose what shape to become as they join with all other companion tetrahedra to formulate the universe. This fact is now convincing physicists that consciousness is required for these decisions to be made.

Like Bohm, Pibram and Sheldrake, emergence theorists are now asking the question: Whose consciousness is behind the choices—a higher intelligence or ours? We already have the necessary tool to fashion Bohm's manual—our consciousness. It follows that the implicate part of our mind (of which we are wholly unaware under normal circumstances) creates and maintains the implicate ground in which the UFolk and the Fairy Folk, materialisations from humankind's collective unconscious, originate.

Whereas our five (explicate) senses limit what we can see before us, at a deep and fundamental level of (implicate) consciousness we see into the Looking Glass world and interpret the circle's hidden messages. One imaginative way to reflect on these incredible theories is to regard a crop circle as a UFO parked in a field. That the formation appears to be an inert imprint on solid ground is a trick of perception whereas, in reality, there is no "ground," only a living, spinning "alien" extrusion from dimensions beyond conscious human comprehension.

The mind exists in both the Explicate and Implicate Orders. We are aware of the workings of that part which inhabits the Explicate. It is the part we use to navigate the physical, mental and emotional pathways along our journey through life. In life we become dimly aware in dreams and visions of the part of the mind that resides in a sub-folder labelled "the Implicate," where there is perfect understanding of what the circlemakers truly wish to convey in their artforms. In the normal course of day-to-day living we are unable to access the information stored in this elusive cabinet but through processes of inner reflection and meditation I do believe that one can learn to train a hidden eye upon its contents. Once this is achieved one can then engage in true and equal partnership with the circlemakers and together, reading from the same page, take the necessary actions to help heal a planet in dire need of tender loving care.

Implicate, substrate, plenum, quasicrystal—these are quantum age terms that describe what has many names, among them: Tír Na nÓg, Annwn, Avalon, Álfheimr, Hy-Brasil, Hyperborea, Wonderland, Olympus, Happy Valley, Shangri-La, Land-of-Make-Believe, Land of Youth, Tir N-aill, the Happy Plain, the Elysian Fields, and, of course, Fairyland. Together, they are merely synonyms for the higher worlds of the earth dimension ordinarily inaccessible to our limited human senses.

During his investigations into fairy lore in the early 1900s, Walter Evans-Wentz concluded that the heaven world of the Celts is not to be found in planetary space but here on Earth. The Celtic mystic believed that the universe comprises two interpenetrating parts: the visible world and the invisible realm of the fairies, which are intelligent beings that reside in the Otherworld and occupy all orders of society and hierarchy. This magical world is a subterranean (dimensional) region that interlaces our earth and which is invisible to humans except under special circumstance. Wentz identified the principle residents of this Otherworld as the Tuatha dé Dannan, the tall and beautiful Good People (*Daoine Maithe* in Irish), a highly cultured race whose members live in the hills of their world, marry and bear children, toil and feast.

The Irish Celts called the folk of the Tuatha dé Dannan the Gentry or, simply, the folk. The Gentry were described to Evans-Wentz as a unique aristocratic race between mankind and the spirit world, noble in appearance and far superior to humans. They range in height and build from child-size to unusually tall, fully grown men and women. They speak in a sweet, silvery voice and play the most beautiful music. The Gentry can take many forms, make things seem other than they are and have the ability to stretch or contract time. A witness told Evans-Wentz of a member of the Gentry that once appeared to him. He was stoutly built and appeared to be only four feet tall but told the witness: "I am bigger than I appear to you now. We can make the old young, the big small, the small big." Crucially, the Tuatha dé Dannan, born from the "waters of heaven or space," a representation of the goddess Anu (later Christianised as Brigit), are extremely gifted in the fields of architecture, science, mathematics and engineering, precisely those skills that are so very evident in the exquisite designs in the fields. If one is seeking an identity for the circlemakers, the master builder-magicians within the Tuatha dé Dannan are as good a choice as any.

> *Do not let it be forgotten that there is a native Mystery Tradition of our race which has its mature aspect in the sun-worship of the Druids and the beautiful fairy-lore of the Celts, its philosophical aspect in the traditions of alchemy, and its spiritual aspect in the Hidden Church of the Holy Grail, the Church behind the Church, not made with hands, eternal in the heavens. All these have their holy places, mounds and pools of initiation, which are part of our spiritual inheritance. Let those who follow the Inner Way study our native tradition, and re-discover and re-sanctify its holy places. Let them keep vigil in the high places when the cosmic tides are flowing, and the Powers of the Unseen are changing guard and the rituals of the Invisible Church are being worked near the earth.*
>
> —Dion Fortune, *Avalon of the Heart*

Jung's opinions on the nature of "alien" energy forms continued to resonate with circle investigators through the years. Colin Andrews and Pat Delgado considered that the circles were created by "an unknown intelligence using an unknown force-field." Fellow investigator George Wingfield, graduate in natural sciences from Trinity College Dublin, did his practical work experience at the Royal Observatory in Greenwich in stellar spectra and the Earth's magnetism. In the 1980s the Wingfield family was living in Wiltshire and became eager circle watchers. Wanting to get to the bottom of this puzzling phenomenon, after much study George Wingfield concluded that the circles were "the product of a non-human intelligence whose nature we still have to investigate as far as we can do that." He set out 20 fundamental characteristics of crop circles, mostly concerning placement and form but the last in the list reads:

> *Intelligent reaction to the circle researchers' discussions and theories, apparently in an attempt to communicate and to lead us in a certain intended direction.*

I concur. The circles are made to be read and interpreted psychically or scientifically. Those observers that have some "shine" about them may come away from their experience with thoughts and feelings about what improvements they can make in their lives to help heal a planet in pain. Scientists, who by and large comprise a community whose members are more intellectually than intuitively gifted, are invited to interpret a design's math and geometry and take collective action to achieve the same objective. Rarely, a great thinker who also believes in the unseen such as scientists Isaac Newton, Albert Einstein, David Bohm and logician Charles Dodgson, comes along and by virtue of their combined left-brain/right-brain flare brings new levels of understanding to complex metaphysical phenomena.

Pure unadulterated circles, genuine extrusions from the etheric world of higher Nature, range from rudimentary geometrical forms to designs of extraordinary complexity. Some have wondered if crop circles are intended to provide mathematical insight, which, once understood, will help mankind to restore its reverence for the Earth. Reflecting on this, Linda Moulton Howe asks: "Could something out there be trying to reinforce the idea that our universe and all its energy and mass are defined by a repeating feedback loop that is mathematical in evolution and powered by consciousness?"[72]

John Michell decried the modern day tendency to confuse the medium with the message, which in the context of crop circle phenomena he regarded as essentially apocalyptic:

> *...There are no known precedents that messages from the gods of Heaven or Earth ever consisted of good news or of congratulations on the happy course of things. Almost always they appear as warnings and omens of approaching difficulties. As a consequence it is hardly surprising that many people associate crop circles with ecological crisis and comprehend them as a spontaneous expression of protest on the part of our mishandled Earth.*

There is no shortage of support from earth watchers for Michell's sobering words. Hopi Indians told Colin Andrews that Mother Earth is speaking to us in symbols directly to man's consciousness through the circles. She is reaching the limits of her endurance to sustain further assaults and is reaching out in an attempt to convince her children to change their behaviour.

---

[72] Howe, L., *Glimpses of Other Realities, Volume II: High Strangeness*, New Orleans. Paper Chase Press, 1998

However, we delude ourselves if we think that Mother Earth needs the presence of humans in order to flourish. Lovelock's Gaia hypothesis that the earth is a self-preserving super organism highlights the fact that the planet does not need billions of humans for its continuing survival. The ancients taught that the neutral lifeforce within animals, plants and minerals keeps the earth in an "existence charge" of perfect balance. For billions of years the planet existed in this happy equilibrium until the Universal Law judged it was time to raise life on earth to the next level of creative expression with the introduction of humans equipped with a new unit called the mind.

The mind's constant conflict with good and evil and one's relentless struggle to forge a path of balance between them generates a tremendous amount of power that feeds back into the Universal Law, thus increasing it. David Bohm illustrated this mutually beneficial process when he referred to man as an "intrinsic feature of the universe, which would be incomplete in some fundamental sense" if a person did not exist to give the universe meaning and allow it to know itself better.

And so, yes, we are good for contributing cosmologically to the beneficial increase in the universal scheme of things but let us not kid ourselves that our planet cannot do without our presence when circumstances demand. Surely, this is a fundamental aspect of the messages in the fields whose authorship is increasingly suspected of having a strong feminine, Mother Nature aspect.

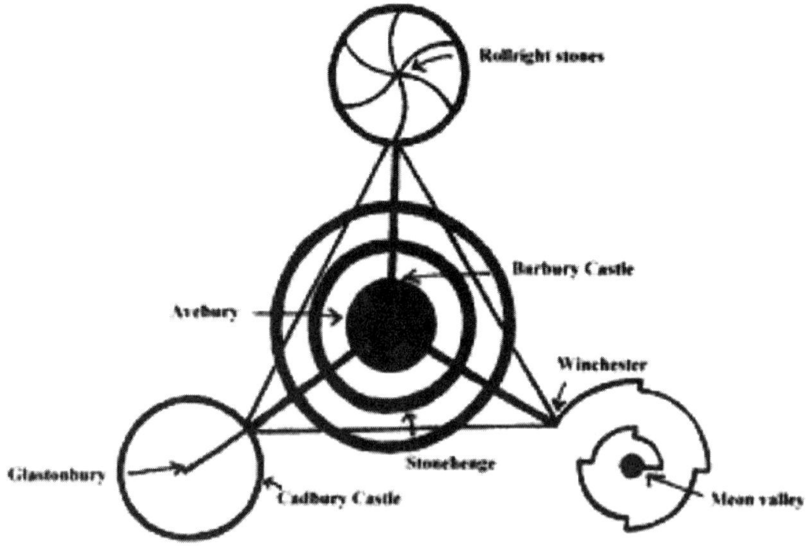

1991 Barbury Castle pictogram superimposed on map of southern England

Carol Cochrane, member of the London-based Centre for Crop Circle Studies, has carried out studies in many formations. Her work indicates that "Isis" is encoded in 90% of the circles, and "Osiris" in 60%. Recurring phrases include, "the answers are in the letters," and "the letters are at all the sites." Isabelle Kingston, a British trance medium who earns considerable respect among circle researchers, offers a psychic solution to the meaning of the "letters." The gifted daughter of a doctor, Isabelle had a successful career in banking and finance before developing her channeling skills. She is a modest person who readily admits she is the unlikeliest person to have any kind of dealings with the Circlemakers. Michael Hesemann is convinced that Kingston warrants attention because she has a convincing record of accurately predicting where and when formations will appear. She correctly predicted the mysterious quintuplet design at Sibury Hill in June 1988 before going on to say that the number of circles would grow enormously. In the following twelve months there were approximately 300 circles compared with 120 in the previous year.

Kingston said that the "old ones" built Silbury Hill as an insurance policy for a time when humanity would expand its energy from the opening up of these centres, hence Hesemann's subsequent remark that Silbury is the "Archimedean point" of the circle phenomenon. Kingston said that the triangle in the Barbury Castle pictogram is an "indication of different dimensions, and the gates to these dimensions are given to us, which are contained in the power of the pyramid. I feel we can learn of a new form of energy through studying the pictograms, which possibly can be used in humankind's future."

Script in circle at Milk Hill Alton Barnes, August 1991—working with 12 linguists, archaeo-astronomer Gerald Hawkins arrived at 18,000 variations in 42 languages. Out of 3 possible solutions, only 1 made grammatical sense: "OPPONO ASTOS," post-Augustus Latin translation: "I oppose acts of trickery (or cunning)." Bizarrely, 6 of the 7 letters have been traced to an obscure Knights Templar-based alphabet code. Who or what is the opposer?

In his 1928 masterwork, *The Secret Teachings of All Ages*, Manly P. Hall included a number of illustrations regarding the Rosicrucian mysteries, one of whose upper part closely resembles the Barbury design. The resemblance between Hall's diagram and the Barbury Castle imagery that appeared in a Wiltshire field 63 years later is so striking that one wonders if the circle maker desired to make a deliberate reproduction. May this provide a clue as to the identity of the circle's creators? Hall described the diagram's upper part as a representation of the realm of the godly, the first divine manifestation symbolized by the equilateral triangle. The 7 outer circles are the angelic world. The diagram's bottom part is the "Ungrund," the Abyss.

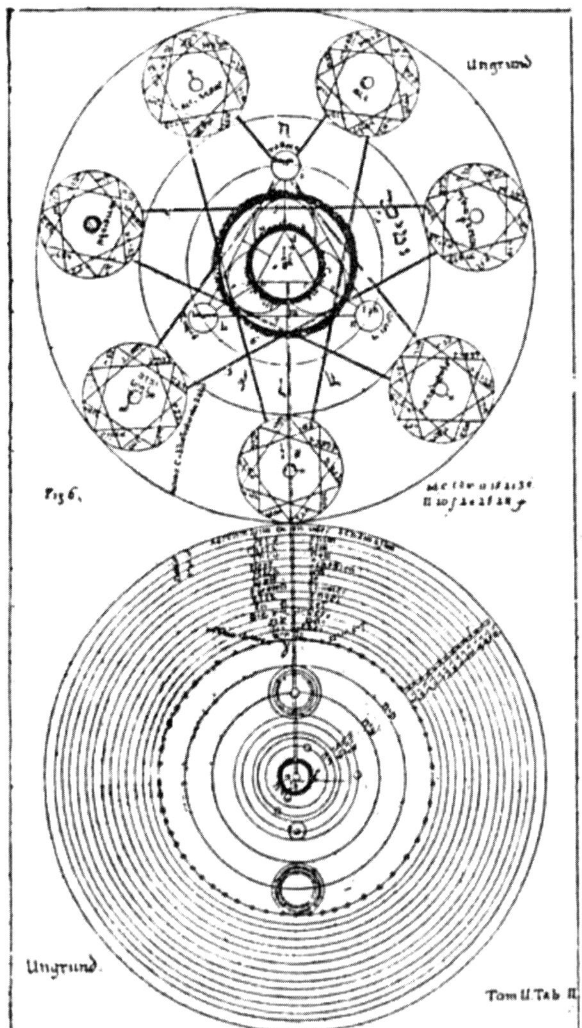

Table VIII figure VI from Manly P. Hall's *Fifteen Rosicrucian and Qabbalistic Diagrams*, *The Secret Teachings of All Ages*, 1928

Kingston's explanation as to the identity of the "old ones" supports the notion that the maker of the Barbury circle was a divine architect, while also paralleling White Eagle's remarks about the ancient Sun-Men, the White Brotherhood, the elementals and, above all, Britain's special place in global esoteric history and its present day influence. Kingston told Hesemann that the circle makers were "The Watchers":

> *"...a term for a cosmic universal consciousness, for beings which are concerned about the planet and what is happening on Earth at present. It is a collective intelligence which guides you mortal humans... linked to angelic beings, part of cosmic consciousness... Britain lies in the centre of the great pyramid of light which encircles your world... You are the immune system of your planet, the healing system which will create the changes...*
>
> *"This country is a testing ground, it has to be right before the whole can be lined up with other dimensions... Circles have appeared as a blueprint for humankind to mark that place as a place of power... There are ley lines running through the Earth and at various points lines of power are energised... This ancient land holds the balance, it is the key to the world. Many of these sacred sites are being cleansed... so that they are channels of new energy.*
>
> *"Spiritual energy from other dimensions is drawn down to the Hill of Silbury, the hill of the Shining Beings* [Sun-Men]*... The energy has been put through thought-processes with light beams so we input power into the Earth's grid. This is to stabilise the energies in the Earth, to stop the Earth destroying you. This has been going on for some time. You have been told of the purpose of Silbury Hill: if we placed the circles elsewhere you would not have recognized it* [i.e. the connection between the energy of ancient sites and that of crop circles].
>
> *"Crop circles have multi-layered meanings, many components, many types of energies coming together, energies of the Earth and of the Universe. They are created by an energy form, a form of consciousness, possibly out of one's own self, possibly from other dimensions. The nature realms and spiritual systems are creating formations, which have a profound effect on people who see and experience them. The crop circles are like a score of music between the Earth and the cosmos. You do not at this time need to learn to read the score. The best is to feel it... the energies being transmitted at this*

time are a combination of all elements and all elemental beings, as well as interplanetary information… Go to the hills and call for the Brethren. Link yourselves wth the Cosmos and draw the energies in to help. Become lightning conductors. Channel the light into the very soil. Transfer it into pure love and wait for the explosion."

The gods in the fields are urging us to wake up and smell the coffee while there is still time. There are indications that they are very much on our side; they want us to succeed in turning things around and reconnecting humankind with the natural world. There is a remarkable theory that crop circles are a method of "earth acupuncture," a healing process administered by unseen physicians to activate southern England's energy lines in accordance with prophecies concerning the emergence of a New Jerusalem. Something is building. The feeling is palpable. Mary and Michael's wild dance across England's sacred landscape generates enormous power, power that the dragon-fixing characteristic of crop circles absorbs and magnifies so that messages achieve maximum potency, readability and comprehensibility. We have a golden opportunity to raise our consciousness and once more sip ambrosia with our Makers on Olympus (or, rather, Silbury Hill).

That is the caring, avuncular side of the gods and humans equation. I believe that we should also be in no doubt that, ultimately, if humankind refuses to change its destructive ways then Mother Earth is more than capable of switching her poles, raising her waves, releasing her quakes, blowing her volcanoes and getting by without us. The ball is in our court but the chair umpire is tapping her timepiece ominously.

The Welsh Dragon

The Mowing-Devil:

Or, Strange *NEWS* out of

Hartford-ſhire.

Being a True Relation of a Farmer, who Bargaining with a Poor *Mower*, about the Cutting down Three Half Acres of *Oats*, upon the *Mower's* asking too much, the *Farmer* swore, *That the Devil should Mow it, rather than He.* And so it fell out, that that very Night, the Crop of *Oat* shew'd as if it had been all of a Flame; but next Morning appear'd so neatly Mow'd by the Devil, or some Infernal Spirit, that no Mortal Man was able to do the like.

Also, How the said *Oats* ly now in the Field, and the Owner has not Power to fetch them away.

Licensed, *August* 22th, 1678.

The strange tale of 1678 in which a Hertfordshire farmer, refusing to pay a local man the going price for mowing his field, swore he would rather the Devil mowed it instead. That night his field was bathed in flame and in the morning the field was perfectly mowed, such that "no mortal man was able to do the like."

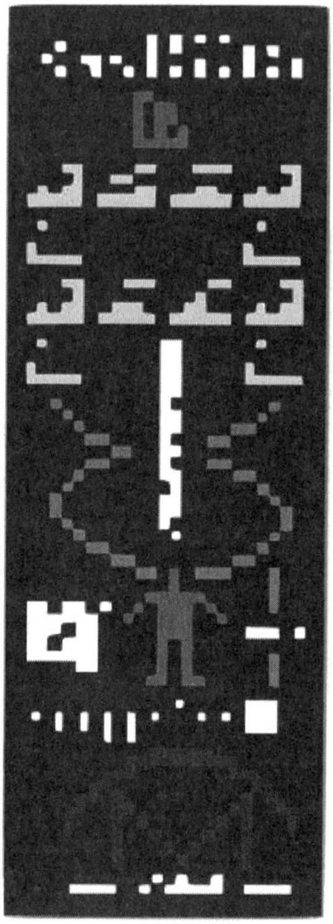

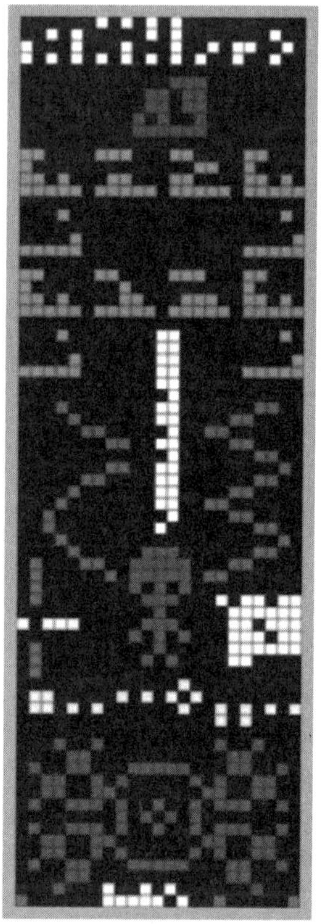

The 1974 Arecibo radio message and apparent response at Chilbolton, 2001

The Arecibo message (left) was transmitted to the globular star cluster M13 as a demonstration of human technological achievement. The response message, right, that appeared in 2001 in a crop circle by Chilbolton radio telescope differs substantially from the original message. The original contained binary encoded information about our base-ten number system, organic elements needed for life on earth, formulae for sugars and bases found in human DNA, the number of base-pairs in DNA, the structure of DNA, a simplified representation of a human being, the average height of a human, the population of earth (in 1974), our solar system (indicating earth as a raised third planet relative to the system).

Significant differences in the Chilbolton message: i) the atomic numbers for life are almost the same, except silicon has been inserted between oxygen and phosphorous; ii) new set of nucleic formulae included, some of which derive from silicon; iii) the DNA structure has changed, indicating an additional strand to our own; iv) a simplified representation of the intended sendee indicates a larger head, more pronounced set of eyes, and drastically shorter average height of 3'4"; v) intended sendee's sun is smaller in size to our own, plus three planets are highlighted instead of the one planet (Earth) indicated in the first message; vi) the "communication device" has changed. Instead it depicts a crop circle that appeared near Chilbolton Observatory in 2000.

James Deardorff, former Senior Scientist at the National Center for Atmospheric Research in Boulder, Colorado, has attempted to calculate the Arecibo response to be less than 2 chances out of 10 billion to be a hoax.

Formation at Milk Hill, 2001, © Handy Marks, public domain

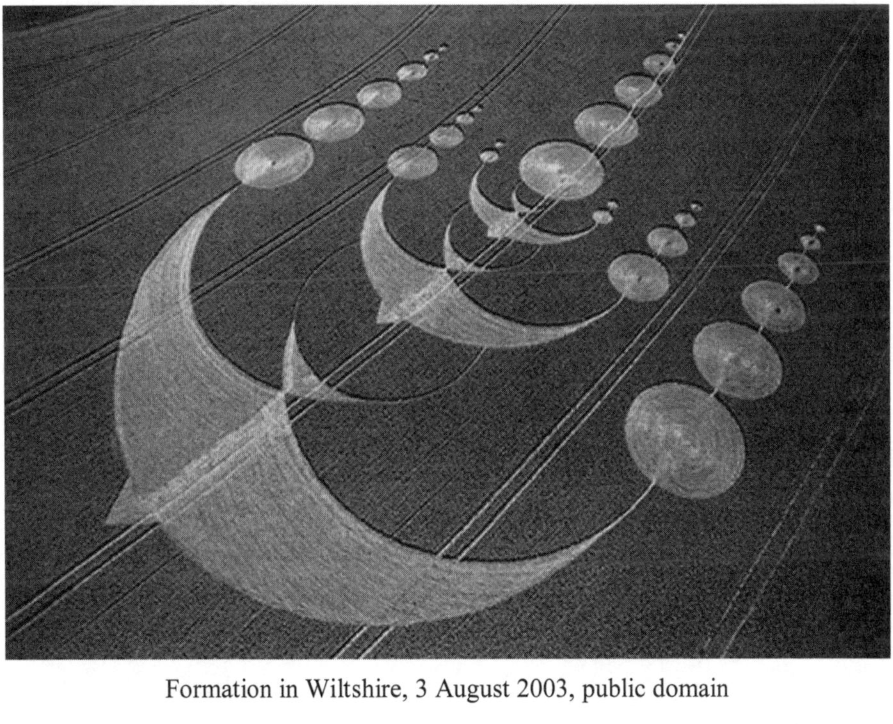

Formation in Wiltshire, 3 August 2003, public domain

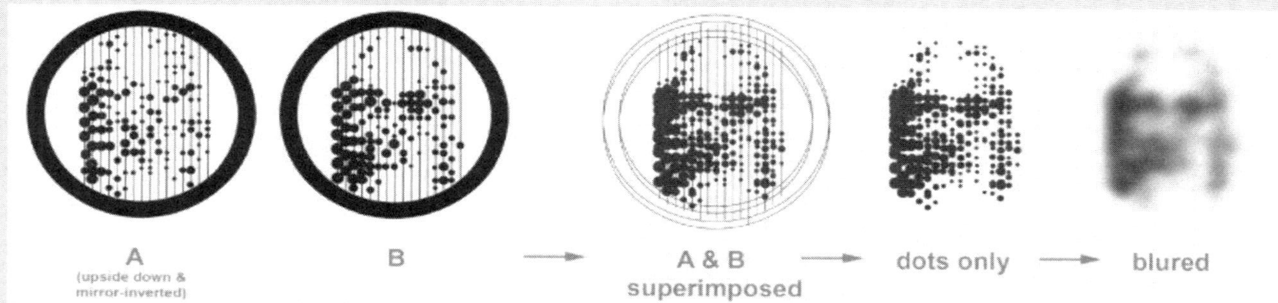

Fig. 4 Seen as two individual designs (Diagram A and B on the left) the two crop circles do not make a lot of sense. But if they are superimposed (Diagram A&B in the middle) a face emerges that resembles the Shroud of Turin (see Fig. 4 below).

Fig. 5 A gradual super imposition of the two crop circle designs with the face on the Turin Shroud.

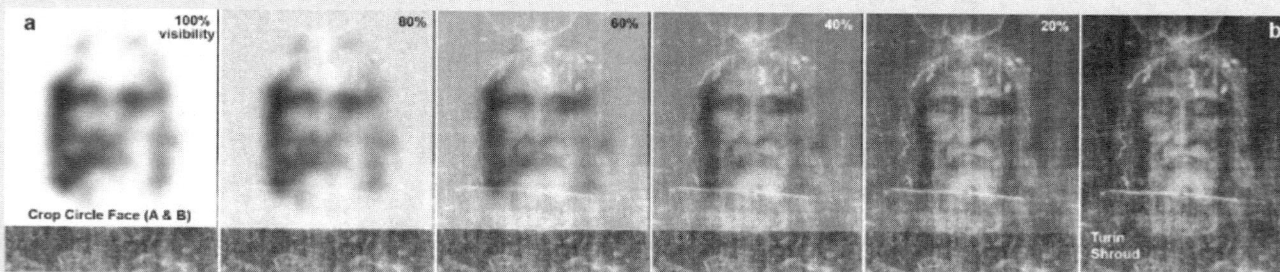

Diagrams © Andreas Müller, kornkreise-forschung.de

Two crop circles appeared in a field in Hungerford 5 August 2010. Superimposing them reveals the image on the Shroud of Turin. This illustration and its sequencing work reproduced with permission of its author, Andreas Müller

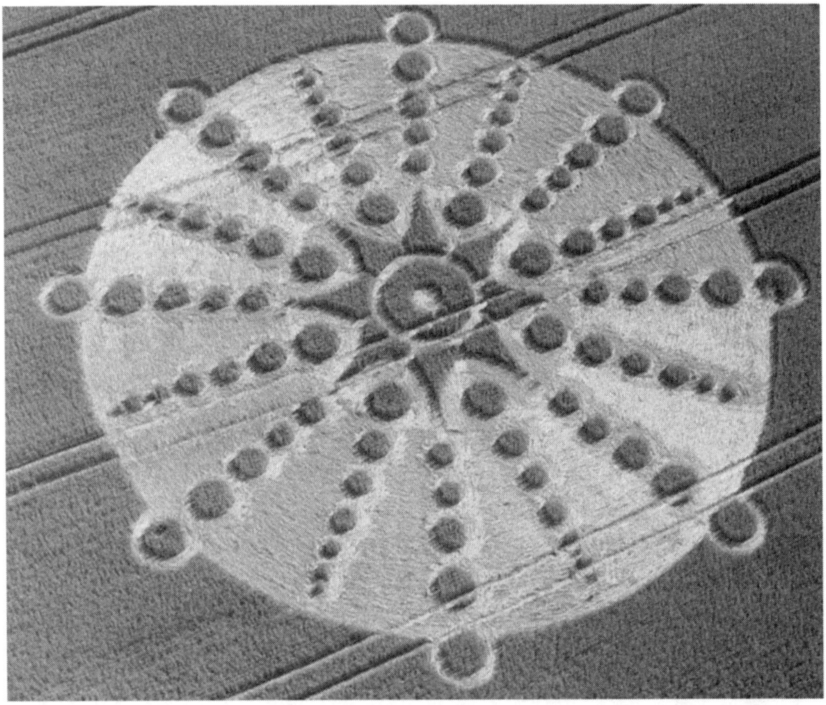

Formation by Old Shaw Village 8/7/2001 – public domain

"Fuji rotation" crop formation, Windmill Hill 4/6/2006 – public domain

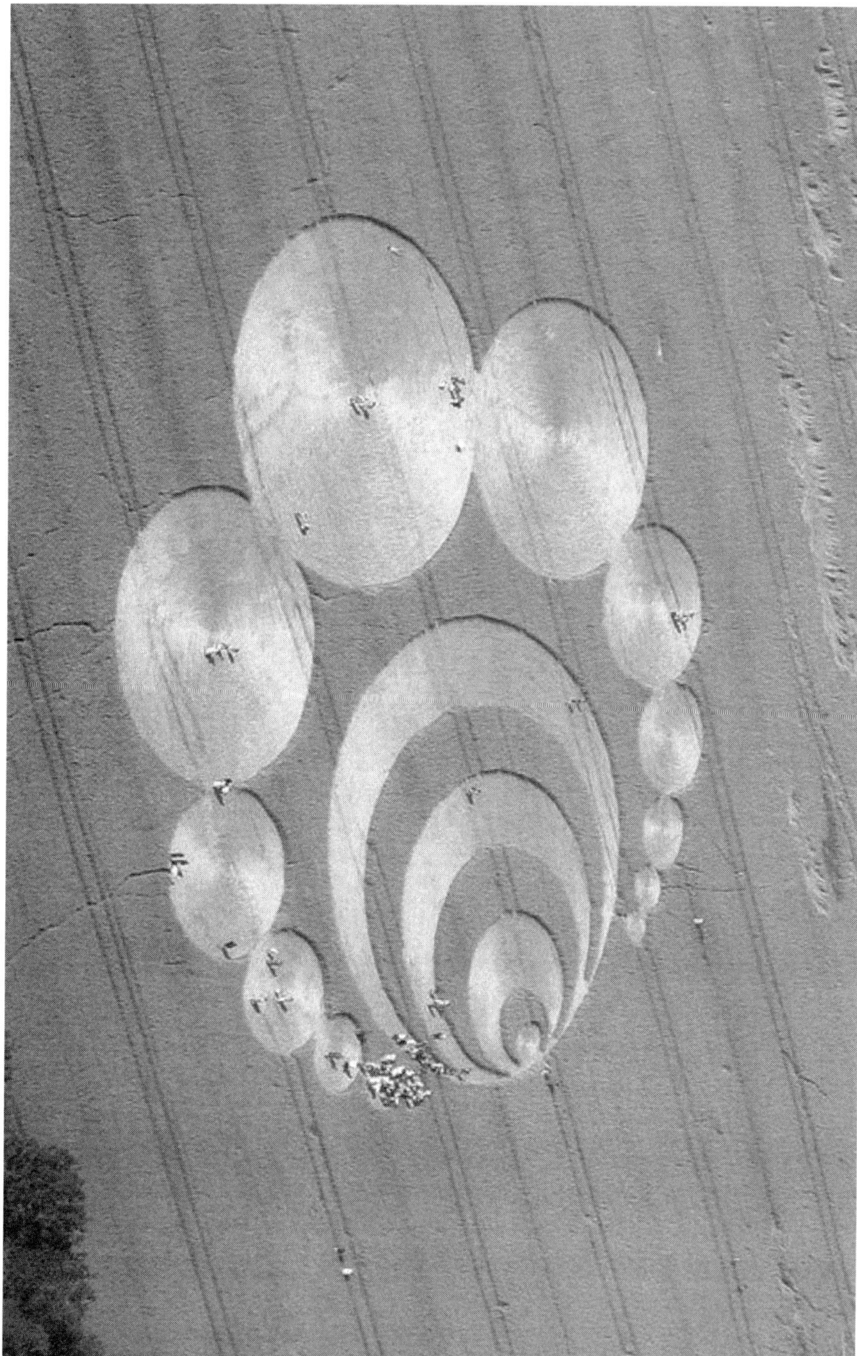

Swiss crop circle, 29/7/2007 – public domain

Chapter 7

Michael, Mary and Alice

Believe in the unseen and it will make itself known.

– an Old Sage

Earlier we bade adieu to Michael and Mary as they followed their respective dragon paths east-northeast out of Wiltshire. Michael's first notable port of call beyond the county is St Michael's Church at Aldbourne in Berkshire. Michael remains in Berkshire for a further fifteen miles, passing through two tumuli near the village of South Fawley before entering Oxfordshire.

Mary passes into Oxfordshire directly from Wiltshire, flowing firstly past White Horse Hill at Uffington and nearby St Mary's Church. The pair makes their next tryst at Wittenham Clumps, two wooded chalk hills (Round Hill, the higher, and Castle Hill) in the Oxfordshire parish of Little Wittenham. Michael and Mary will not meet again for a further 55 miles until they arrive at Royston in Hertfordshire.

The view from The Clumps was described by the artist Paul Nash who first saw them in 1911, as "a beautiful legendary country haunted by old gods long forgotten." The name Wittenham Clumps actually refers to the summits of these hills, more properly named the Sinodun Hills as Miller and Broadhurst labelled this nodal point in the southwest of Oxfordshire. Another local name for the Clumps is "Mother Dunch's Buttocks," after a local Lady of the Manor named Dunch. On Sinodun Hill is a hollow named the Money-Pit and a clump of trees named the Cuckoo Pen. The Money-Pit is supposedly the location of a treasure hoard guarded by a raven. The Cuckoo Pen gets its name from the local belief that a trapped cuckoo would ensure eternal summer.

After a flight of eight miles, via Churn Knob round barrow, Blewburton Hill hillfort and a fairy mound in North Moreton village, Michael arrives at St Michael and All Angels Church at Clifton Hampden. Clifton Hampden is doubly significant for our journey from Cornwall to Norfolk. Firstly, the village lies precisely on the St Michael ley corridor; that is, it sits on the notional mean line between the ley's male and female energy currents. Secondly—a hitherto unreported feature of the alignment—Clifton Hampden occupies the eastern Golden Ratio point upon the terrestrial St Michael ley.

I did not make the discovery because I was actively looking for the line's Golden Ratio points but because I was focused on the village in the context of its proximity to the geographical origin of the first telling of Lewis Carroll's *Alice* story. I had found myself wondering if it was more than coincidence that this tale was born just up the road from the ley point at Clifton Hampden. Why might the story of Alice be important when reflecting on the magical characteristics of the Michael alignment? Because Grace Cooke revealed that the true guiding force behind its authorship were the nature spirits—the sylphs of the air.

Broadhurst and Miller describe St Michael and All Angels as one of the most beautiful churches along the St Michael ley. Built on a steep mound, it is surrounded by archetypal green and pleasant English countryside by the Thames. From the lower slopes, wrote the pair, the church looks like a place from a "fairy tale." To reach the entrance requires climbing 33 steps, a significant esoteric and masonic number. A beautiful wooden carving of St Michael enhances its charming interior. The two dowsers traced the precise centre point of the Michael current to a stone pillar in a field by the church.

St Michael and All Angels Church at Clifton Hampden

Lewis Carroll wrote in his diary of a "golden afternoon," Friday, 4 July 1862, when he first told the story of Alice to his party of attentive listeners. (Curiously, in the pre-Gregorian Julian calendar this date would have fallen on 23 June during the Summer Solstice.) Carroll embellished the details in an article, *Alice on the Stage*, which he wrote in 1887 for *The Theatre*:

> *...full many a year has slipped away since that 'golden afternoon'... but I can call it up almost as clearly as if it were yesterday – the cloudless blue above, the watery mirror below, the boat drifting idly on its way, the tinkle of the drops that fell from the oars as they waved so sleepily to and fro...*

Alice herself later wrote:

> *...the beginning of Alice was told one summer afternoon when the sun was so burning that we had landed in the meadows down the river. Deserting the boat to take refuge in the bit of shade to be found... under a new-made hayrick.*

It has been suggested that both Carroll and Alice may have confused the date or perhaps conflated it with the telling of another Alice tale for that particular day was cool, cloudy and rainy.

Carroll was christened Charles Lutwidge Dodgson in 1832: Charles after his father, Lutwidge after his mother, his father's first cousin, Frances née Lutwidge whom Charles senior married in 1830. From a young age C.L. Dodgson wrote poetry and short stories and contributed frequently to the family magazine, *Mischmasch*. Between 1854 and 1856, his work, most of it humorous in style, appeared in the national publications, *The Comic Times* and *The Train*, as well as in smaller magazines such as the *Whitby Gazette* and the *Oxford Critic*.

In 1856, Dodgson published his first piece of work under the name that would make him famous. A romantic poem by "Lewis Carroll" called "Solitude" appeared in *The Train*. This pseudonym was a play on his birth name: Lewis was the anglicised form of Ludovicus, the Latin for Lutwidge, and Carroll an Irish surname similar to the Latin name Carolus, from which comes Charles. The tortuous transition went as follows: "Charles Lutwidge" translated into Latin as "Carolus Ludovicus." This was then translated back into English as "Carroll Lewis" and then reversed to make "Lewis Carroll." The pseudonym was chosen by *The Train's* editor Edmund Yates from a list of four submitted by Dodgson, the others being Edgar Cuthwellis, Edgar U.C.

Westhill and Louis Carroll.

Dodgson and his friend, the Reverend Robinson Duckworth (Fellow of Trinity College), rowed in a boat with the three daughters of Henry Liddell, the Vice-Chancellor of Oxford University and Dean of Christ Church. They were Lorina Charlotte Liddell aged 13 ("Prima" in *Alice in Wonderland's* prefatory verse), Alice Pleasance Liddell aged 10 ("Secunda"), and Edith Mary Liddell aged 8 ("Tertia"). Duckworth later related that Alice acted as "cox" of their gig while he rode stroke and Dodgson bow during the "Long Vacation" voyage to Godstow for tea in the hayricks on the riverbank.

The boat trip began at Salter's boatyard (still present) by Folly Bridge in Oxford and ended five miles away at Port Meadow near Godstow. Until the late 17th century Folly Bridge was known as South Bridge and formed part of a long causeway, Grandpont, which stretched along most of the line of Abingdon Road. In the 13th century, the noted alchemist Roger Bacon lived and worked at "Friar Bacon's Study," which stood across the north end of the bridge until 1779 when it was removed to widen the road. It is believed that Folly Bridge may be derived from the name of a one-time tenant in Bacon's study.

Folly Bridge, Oxford

Godstow Old Bridge

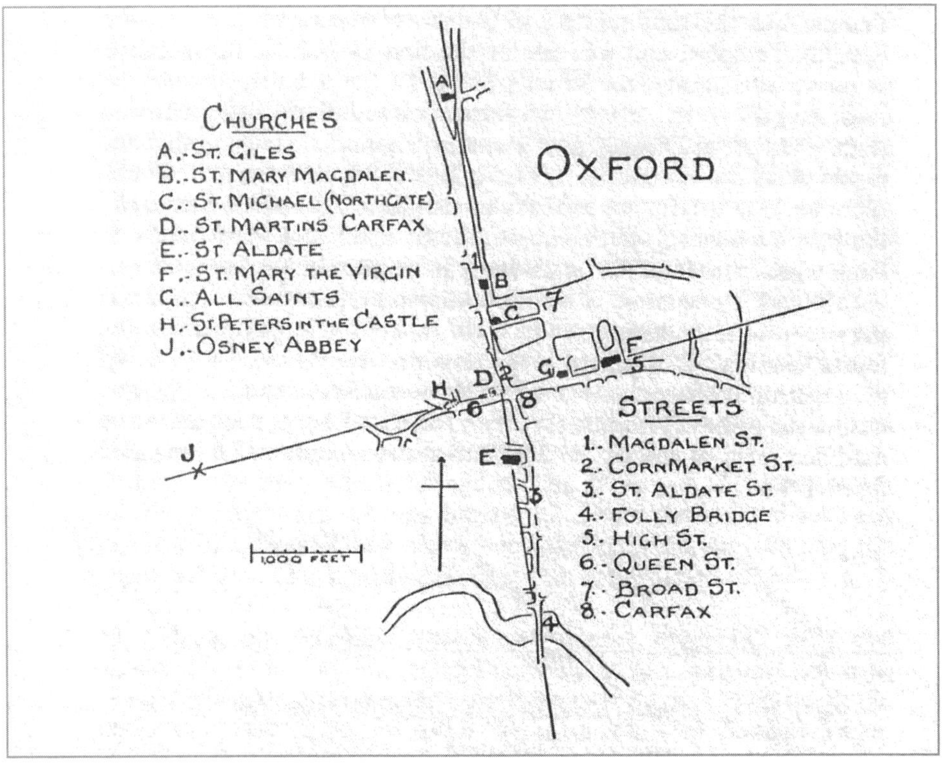

Alfred Watkins' alignments of Oxford's churches

Before long, the boat and its occupants arrived on a peaceful stretch of the Isis where trees overhang the banks. The Isis is the historical name for the stretch of the Thames beginning from its source in the Cotswolds to the place where it joins with the River Thame at Dorchester, two miles southwest of Clifton Hampden. Leaving Oxford behind, the boat party shortly passed through Osney Lock.

At some point thereafter Carroll began telling the girls a story that featured a bored little girl named Alice who goes looking for an adventure. As Carroll wrote years later, he had begun by sending his "heroine straight down a rabbit-hole without the least idea what was to happen afterwards." Presently, the party arrived at Port Meadow, a vast open space used for grazing, graced today by geese, ducks and the occasional blue heron. Nearby lay the hamlet of Godstow. A picnic was laid out and Carroll went on with his story. Only through the prodding and interruption of the children did it move forward to a conclusion. The girls loved it. Alice Liddell, perhaps especially taken by the story, pressed Carroll to write it down for her. Carroll began writing the manuscript the next day, although that earliest version is lost to history. Carroll and the girls took another boat trip a month later when he elaborated the plot of the story of Alice (perhaps the actual occasion of the "golden afternoon"?). In November, Carroll began working on the manuscript in earnest.

The distance from Port Meadow to Clifton Hampden is 8¾ miles. Confident that the village and its "fairy-tale" church sit comfortably within Michael and Mary's field of influence, I checked the GPS co-ordinates of Carn-lês-Boels, Hopton-on-Sea and Clifton Hampden to identify if a mathematical relationship exists between them:

A) Carn-lês-Boels, Cornwall
50.05033° N, 5.6947° W

B) Hopton-on-Sea, Norfolk
52.5460° N, -1.7274° E

C) Clifton Hampden, Oxfordshire
51.6580° N, 1.2075° W

A to B=364 miles (1 mile less than Jiro Olcott's measure)

A to C=224 miles,

AB/AC=1.618=the Golden Ratio, its Greek mathematical symbol being Phi (uppercase Φ, lowercase φ or ϕ)

I was taken aback by the finding, which appeared to set apart Clifton Hampden as a place of special interest along the St Michael ley. There may be many reasons for this but one to consider is the locality's proximity to the first telling of the Alice story. Lewis Carroll initially called his tale *Alice's Adventures Underground*, which suggests that Carroll was not describing just any old world of enchantment.

In his address to the British Association in September 1999, Dr Tony Cooper referred to geological features in North Yorkshire, which, in his opinion, inspired Carroll's classic tale. Carroll was born in Cheshire but when in 1843 Prime Minister Robert Peel awarded his father the Crown living of Croft-on-Tees, the family moved to Yorkshire. Here Carroll lived until 1846 when he enrolled as a pupil at hated Rugby School. At Croft Carroll met long-haired Mary Hilton Badcock, daughter of a local canon, and later took photographs of her. Carroll's illustrator John Tenniel adapted these for the figure of Alice in the first edition of *Alice in Wonderland* (Alice Liddell was not Tenniel's model; she always wore her hair in a fringe). In his talk, Cooper referred to Hell Kettles, three ponds in Croft. Tradition says that they are bottomless but, in fact, are just 22 feet deep. He suggests that the ponds at least partly inspired this passage from the first chapter:

> *The rabbit-hole went straight on like a tunnel for some way, and then dipped suddenly down, so suddenly, that Alice had not a moment to think about stopping herself falling down what seemed to be a deep well. Either the well was very deep, or she fell very slowly, for she had plenty of time as she went down to look about her, and to wonder what would happen next.*

Although other water bodies overlie the area's limestone formation, Hell Kettles is the only site in County Durham where exists open water fed by calcareous springs. We have noted the same geological feature in tracing the source of Swallowhead Spring's waters near the Avebury complex and the region's superabundance of remarkable crop circles. Cooper then spoke of a second pertinent geological feature. Running beneath two-thirds of Ripon, including Mary Badcock's's family home, Ure Lodge, is a complex water-filled cave system. This two-mile wide gypsum belt stretches from Hartlepool to Doncaster and is filled with dozens of craters and deep shafts of which Carroll, a young man with a sharp and inquiring mind, was most likely aware. A collapse in 1834 four hundred yards northeast of Ure Lodge left a 60-foot deep and 30-foot wide shaft with solid rock exposed on all sides. It undermined a number of gardens, including the field opposite Ure Lodge, and dumped domestic clutter at its base. Moreover, the Maitlands family, who were other close friends of the Dodgsons, lived at Littlethorpe near Ripon, the site of a major geological collapse in 1796. Cooper believes that this local knowledge and, specifically, the particulars of the Ure Lodge collapse, inspired this passage:

> *Down, down, down. Would the fall never come to an end?"I wonder how many miles I've fallen by this time?" said she aloud. "I must be getting somewhere near the centre of the earth. Let me see: that would be four thousand miles down, I think." Down, down, down: there was nothing else to do... when suddenly, bump, bump! Down she came upon a heap of sticks and shavings, and the fall was over.*

Theses geological events are especially interesting when we look at the experiences of writer Alec Maclellan who described a terrifying experience at Grassington Moor,[73] twelve miles or so from the gypsum belt cave system, a distance barely relevant in geological terms.

While on a field trip, Maclellan saw a cave near the village of Kettlewell (the "Kettle" motif once again). Inexplicably, Maclellan felt very uneasy but pushed on into the cave and eventually saw a glowing green light pulsating further down the passageway. He then heard a humming noise and the ground beneath him began to vibrate violently while the green light pulsated with ever increasing vigour. Becoming more and more fearful and convinced that something was coming towards him, Maclellan panicked and dashed back up to the surface.

Alice at the Mad Hatter's Tea Party

[73] McLellan, A., *The Lost World of Agarthi: the Mystery of Vril Power,* 1982

Afterwards Maclellan researched the area and its history and came across the work of writer Charles James Cutcliffe-Hyne who had created the tough fictional adventurer, Captain Kettle. Cutcliffe-Hyne had lived in Kettlewell and was obsessed with the legend of Atlantis. In 1889 he wrote a book called *Beneath Your Very Boots*, today so rare that the only copies are to be found in a handful of university libraries. The book tells a story about a subterranean kingdom based on actual accounts he had uncovered about a hidden world beneath Wharfedale.

Maclellan obtained the book and saw that Cutcliffe-Hyne's accounts of the adventures of a certain Anthony Haltoun exactly matched his own, except that Haltoun did not have time to flee the passage. He fainted and when he came round saw that he was in the company of a party of men, members of a race who described themselves as the Nradas, a fair-skinned, blond-haired people who had lived in peace below ground since prehistoric times.

The book goes on in more detail and, although written as a fictional fantasy, contains convincing particulars of true-life detail and legend. The description of the Nradas' power source is very close to Lord Bulwer-Lytton's 19th century story, *The Coming Race*,[74] which describes a mysterious "Vril" power wielded by a subterranean people. Philosopher René Guénon used Lytton's book as the basis of his hostile account of the Theosophical Society in articles that he wrote concerning the mythical Underworld of Agartha. Guénon's decision to write the articles under the pen name "Narad Mani" suggests that he was aware of Cutcliffe-Hyne's book.

There is abundant hollow earth literature on green lights, green children and other like phenomena. Najm Kobra speaks of green as the colour of the pole. The pilgrim at first finds himself in a deep well and then is suddenly illuminated by an extraordinary green light that at first shines at the mouth and presently suffuses the whole of the well so that one is travelling up a luminous shaft "of green light because it has become the place to which descend the Angels and the divine Compassion." Iranian philosophers refer continually to the colour green: emerald rocks, emerald cities and the Green Island where the hidden Imam lives, a place mindful of Avalon's Island of Apples where Arthur sleeps in eternal vigil.

Carroll's description of Alice's fall into Wonderland calls to mind the mythic hero's archetypal descent into the otherworld. It is a representation of a journey described in many cultures to the omphalos or world axis point, a major element of the mythologised landscape.

---

[74] Bulwer-Lytton, E., *Vril: the Power of the Coming Race,* 1877

One can liken it to Persephone's descent into the lower world, a feature of the mysteries of Eleusis (meaning gateway or passage). When Persephone's mother, Demeter, discovered what had happened she disguised herself as a hideous woman in her quest to retrieve her daughter from her imprisonment by Hades. Consider here comparisons with Carroll's less than comely characters: the furious Queen of Hearts who has no conversation other than to demand "off with their heads," and the ugly Duchess and her pig-baby.

Devereux[75] explores this theme in his description of Henry Corbin's studies of ancient Iranian tradition. Persian mystics developed a model of the world, which featured a synthesis of the ancient Zoroastrian traditions of paradise, the omphalos, the mind and the "Interworld." The Interworld, the return to the Garden, geographically represents the idealised image of Paradise, which is dominated by a central mountain, trees and springs, and the four cardinal rivers.

Paradise comes from ancient Iranian "pairidaeza," a walled garden. It symbolises the earth in all its manifestations, physical to celestial. In its purest form, paradise is structured upon a quincunx arrangement of trees (one at each corner of a square and a fifth in the centre), positioned round a central body of water. In the Mazdean system, flowers correspond to different spiritual entities. Carroll's Wonderland story of the garden of live flowers mirrors these paradise archetypes of Persian mysticism.

In the Zoroastrian system the Interworld is known as the "Eighth Climate," one of eight mythic spaces aligned with the physical world and whose boundaries are established by reference to annual solar positions. The omphalos nature of this visionary geography requires that while one considers physical landscape in horizontal terms, equally one should visualise the visionary sphere in vertical terms. Here in this mythical landscape is the cosmic mountain, Qaf, the Mother of all Mountains, which marks the boundary between the visible and invisible worlds. Its summit supports an emerald stone, the smaragdina.

The 17th century Islamic mystic Muhsin Fayz Kashani taught that "this intermediate world... is the world through which spirits are embodied, and bodies spiritualised." We may only perceive this world through our imaginative and intuitive faculties. In sleep, the interworld is accessed through an alert form of consciousness, lucid dreaming, in which one "awakens" within a dream and experiences three-dimensional space in a magical supersensory world.

This is much like Alice's experience when, prior to falling into

[75] Devereux, P., *Symbolic Landscapes,* Gothic Image Publications, Somerset 1992

Wonderland, she had been feeling “very sleepy and stupid” but was not too dozy while dwelling on the pleasures of making a daisychain to observe a White Rabbit hurrying by. On the next occasion of Alice’s supersensory travels, before stepping through the drawing-room mirror into the Looking Glass world she had been “sitting curled up in a corner of the great arm-chair, half talking to herself and half asleep.” Wordsworth captured this special state of consciousness in his ode, *Intimations of Immortality from Recollections of Early Childhood*:

There was a time when meadow, grove and stream,
The earth, and every common sight,
To me did seem
Apparelled in celestial light,
The glory and freshness of a dream

The Persian concept of the eight mythic spaces and their solar boundaries that interconnect with our physical world is reflected powerfully in the chess symbolism underlying the Looking Glass narrative. Manly P. Hall believed that chess is the most significant of all games and represents the vital elements of life and philosophy. The chessboard’s 64 squares, alternately black and white (positive-negative, male-female, white dragon-red dragon, yin-yang, king and queen, Michael and Mary...), symbolize one’s mysterious passage through life. Upon it move strangely carved figures, each according to fixed law. The white king is Ormuzd; the black king is Ahriman. These opposing forces engage in the eternal battle between Light and Darkness.

At the human scale, the kings represent the spirit; the queens the mind; the bishops the emotions; the knights the vitality; and the castles the physical body. The pieces on the king’s side are positive in polarity; those upon the queen’s, negative. The pawns are the sensory impulses and perceptive faculties—the eight parts of the soul. The white king and his suite symbolize the true Self and its positive allies during one’s spiritual journey. The black king and his retinue represent the false Ego and its legion of negative attachments and earthly desires that befog one’s journey through life. The game of chess thus sets forth the eternal struggle of each part of man’s divine compound nature against the substanceless shadow of itself. When one’s soul force (a pawn) achieves passage from its end of the chessboard to its opponent’s, it becomes a queen. Alice’s advance from the forest of the White Knight secures her the prize of a golden crown; a synonym for the gifts one accrues through patient action and taking life one step at a time no matter what its challenges.

RED

WHITE

White Pawn (Alice) to play, and win in eleven moves

	PAGE		PAGE
1. Alice meets R. Q.	160	1. R. Q. to K. R.'s 4th	165
2. Alice through Q.'s 3d *(by railway)*	167	2. W. Q. to Q. B.'s 4th *(after shawl)*	192
to Q.'s 4th *(Tweedledum and Tweedledee)*	170		
3. Alice meets W. Q. *(with shawl)*	191	3. W. Q. to Q. B.'s 5th *(becomes sheep)*	197
4. Alice to Q.'s 5th *(shop, river, shop)*	197	4. W. Q. to K. B.'s 8th *(leaves egg on shelf)*	203
5. Alice to Q.'s 6th *(Humpty Dumpty)*	204	5. W. Q. to Q. B.'s 8th *(flying from R. Kt.)*	223
6. Alice to Q.'s 7th *(forest)*	217	6. R. Kt. to K.'s 2nd (ch.)	230
7. W. Kt. takes R. Kt.	229	7. W. Kt. to K. B.'s 5th	244
8. Alice to Q.'s 8th *(Coronation)*	245	8. R. Q. to K.'s sq. *(examination)*	248
9. Alice becomes Queen	246	9. Queens castle	253
10. Alice castles *(feast)*	247	10. W. Q. to Q. R. 6th *(soup)*	256
11. Alice takes R. Q. and wins	261		

Author's Note

As the chess-problem, given on the next page, has puzzled some of my readers, it may be well to explain that it is correctly worked out, so far as the *moves* are concerned. The *alternation* of Red and White is perhaps not so strictly observed as it might be, and the 'castling' of the three Queens is merely a way of saying that they entered the palace: but the 'check' of the White King at move 6, the capture of the Red Knight at move 7, and the final 'check-mate' of the Red King, will be found, by any one who will take the trouble to set the pieces and play the moves as directed, to be strictly in accordance with the laws of the game.

The new words, in the poem 'Jabberwocky' (see page 152), have given rise to some differences of opinion as to their pronunciation: so it may be well to give instructions on *that* point also. Pronounce 'slithy' as if it were the two words, 'sly, the': make the 'g' *hard* in 'gyre' and 'gimble': and pronounce 'rath' to rhyme with 'bath.'

Christmas, 1896

The Looking Glass chess game and Carroll's notes

"... and now for the last brook, and to be a Queen! How grand it sounds!' A very few steps brought her to the edge of the brook. 'The Eighth Square at last!' she cried as she bounded across, and threw herself down to rest on a lawn as soft as moss, with little flowerbeds dotted about it here and there. 'Oh, how glad I am to get here! And what is this on my head?' she exclaimed in a tone of dismay, as she put her hands up to something very heavy, that fitted tight all around her head. 'But how can it have got there without my knowing it?' she said to herself, as she lifted it off, and set in on her lap to make out what it could possibly be. It was a golden crown."

So intimately does Carroll describe Alice's underground adventures, so embedded have they become in popular consciousness and so closely did he build on local "otherworldly" legends, that one seriously wonders if the Oxford don was writing from personal experience. During a discourse on nature spirits White Eagle once said:

Did we tell you of the ability of... elemental creatures to grow to a great size if necessary, or to diminish their size? This is one of their attributes. That remarkable book 'Alice in Wonderland' deals with this happening. Do you think that book came only from the mind of its writer? Do you not see that such a story originated from the sylphs trying to teach humans great mystical truths? If you want to learn mysticism... read your fairy stories again. You will learn some beautiful truths if you ponder on what they have to tell you.

Swiss physician, alchemist and astrologer, "Paracelsus," (Philippus Aureolus Theophrastus Bombastus von Hohenheim, 1493-1541) devoted much of his life to a study of the elementals. He believed that each of the four primary elements (earth, fire, air, and water) consists of two parts: a subtle, vaporous etheric principle and a gross corporeal substance. According to Paracelsus, the Earth is not just our visible spinning ball but it comprises other, more subtle dimensions that are home to the higher powers of Nature. He explained that just as visible nature is populated by a vast number of living creatures its invisible spiritual etheric counterpart is similarly populated by unique life forms. He gave these forms the name elementals. Later, they became known more widely as nature spirits.

Paracelsus divided these beings into four distinct groups: gnomes (of the Earth), undines (Water), sylphs (Air) and salamanders (Fire). Crucially, Paracelsus taught that they are living entities, many resembling human beings. Members of each group are fashioned out of the corresponding ether in which they exist. It is believed that the sylphs, salamanders and nymphs had much to do with the oracles of the ancients; that, in fact, they were the ones who spoke from the prophetic depths of the earth centres such as Delphi and Dodona and from the air above.

The sylphs of the air, the fairy race that sought, through Lewis Carroll, to teach humankind "great mystical truths," are composed from the finest ether of the four elements. They are highest form of all the elementals, their native element being the finest in vibratory rate. They are called the riders of the night, the wind-born, the storm angels and the air-devas. They sound very much like our friends, Michael and Mary, and their unbridled dragon flights across the English countryside.

The sylphs' leader is Paralda who dwells on the highest mountain of the earth. These fairies of the high places have no fixed domicile but wander from place to place, invisible but ever-present powers in the intelligent activity of the universe. They move from castle to castle built out of the ether of the air element, which is the reflection of the mental plane. Paracelsus taught that the sylphs sometimes assume human form but for only short periods. Their size varies but in the majority of cases they are no larger than human beings and often considerably smaller.

The sylphs work directly with the airy elements of man's body such as the gases and ethers that gather within it, and indirectly with the nervous system. They live hundreds of years, often attaining a thousand years and never seeming to grow old. The Greek Muses are believed to have been sylphs for these spirits are said to gather around the mind of the dreamer, the poet and the artist (such as Carroll) and inspire one with their intimate knowledge of the beauties and workings of Nature. The peculiar qualities common to men and women of genius are supposedly the result of the cooperation and influence of sylphs.

It is said that the sylphs have occasionally accepted humans into their presence, even into their communities. May young Charles Dodgson have been afforded this rare honour? White Eagle spoke of children, recently born from the spirit world where the elementals abide, who preserve the ability to see their former companions in fairyland. He gave an example of a girl who insisted that her account of seeing a little man on the hearth making the fire burn was true. She spoke animatedly of "the little king and queen" of gnome-land, whom she visited in her sleep and was able to describe most vividly.

That Carroll had a similar experience in childhood, which planted a seed, later to germinate and pierce the veil of the physical during a "golden afternoon," cannot be ruled out. Carroll never recorded such an instance but perhaps hinted as much in the closing lines of the poem that prefaces *Alice in Wonderland*:

Alice! A childish story take,
And with a gentle hand
Lay it where Childhood's dreams are twined
In Memory's mystic band,
LIke pilgrim's wither'd wreath of flowers
Pluck'd in a far-off land.

The seed lay dormant for many years. At the appointed time of germination all that was needed was a trigger to pull forth the shoot. The work of psychic researcher and crop circle investigator Andrew Collins may provide detail on the nature of this trigger. As I noted in *Jack the Ripper's New Testament*, in 1862 Arthur Hughes, an artist associated with the pre-Raphaelite Brotherhood, painted a stylised portrait of a woman: *The Lady with the Lilacs*. In the painting the redheaded subject is standing beneath a lilac tree. Around her neck is a five-point "Star of Isis" pendant suspended from a double chain. The art world's general opinion is that Hughes's wife, Tryphena, modelled the subject. Carroll is believed to have seen the partially completed painting in July 1863 during a first visit to Hughes' studio. Struck by the painting, Carroll asked Hughes to re-work it for his own collection, a task that the artist completed 8 October. Carroll's diary records that he took formal possession of the painting on the 12th.

The story that Carroll fell in love with *The Lady with the Lilacs* after seeing it in partly finished format in Hughes' studio is challenged by a remark in Leonard's catalogue raisonné, which describes the provenance as "Commissioned in 1863 by Lewis Carroll." That Carroll saw a work-in-progress, liked what he saw and asked the artist to finish it off does not meet the usual criteria of a commission. What it does suggest is that Carroll had a special interest in the subject and instigated the sitter's representation in oils. By all accounts, *The Lady with the Lilacs* was the only painting that Carroll ever owned.

A body of opinion has emerged which suggests that the subject in the painting is a woman named Mary Heath, a possibility that Roberts in his correspondence with me has not ruled out. In a subsequent email exchange, Roberts also noted Hughes' "odd" inclusion of the Star of Isis in *The Lady with the Lilacs*, as it had not been used in the artist's previous pictures. It is clear that Roberts has doubts about the sitter's identity. Had Carroll, a man who populated his library with books on occult and spirit phenomena, known of Mary Heath and desired to immortalise her in a work of art in a specially commissioned portrait that provided clues to a secret life in Victorian England?

Andrew Collins and his colleagues have presented a fascinating account of Mary Heath's life. She is believed to have been born in France around 1840, the illegitimate daughter of wealthy and eminent printer and designer, Thomas de la Rue. Mary first came to London around 1855, possibly under the guardianship of the Dalziel brothers: engravers for Lewis Carroll's illustrator, John Tenniel, and illustrators for Madame Michelet's nature works.

In this period Heath was introduced to a number of individuals in pre-Raphaelite circles. Collins speculates that Carroll, then aged twenty-three, was among those that were smitten by the teenage member of the influential Guise-Lorraine family, which had championed Mary Queen of Scots. The family is also a scion of the Merovingian line of kings, which, according to legend, originated from a child born to Jesus and Mary Magdalene who was brought to France in a rudderless boat by Mary after the crucifixion. Collins' work indicates that Mary Heath later returned to France where her family provided her with the names of contacts and societies in England that shared similar beliefs and allegiances. When she returned to England the de la Rue family asked Mary to meet with them and establish through their support a new group of like-minded mystical Christians, a group that became known as the Fire Phoenix.

A photograph said to be of Mary Heath, Arthur Hughes' "Lady with the Lilacs"

Mary revealed these confidential matters to her artist friend Arthur Hughes, who, according to Collins, firstly incorporated her image into a painting that he initially called *A Mother's Grave.*

Carroll's first encounter with young Mary would have taken place around seven years before the famous boat trip on the Isis. His attentive listeners that July day said that their storyteller told the tale in such rounded fashion that it was as if it were already largely thought out. Any mystery of how Carroll might have made up on the spot the complete story, despite professing that he had not "the least idea what was to happen afterwards," is explained if he was narrating a work that had already been incubating in his imagination for many years.

On Mary's return from France, Carroll would have met a powerful young woman steeped in mystical learning and esoteric tradition, who shared his sincere belief in the worlds of spirit, fairy folk and enchantment. The fusion of two open-minded imaginative individuals would spark a sleeping seed sewn by a magical childhood adventure that germinated and bloomed, phoenix-like, into Alice's tale told on a "golden afternoon" (not a remark about the weather but of a time of revelation), so that all may understand we are not alone. Carroll told his tale within the geographical bounds of the fiery corona that encircles the Michael and Mary currents. Moreover, their line of flow in the locality corresponds to the most harmonious point of proportion along the entire southwest to northeast direction of the St Michael ley.

It is my contention that the creators of the ley, its twin currents and its remarkable outcroppings—stone circles, Glastonbury Tor, the zodiac, the Avebury complex, Silbury Hill, crop circles and, undoubtedly, many marvels yet to come—are the elemental citizens of a higher nature world that permeates our own and which, at special times, we, like Carroll, can glimpse, even enter, for learning and insight into the truth of "things are never what they seem."

Ancient wisdom described the elementals as nature's living essence, the pulse of the Universal Law through which men and women find their spirit and a corresponding sense of oneness with creation and immortality. As blood flows through the veins of animals, so do the elementals flow through the unseen arteries of Mother Nature, the divine spirit of Gaia who was worshipped so devoutly in the long distant past, not least in ancient Britain, which achieved a status of especial favour by virtue of its enduring reverence for the Goddess and her inexhaustible gifts. In Carroll's tale of the little girl drawn down the rabbit hole and through the looking glass, Alice symbolises not only the goddess and her sovereignty and love for the natural world but, microcosmically, the sylphs of the air that work tirelessly to maintain its beauty and form.

The Michael and Mary currents pass through three times as many St Mary, St Margaret and St Mary Magdalene churches than those that celebrate the Michael and George dragon-slayers. It is the ley's feminine essence that dominates its overall polar nature. Its lesser masculine stream plays its vital part in fixing and regulating the fiery goddess energy so that its cosmic power does not consume her offspring.

The Mother Goddess is and always has been an image that evokes a perception of the universe as an organic, living and sacred whole in which humanity and all life on Earth participate as "her children." Ann Baring and Jules Cashford[76] liken the relationship to the weave of a cosmic web, all in its net sharing in the sanctity of the original source. At some point in the distant past the feminine principle, which manifested in mythological history as the "goddess" and her qualities of feeling, instinct and intuition became lost as a sacred expression of the unity and cohesion of life. Thankfully, it never really died but continued in a figurative sense as exemplified, for example, by Zeus marrying the old mother goddesses who continued to rule and take responsibility for the timeless processes of childbirth, fertility and spiritual transformation. The authors liken this eternal feminine principle to an active imaginative force, a medium that Bohm in his quantum model of the Implicate Order described as an "ocean of energy."

It is invariably true, Baring and Cashford remind us, that wherever there appears an arrangement of stones in a circular, spiral or serpentine form as at Glastonbury, Avebury, Silbury Hill and Stonehenge, or wherever a cave or hollow has been marked as the place of birth or revelation, there dwells the tradition of the Mother Goddess. In such places she is worshipped as both the giver of life and the recipient of the souls of the incoming departed. She transforms life by first bringing it out of herself and then by taking it back in a perpetual cycle of time. She is the coiling serpent tracing the labyrinthine spiraling of the lifeforce as it passes from spiritual space to Earth space. The umbilical cord connecting mother and child, a new life form that has emerged from a spirit world beyond our imagination, resembles intertwined double snakes. Because of its power to slough its skin and grow a new one, the serpent has always represented the goddess's power of renewal, especially her magical power of restoring life to the dead.

The source of the Mother Goddess's transformational power, the

[76] Baring, A., & Cashford, J., *The Myth of the Goddess*, Penguin, 1993

watery womb of life in which all life is contained, is beyond human understanding. Thanks to Carroll we are left with a permanent reminder that if we have the courage and confidence to believe in the invisible it will make itself known. Michael and Mary are powerful representions of the higher lifeforms that populate a world that is always a little bit out of sight but can be occasionally glimpsed from the corner of a half-open, languid eye. Pull back the drapes and what might one see?

> *"All at once the flat, undistinguished pasture peeled away and was replaced by a giant chessboard that stretched as far as the eye could see and spilled over the horizon. Charles felt as if he was observing the extraordinary scene as if through a large gilt-framed drawing room mirror.*
>
> *Illuminated by pulsing kaleidoscopes of light, the chessboard squares were filled with scenes more beautiful than the imagination can conjure. Charles had the extraordinary feeling that the landscape was revealing the true essence of nature, which, in his understanding, was the smiling face of God. Before him was nature first born—the first and greenest hillside; the first and most verdant wood; the first and most sparkling stream; and the first and most highly perfumed rose.*
>
> *The lines between the squares were fast flowing streams of silvery liquid light spanned at intervals by humpbacked bridges. The streams' delicate fire-tipped waves leaped and bobbed as if dancing a frenzied jig. The beating wings of a great host of fairies combined with the music of flutes, strings and bells to create a harmonious symphony over the heavenly landscape.*
>
> *A dazzling company of light-beings moved gracefully around the board. One would spread their arms and before them would appear a great sparkling pyramid of light and energy. Another would bring into form a brilliant shining cube and set it spinning on a single point. And so the pageant went on, fantastical geometric forms appearing briefly, only to be replaced by other breathtaking shapes and solids in dazzling rays of living colour.*
>
> *A light-being of regal poise and tall stature raised a hand as if acknowledging the presence of the young observer. Charles "knew" that this was the Queen and waved back cheerily. The Queen came forward, extended a white-sleeved arm and handed Charles a basket of apples.*
>
> *"One each for your family, Charles," the Queen said*

> *sweetly. "They are delicious. Plant the seeds in your orchard. You will have the best apples in all of England. It is time for us to go now, Charles, but you will always remember us. You will write about it one day. Farewell."*[77]

Like Wiltshire, Oxfordshire is blessed with a wealth of mysterious and unexplained riches. Situated on the Ridgeway at Uffington, 20 miles northeast of Avebury, lies Dragon Hill, reputed to be one of the most mystical power spots in Britain. Like Silbury Hill and Merlin's Mount, Dragon Hill is a manmade structure with a flattened summit.

Wherever there is a -ton, -tot or -tor in a placename, it usually indicates the presence of a sacred mound. Some researchers have associated these "tot" hills with the Egyptian god Thoth (the Greek Hermes), the god of magic. Dragon Hill's surrounding streaks of bare chalk bear testament to a place where in legend a dragon was slain, its blood falling upon the earth making the ground barren. Overlooking the hill is the famous chalk White Horse that overlooks the eponymous Vale. Its beak-like head suggests that the effigy might not be a representation of a horse but of a dragon figure. It is situated not far from the Neolithic chambered barrow of Wayland's Smithy.

Wayland's Smithy is a Neolithic burial-chamber in a long barrow edged with stones. Beneath its mouth is a smaller long barrow of earlier date, with burials in a wooden chamber. It was said to be the haunt of the blacksmith of the god Wieland, a figure from German and Scandinavian mythology. In his youth Wieland and his brother Eigil, the original hero of the William Tell legend, had an adventure with women of an unusual race, the legendary "Swan Maidens" from whom Wieland learned the art of flight. Hearing of his skill as a blacksmith, a local king crippled Wieland and imprisoned him on an island where he was put to work. The word Smithy signifies the locale's importance as an ancient place of initiation during which the truthseeker, having found the circle of initiates, was magically re-shod so that they might "travel" onwards, a ceremony referenced in ancient mystical teachings in the myth of the "God-shod feet," sometimes symbolised by golden shoes.[78]

Paul Devereux writes of a two-mile long corpse road between Noke and Islip, five miles northeast of Oxford. Formerly, corpse roads provided a practical means for transporting the deceased, often from remote communities, to cemeteries that had burial rights, such as parish churches and chapels of ease. In Britain, they were variously known as

---

[77] Finlay, G., *The Looking Glass Ripper*, Create Space Independent Platform, 2015.
[78] Michell, J., *The Flying Saucer Vision*, Abacus, 1974

a bier road, burial road, coffin line, coffin road, corpse way, funeral road, lych way, lyke way, or procession way. Such “church-ways” have produced a great deal of associated folklore regarding ghosts, spirits and wraiths. Occasionally would be glimpsed a corpse candle or light in the form of a flame or ball of light, often blue, that was seen to travel just above the ground between the cemetery and a house where lived a person on the point of death.

Islip is proud to have been the birthplace of Edward the Confessor in around 1005. The tiny village of Noke, two miles east of Islip is one of the Seven Towns of Otmoor, the others being Beckley, Oddington, Charlton-on-Otmoor, Horton-cum-Studley, Murcott and Fencott. Before Enclosure in the early 1800s any cottager who lived in one of the “Seven Towns” had right of grazing for their cattle, sheep and geese on the moor. It crosses Otmoor, a “curious area of almost wild fenlike desolation,” a forgotten land seemingly cast under a magic spell.

Binsey village on the opposite side of the Isis from Port Meadow and about a mile southwest of the ruins of Godstow Abbey is noted for its 12th century parish church of St Margaret. Just outside its west end and belltower stands St Margaret’s Well, which is the model for the “Treacle Well” in Alice’s Wonderland adventures. It is a holy well dedicated to St Frideswide, patron saint of Oxford. According to legend, Frideswide fled to Binsey to escape marriage to a king of Mercia, whose pursuit of her was halted when he was struck blind at the gates of Oxford. Frideswide’s prayers brought forth a healing spring, whose waters cured his blindness (the old English word “treacle” meant “healing unguent”). The site became a popular pilgrim destination.

Alice’s county has been host to a number of highly impressive crop circles. Some regard the 2005 formation at Waylands Smithy as a representation of a Mayan calendar containing two key dates. One is the date of the circle’s formation in the Oxfordshire countryside, 9 August 2005, provided, it is surmised, so that analysts might have an easy check and base point for their calculations. The second is 21 November 2007, a seemingly arbitrary date until associated with the earlier occasion of Comet Holmes and its conjunction with the bright star Mirfak in the constellation of Perseus. As shown in photographs taken at the time, Comet Holmes, after its outburst, showed a bright, blue-green halo or coma. Most observers called it a “new star in Perseus.” It has since been speculated that the outburst of Comet Holmes fulfilled a Hopi prophecy: “a new blue star will suddenly appear in our sky, just before the end of one age and the beginning of another.”

Top: diagram of "Mayan Calendar," Waylands Smithy, 9August 2006
Bottom: Woolstone Hill formation, Uffington, 13 August 2005

Four days after the "Mayan Calandar" circle appeared at Waylands Smithy, a breathtaking formation materialised at Woolstone Hill near Uffington. The superb design was 400 feet in diameter and took the form of a central hexagram surrounded by sixteen squared spirals with seventy-two feathers contained within a ring. It is one of the most complex crop circle formations in terms of construction ever to be seen in England, a full-on slap in the face to those who insist that crop circles are made by human hands.

In just a few hours of darkness, "Doug and Dave" pranksters would have had to construct the six central diamond shapes; surround these with a 44m circle; divide its circumference into 12 for the (invisible) radial construction lines (to enable the positioning of the diamonds' outer points, mid-points and exact centres); describe guideline circles, one of 22m diameter, and a further circle slightly larger (both invisible) for the diamond mid-points centres (bearing in mind that the radii for the diamond centres are not the same as for the mid-points); lay the crop in precise swirls around the diamond centres to create the 24 walls of standing crop; outline these walls by laying the crop in 24 straight lines on the outside of the walls; set out the four tangents to the 44m diameter circle at exactly 90 degrees to each other to form the inner edges of the large rectangle; divide the length of each of the four tangent grooves into exactly three equal parts, these 'thirds'establishing the dimensions of the sides of the 16 small spiral blocks and the overall size of the great rectangle; create the 16 blocks, this stage being the construction's most difficult operation (the 15 x 15 invisible pixel grid has to be established such that the precise sizing, spacing and sequencing rotations of the spiral bars in the blocks is done with zero error); create the outer edge of the great circle of radius 55.8m; create the circle which coincides with the corners of the big rectangle and carries the 78 divisions for the 'feathers' (extremely difficult for a human team seeing that 78 does not reduce to convenient factors); next, the superhumanly difficult part where the feathers have to be cut by making very narrowly laid grooves in perfect alignment with the circle centre, while ensuring the grooves do not cut into either the great rectangle or the central diamond pattern; finally, round off the ends of the feathers to a uniform small radius, a relatively simple exercise but for human hands very time-consuming. Phew!

Northwest of Oxford is a farm region that includes the villages of March Baldon, Toot Baldon, Big Baldon and Little Baldon. The entire region's population is less than 500 people. On 30 July 2006 there appeared in a wheat field in Toot Baldon a beautiful formation.

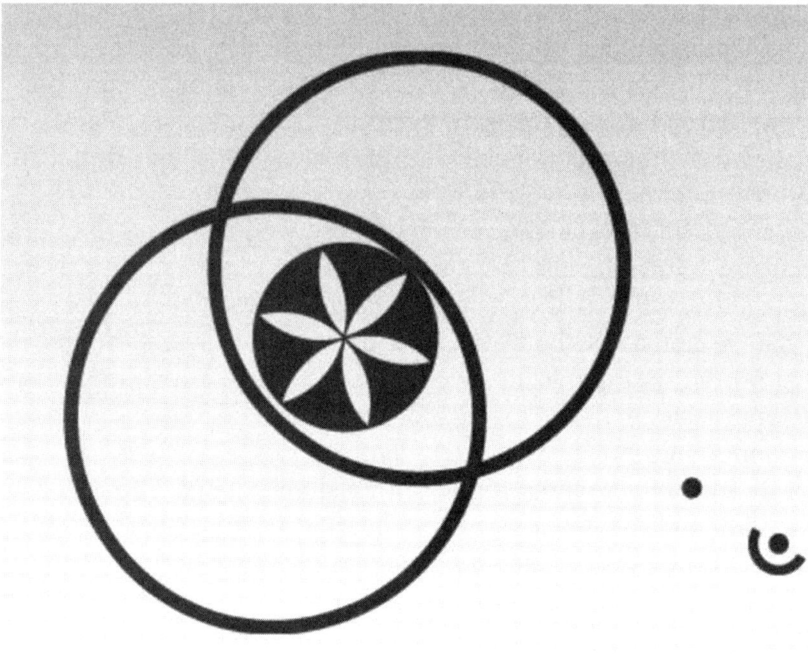

Diagram of Toot Baldon formation, note "signature" bottom right

It took the form of a "Flower of Life" nestled within a Vesica Piscis. Toot Baldon is located at the top of a hill; "toot" means lookout. Mark Fussel and Stuart Dike at Cropcircleconnector.com had received an alert about the formation. The first to check it out were Ellis Taylor, Geoff Ambler and Ross Holcomb. Ross wrote: "Toot Baldon, Oxfordshire, Wheat, Two intersecting 400-foot circles with 60-foot-wide seed of life in centre of Vesica Piscis, (comprising) two five-foot-wide intersecting rings measuring approximately 400 feet around (132 feet in diameter). There is a circle centered in the resulting Vesica Piscis, which measures about 60 feet across. Within the centre of the circle is a 6-petaled 'seed of life' formation. The southernmost ring is laid in a counterclockwise direction. The northernmost ring is split down the middle by a thin line of standing crop with the inner half of the ring flowing clockwise, the outer half of the ring flowing counterclockwise."

Michael and Mary continue their journeys through Oxfordshire towards the eastern part of the St Michael ley. After leaving Clifton Hampden, Michael passes through churches at Marsh Baldon, Garsington and Cuddesdon and Rycote before entering the county of Buckinghamshire four miles later. Mary, meanwhile, after leaving Sinodun Hill makes her final noteworthy visit in Oxfordshire at Dorchester-on-Thames before making her way to All Saints Church at Marsworth in the next county along the line.

Dorchester was once a place of very significant importance, and a site of continous settlement for 6,000 years. It hosts two significant sites in England's prehistoric landscape: a Cursus and a Henge. Both were both built directly on the path of the St. Michael ley.

The Neolithic Cursus at Dorchester, partly excavated in 1947-52 and 1981, is known today only by crop-marks, the most notable being a double ring henge called the "Big Rings." Bones found there were carbon-dated to circa 3000 BC. The Cursus has largely been destroyed by gravel quarrying and the construction of the Dorchester bypass. It comprised two broadly parallel ditches circa 60m apart, running for at least 1600m metres in a northwest-southeast direction. The Cursus was aligned on the midwinter sunrise and would have been recognized as an important ceremonial site for several hundreds of years.

Dorchester Big Rings (Henge) was discovered in 1938 and later also destroyed by gravel quarrying. The site comprises two concentric ditch circuits, with roughly opposed entrances to the north-northwest and south-southeast. The outer ditch has a maximum diameter of 193m, the inner of 125m. Few finds came from the outer ditch: some flints, plus a few Iron Age sherds. The inner ditch was a little more productive, including finds of Beaker sherds, struck flints and animal bones. A pit beside the north entrance dug into the inner ditch also contained Beaker and Iron Age sherds.

The Henge was probably built sometime in the middle of the second millenium BC. It was an important prehistoric ritual site and most likely had relevance to the adjacent cursus. A number of important mortuary and ritual sites were also built close to the site over a period of nearly two thousand years. Christopher Knight and Alan Butler have suggested that the Henge may bear evidence of use of a 366th division of the globe in prehistoric times. The Big Rings once shared the exact same circumference of 366 megalithic yards with the original Henge at Stonehenge.

Professor Alasdair Whittle of Cardiff University has described the area under threat as "a complex prehistoric landscape, with a startling concentration of Neolithic and Bronze Age monuments, among other features, which collectively constitute an archaeological resource of national significance, comparable in importance for example to those around Avebury and Stonehenge."

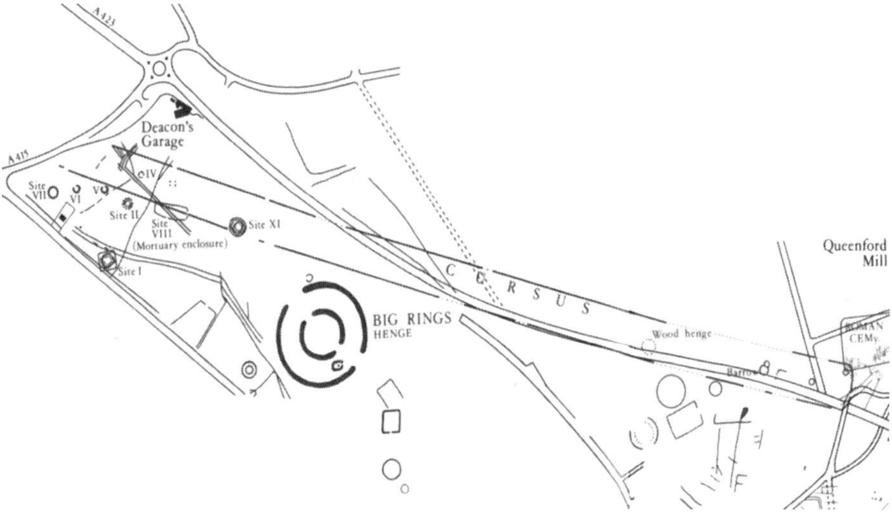

Above: Dorchester Cursus

Below: the Dorchester "Big Rings" Henge photographed in 1933

While Professor Roger Mercer from Edinburgh University describes Dorchester's stretch of the River Thames as "an area of quite extraordinary richness in terms of prehistoric activity not only in its British context but when compared with an equivalent area in North-West Europe."

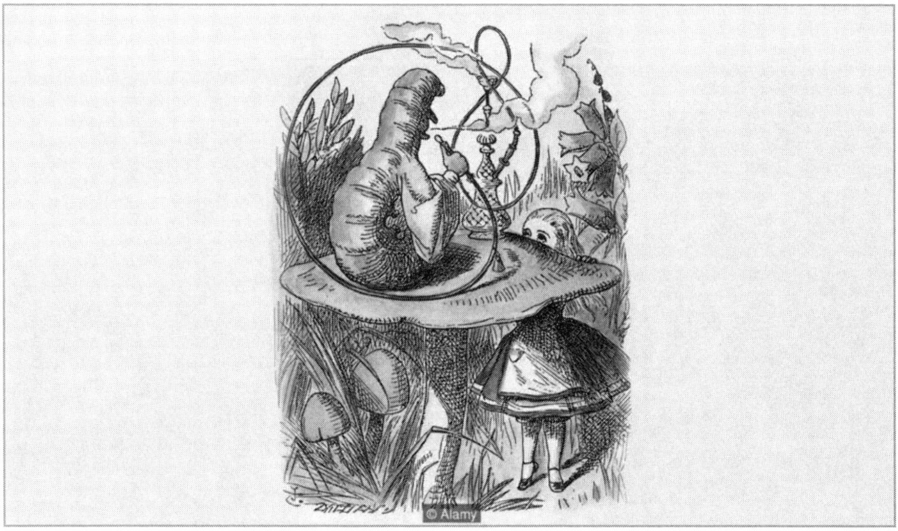

Alice meets the the hookah-smoking Wonderland caterpillar

We now pass into the Eastern section of the St Michael ley. Here Michael and Mary traverse a relatively flat region not known for its stone circles, zodiacs, enigmatic hills and henges but one blessed, nonetheless, with its own unique personality and surprising features.

Alice meets the the White Knight in the Looking Glass forest:
"What does it matter where my body happens to be?" said the White Knight. "My mind goes on working all the same."

Lewis Carroll's own drawings for *Alice's Adventures Underground*

"When I used to read fairy tales, I fancied that kind of thing never happened, and now here I am in the middle of one!" said Alice in the White Rabbit's house.

Chapter 9

East of the Line

The section of the Michael ley from Oxfordshire's eastern border to Hopton-on-Sea is 120 miles, one-third of the line's total length. Within their invisible corridor, Michael and Mary weave their idiosyncratic flightpaths through parts of Buckinghamshire (approximately 14 miles), Hertfordshire (18 miles), Bedfordshire (5 miles), Cambridgeshire (18 miles), Suffolk (60 miles), and Norfolk (5 miles).

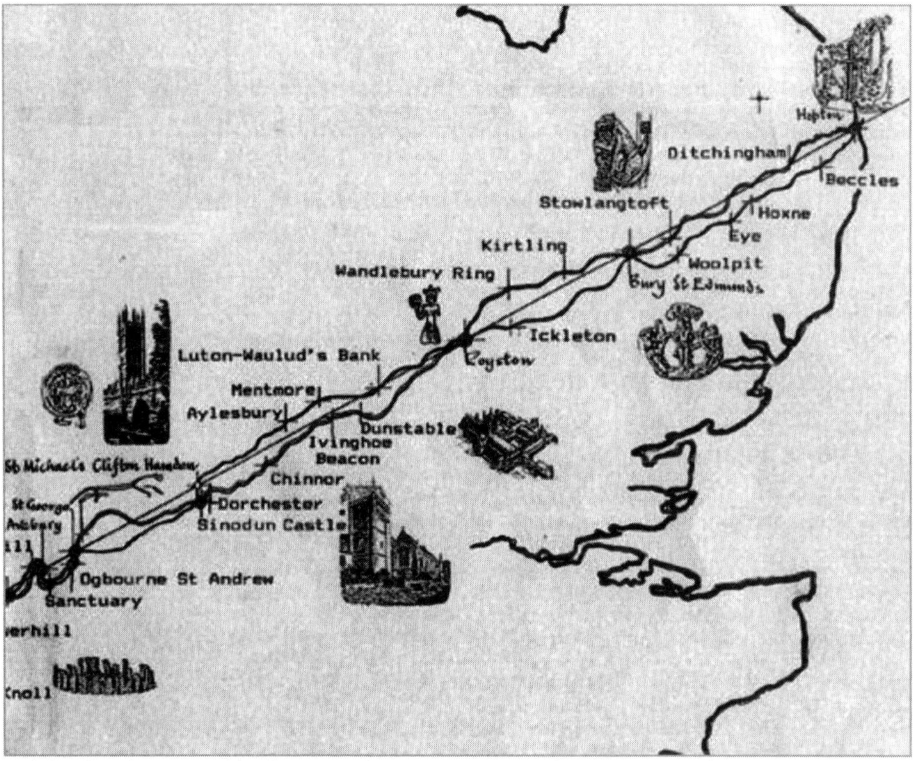

Michael and Mary paths from Avebury to Hopton—for context, Chinnor is the line's exit point out of Oxfordshire; Ivinghoe Beacon is in Buckinghamshire; Waulud's Bank and Dunstable, Bedfordshire; Royston, Hertfordshire; Wandlebury Ring, Ickleton and Kirtling, Cambridgeshire; Bury St Edmunds to Beccles and places between, Suffolk; end of the line Hopton-on-Sea, Norfolk.

Ivinghoe Beacon seen from the Ridgeway

Buckinghamshire is notable for its open countryside and natural features, including in its southern part the Chiltern Hills, officially designated in 1965 an Area of Outstanding Natural Beauty covering an area of 322 square miles. The Chiltons, as they are popularly known, form a chalk escarpment across Oxfordshire, Buckinghamshire, Hertfordshire and Bedfordshire. The hills decline slowly in prominence in northeast Bedfordshire. The 87-mile Ridgeway Path, which, as noted earlier, occupies an important position in Wiltshire's mystical landscape, runs into the county before terminating at Ivinghoe Beacon, a prominent hill in the Chilterns by Ivinghoe village where Mary passes through the church that bears the Saint's name.

The southern end of Bedfordshire is on the chalk ridge of the Chilterns Hills. The remainder is part of the drainage basin of the River Great Ouse and its tributaries. Hertfordshire's eastern regions are predominantly rural and arable, intermixed with villages and small- to medium-sized towns. Royston is one of the few major settlements in this regard. The physical geography of eastern Hertfordshire is less elevated than the far west, but with lower rising hills and prominent rivers such as the Stort.

Large areas of Cambridgeshire are very low-lying. Holme Fen, a Site of Special Scientific Interest near Holme, is notable for being the United Kingdom's lowest physical point at 9 feet below sea level. To illustrate its relative extreme flatness, the county's highest point is in the village of Great Chishill at just 480 feet above sea level. Like

Cambridgeshire, much of Suffolk is low-lying but has proportionately more hills than its westerly neighbour. It comprises largely arable land with the wetlands of the Broads in the north. The coastal strip to the East contains an area of heathland known as "The Sandlings" which runs almost the full length of the coastline.

The relatively unremarkable eastern countryside is not lacking in features of interest. The Waulud's Bank earthworks in the northern part of Luton in Bedfordshire are situated on the edge of Leagrave common. The River Lea runs alongside on the western side, its source located within the vicinity of the surrounding marsh. Archaeological excavations date the site to around 3000 BC in the Neolithic period, the same date for the construction of the Dorchester Big Rings. The source of the River Lea is known as the "Five-Springs" and lies in the northwest corner of Waulud's Bank.

In legend, the Celtic god Lug (or Lud or Lyg) presided over the springs; the name "Lea" may be derived from this name. "Luton" may derive from "the town on the river of Lugus." Waulud may derive from Wayland, the Norse god of smithies, in which case the Luton earthwork shares its name with the Wayland's Smithy long barrow to the southwest in Oxfordshire referenced earlier.

Royston Cave, a manmade structure, is located beneath the crossroads formed by Ermine Street and the Icknield Way in Katherine's Yard, Royston. The Cave is a circular, bell-shaped chamber cut into the chalk bedrock. It is 26 feet high and 17 feet in diameter with a circumferential octagonal podium. It is unique in Britain for its numerous mediaeval wall carvings; comparable examples exist only in the former Czechoslovakia and Israel. Some of the figures are thought to be those of St. Catherine of Alexandria, St. Lawrence and St. Christopher. It has been speculated that the Cave was used by local Freemasons and, much earlier, by the Knights Templar, who founded nearby Baldock. Although claims have been made that the Templars held a weekly market at Royston, the market charter was in fact granted to the Augustinian Canons of the town.

It is thought that the cave was divided into two levels by a wooden floor, the evidence consisting of a single posthole and what may be beam slots to secure the platform to the walls. Two figures close together near the damaged section may be all that remains of a known Templar symbol: two knights riding the same horse. Other theories hold that the Cave served as a prison or was used by Augustinian monks from the local priory, who would have required a cool store for their produce, a chapel for their devotions or an anchorite cell.

Drawings on the walls of Royston "Templar" Cave, Hertfordshire

A ditch in Wandlebury Hill Fort, Cambridgeshire

Wandlebury Hill Fort, otherwise known as the Wandlebury Ring, lies in the Gog Magog Downs southeast of Cambridge. The Iron Age fortification was constructed in about 400 BC, consisting of a substantial outer ditch and an inner rampart bank of chalk rubble and soil that encloses a circular area of about 6 hectares. A second ditch and bank circuit was added on the inner side of the first rampart in the 1st century BC, and a low counterscarp bank added around the perimeter. The inner ring had a wooden palisade to deter invaders. Wandlebury was a border settlement and there is evidence that it was occupied by the Romans.

The fort and surrounding hills are shrouded in legends. Gervase of Tilbury said in his *Otia Imperialia*, "...if a warrior enters this level space at dead of night by moonlight and calls out 'Knight to knight, come forth,' he will at once be faced by a warrior armed for fight, who charging horse against horse, will either dismount his adversary or himself be dismounted." A knight named Osbert once tested the story and legend has it that he defeated the knight who appeared to him but was wounded in the thigh by his opponent's javelin. This is mentioned in Sir Walter Scott's 1808 poem *Marmion* featuring King Alexander III jousting with a goblin knight.

After departing Oxfordshire, Michael travels to Haddenham in Buckingham, his specfic path taking him to St Mary's Church on the edge of the village by thatched cottages and a duckpond. Leaving the village behind, Michael passes directly through the ruined tower of Dinton Castle, described by Miller and Broadhurst as a romantic octagonal-shaped structure embedded with fossils, including trilobites and ammonites. Eighteenth century fossil collector John Vanhatten built it as a folly. Next, Michael makes for the very old Stone Church in the grounds of Hartwell House and passes through churches at Walton, Bierton and Hulcott before arriving in the county of Bedfordshire. Here, Michael favours churches at Mentmore, Slapton, Eaton Bray and Totternhoe before reaching the monastic church of Dunstable Priory in Bedfordshire. Michael passes through its large doorways and impressive arches.

Subsequently, Michael follows the Icknield Way Path, and runs through Waulud's Bank in the north of Luton town. Running on, Michael passes through Ickleford and Letchworth before joining Mary at Royston Cave, its inverted womb shape described by Miller and Broadhurst as like a mythical entrance to the Otherworld. Leaving the Cave, Michael flies along the Icknield Way in Cambridgeshire before passing through St Mary's at nearby Ickleton, the only church in Britain with a bare-breasted Mary Magdalene.

"The Doom" mediaeval wall painting St Mary's Ickleton, Mary Magdalene on left

Michael then runs on through churches at Hadstock, Withersfield, Great Thurlow, Stradishall, Wickhambrook and Chedburgh villages. A few miles later, Michael skirts around Ickworth House built in the early nineteenth century. It is one of England's more unusual houses whose architecture provokes extremes of opinion. It has been described unflatteringly as resembling "a huge bulk, newly arrived from another planet." The stately home is now being architecturally reassessed and recognized as the only building in England comparable with the monumental works of the neoclassical masters, Boullée and Ledoux. Michael flits through Ickworth's splendid park, designed by Capability Brown, where he passes through the porch and tower of the estate's neglected private chapel before arriving in Bury St Edmunds.

Until the Dissolution of the Monasteries, the Abbey of Bury St Edmunds was among the richest Benedictine monasteries in England. It was a centre of pilgrimage as the burial place of the Anglo-Saxon martyr-king Saint Edmund, killed by the Great Heathen Army of Danes in 869. Evidently hating Edmund, the Viking raiders shot arrows into him until he bristled like a hedgehog. They then cut off his head and threw it deep into the briars in the forest. Local legend recounts that while Edmund's men were searching for his body they heard a voice shouting, "Here, here, here." They followed the sound and found the head guarded by a wolf. When the head was put back with the body it miraculously became reattached. This was felt to be a sign of sainthood and miracles were subsequently attributed to Edmunds's healing power.

The statue of Edmund's wolf, Bury St Edmunds

The ruins of the abbey church and most other buildings are merely rubble cores but two very large mediaeval gatehouses survive, as well as two secondary mediaeval churches built within the abbey complex.

Miller and Broadhurst traced the two currents. Michael runs through Churchgate Street before moving through the Norman Arch into the abbey. There, the dowsers expected to find a node in the remains. Instead, they were surprised to find that the pair came together in the choir in the North-South transept but, in their words, "kissed" not crossed. The Michael current then proceeds along the axis of the abbey buildings, before moving firstly through the West Front and then the town's great Norman tower opposite the Masonic Lodge in Chequers Streets.

After leaving the cathedral city, Michael travels through Woolpit and the churches of several other Suffolk places before arriving in the village of Eye where the serpent snakes his way through a ruined castle atop a steep mound, once the site of a Norman keep. Thirty miles later, having passed through churches in Hoxne, Weybread, Withersdale, South Elmham, Beccles and Somerleyton Park, Michael enters Norfolk and ends the terrestrial part of its journey through England at the ruined church of St Margaret's at Hopton-on-Sea.

Meanwhile, the female fire energy has scorched its own flightpath on its route from Oxfordshire's villages to the eastern seaboard. After departing from All Saints Church in the Buckinghamshire village of Marsworth, Mary visits Bedfordshire's Whipsnade Park Zoo and the local St Mary Magdalene Church. She then drops by St Mary's at Wallington in Hertfordshire, a church that bears a memorial plaque to Eric Blair, better known to the world as George Orwell.

After seven miles, Mary passes through Royston and then enters Cambridgeshire. Here in fen country, Mary makes brief acquaintance with churches in Melbourn, Foxton, Newtown and Great Shelford before flying over the Gog Magog Hills and Wandlebury Ring hillfort. Thereafter, Mary passes through churches at Dullingham, Stetchworth, Little Ditton, Kirtling and Westley Waterless, whose guide book says that its dedication to St Mary the Less may be derived from "St Mary in the Leys." Twelve miles later, via Kirtling Manor, Ousden, Little Saxham and Westley, Mary arrives in Suffolk at Bury St Edmunds where, meeting Michael, she runs through the Abbey gardens and its mediaeval gatehouse. In the last leg of her aerial adventures eastward across the countryside, Mary makes a 50-mile flight to the village of Hopton-Sea but not before passing through no fewer than 21 churches before meeting Michael at St Margaret's church.

Bury St Edmunds Abbey ruins

It is pleasing to report that the St Michael ley's eastern tranche is no stranger to episodes of high strangeness.

One day during harvest time in the reign of King Stephen (1135–1154), the villagers of Woolpit discovered by one of the wolf pits that gave the village its name two green-skinned children. They were found to be brother and sister. Apart from their unusual skin colour the siblings were of unremarkable appearance although their clothing was unfamiliar and they spoke in an unknown language. Villager Richard de Calne took the children into his home where for the first few days they refused all food until they saw some raw broad beans, which they consumed eagerly. Eventually, the children learned to eat other food and lost their green pallor.

After a while the boy, the younger of the two, turned sickly and died. His sister was baptised shortly afterwards and given the name Agnes. After she learned to speak English the girl explained that she and her brother had come from a land where the sun never shone and the light was like twilight. She named it Saint Martin's Land, a subterranean world where everything was green, including its inhabitants.

"Agnes" was unable to account for how they had left their mysterious homeland and arrived in Woolpit. All she could remember was that they had been herding their father's cattle and became lost after they followed the cattle into a cave. After being guided out from the cave by a loud noise, identified as the Abbey bells of Bury St Edmunds six miles from Woolpit, they found themselves by the pit where they were found. Agnes was employed for many years as a servant in the Calne's household where she was considered to be "very wanton and impudent." She eventually married a royal official named Richard Barre from King's Lynn.

"Black Shuck" is the name given to a ghostly black dog, which is said to roam the coastline and countryside of East Anglia, one of many ghostly black dogs recorded in folklore across the British Isles. It is sometimes recorded as an omen of death but, in other instances, is described as companionable. It is likened in size to a calf or horse. The name Shuck derives from the Old English word scucca: devil or fiend. In his 1850 journal *Black Shuck*, the Reverend E.S. Taylor described "Shuck the Dog-fiend": "This phantom I have heard many persons in East Norfolk, and even Cambridgeshire, describe as having seen a black shaggy dog, with fiery eyes and of immense size, and who visits churchyards at midnight." W.A. Dutt in his 1901 *Highways & Byways in East Anglia* describes the creature:

He takes the form of a huge black dog, and prowls along dark lanes and lonesome field footpaths where, although his howling makes the hearer's blood run cold, his footfalls make no sound. You may know him at once, should you see him, by his fiery eye; he has but one, and that, like the Cyclops', is in the middle of his head. But such an encounter might bring you the worst of luck: it is even said that to meet him is to be warned that your death will occur before the end of the year. So you will do well to shut your eyes if you hear him howling; shut them even if you are uncertain whether it is the dog fiend or the voice of the wind you hear. Should you never set eyes on our Norfolk 'Snarleyow' you may perhaps doubt his existence, and, like other learned folks, tell us that his story is nothing but the old Scandinavian myth of the black hound of Odin, brought to us by the Vikings who long ago settled down on the Norfolk coast.

The Peterborough Chronicle (a version of the Anglo-Saxon Chronicle) recorded an incident that took place in Peterborough Abbey in 1127. It describes a sighting by multiple observers of "a great number of huntsmen hunting." The witnesses' description is reminiscent of the dreadful Ringraiths in Tolkein's *Lord of the Rings*:

The huntsmen were black, huge and hideous, and rode on black horses and black he-goats... the hounds were jet black with eyes like saucers and horrible. This was seen in the very deer park of the town of Peterborough and in all the woods that stretch from that same town to Stamford, and in the night the monks heard them sounding and winding their horns. Reliable witnesses who kept watch in the night declared that there might well have been as many as twenty or thirty of them winding their horns as near they could tell. This was seen and heard from the time of his arrival all through Lent and right up to Easter.

In August 1577 Black Shuck appeared in churches at Bungay and Blythburgh in Suffolk. At Blythburgh the dog-fiend burst in through the doors of Holy Trinity Church to a clap of thunder. He ran up the nave, past a large congregation, killed a man and boy and caused the church steeple to collapse through the roof. As the dog left, he left scorch marks on the north door, which can be seen at the church to this day. Later that same day, Black Shuck ran into St Mary's Church in Bungay and killed two worshipers. Abraham Fleming described the scene in his contemporary account, *A Straunge and Terrible Wunder:*

An artist's impression of Big Shuck

> *This black dog, or the divel in such a likenesse (God hee knoweth al who worketh all), running all along down the body of the church with great swiftnesse, and incredible haste, among the people, in a visible form and shape, passed between two persons, as they were kneeling uppon their knees, and occupied in prayer as it seemed, wrung the necks of them bothe at one instant clene backward, in somuch that even at a moment where they kneeled, they strangely dyed.*

Four miles west of Woolpit is the village of Rougham. Although tiny, Rougham punches far above it weight as an "X-Files" location for more than 20 reported time-slip incidents. In October 1926, vicar's daughter Ruth Wynne was tutoring for a young lady named Eveleyn Allington. On the day in question, the two girls decided to take a walk to the church at Bradfield St George, a mile and half south of Rougham. Their path took them through a farmyard close by Colesville Grove, a new route for their regular strolls together. When they passed through the farmyard and reached the road they saw a high wall of greenish-yellow bricks. They followed the road round and came upon tall wrought iron gates set in the wall. Behind the wall and towering above it was a grove of tall trees. From the gates, a drive led into the trees to what was evidently a large house. They could see a corner of a roof above a stucco front inset with windows of a Georgian design. On the next occasion that they walked the same route they were dumbfounded to find that the wall, gates and imposing Georgian house were nowhere to be seen. In their place flanking the road was a ditch and a wild area of weeds overgrown with earth inside the grove of trees they had seen on their previous visit. According to a study of eighteenth century maps, the Grove was laid out as the estate of a large house between 1783 and 1813.

In 1940, Edward Bentley and his boss, men's clothing outfitter Aubyn Davies, were out and about in Davies' car delivering catalogues. They were in the neighbourhood of Wynne and Allington's 1926 walk. They were driving down Kingshall Street when Bentley saw a house and told Davies they had missed one. Davies reversed the car but when they reached the spot the house had vanished.

In 1974, 14-year old Sandra Hardwick was heading home on her bicycle just before dusk. As she approached two bungalows that occupied the east side of Kingshall Street she suddenly saw a house on her right. In the meantime it had become unnaturally quiet. The house seemed very brightly illuminated "like the sun had come out on a bright summer's day." "It was beautiful," she later said, "thatched roof, windows open, and a garden with yellow and pink flowers, a fence and a gate." The curtains to the windows were billowing in the wind. Suddenly feeling terrified, Hardwick pedalled furiously home.

Old map of Rougham and neighbouring villages incorporating the anomaly sites

Gypsy Lane, a track that leads off Kingshall Street, has also been the site of bizarre events. Edith Rose whose family occupied one of the two bungalows was doing crochet work in the room that looked out onto the lane. Suddenly, half of the room went intensely black. Edith could not see her hand when she placed it in the dark zone. Another time, a group of monks were seen walking past the living room window. The family's horses would refuse to traverse Gypsy Lane, often breaking free and bolting in panic.

Nearby residents Bob and Win Barker frequently reported seeing balls of light in their bedroom. The lights would emerge from a wardrobe on the right of the room and travel to the left, about two feet below the ceiling and then disappear into another bedroom.

An elderly lady and her two daughters have a good view of the fields leading up to Rougham Church. On many occasions they have seen a strange arc of light emerge from the ground and form a kind of rainbow. They last witnessed the phenomenon in 2011.

Others have witnessed in the fields by Colesville Grove a wheel-shaped vortex whizzing by them in a circular motion accompanied by a rushing noise. They report feeling very ill afterwards. It is speculated by investigators that the Grove is the centre of a zone in which a strange energy holds sway. It can cause people to see visions from the past. The zone appears to be at least thirty miles in diameter, based on two separate accounts of high strangeness.

Alone in the Suffolk woods…

Teenager Chris Jensen was with a school friend between classes when he saw a group of children in the uniform of the middle school, St James, near the West Front of St Edmundsbury Cathedral in Bury St Edmunds, five miles from Rougham. Bizarrely, Jensen saw among this group his younger self. Immediately, he became extremely ill, sick and dizzy and suffered such a severe headache that he had to be sent home.

The second event concerned the experiences of three army cadets while they were undertaking a training exercise. In the course of the training the troops entered the village of Kersey, fifteen miles south of Rougham. On doing so, they were amazed to find that they had entered the village just as it had been in the Middle Ages when it was ravaged by the plague. Antiquarian research confirmed the presence of a butcher's shop precisely where they saw it.

Investigators have likened events in Rougham and its extended hinterland of influence to phenomena associated with "Die Glocke," the infamous "Nazi Bell" reportedly built by Hitler's scientists in the latter part of WWII. All kinds of sensational claims have been made about the purpose of Die Glocke, including its alleged ability to generate images from the past and to open dimensional gateways. The Nazi scientists' tests on the Bell were split into "vortex compression" and "magnetic fields separation." Evidence suggests that the Bell was intended to serve either as an anti-gravity device, which would carry a new generation of chemical weapons (the secret work was designated "Decisive for the War"), or time-travel. During the tests period five scientists died after suffering sickness, dizziness, lack of coordination, a metallic taste in the mouth, headaches and muscle cramps, just as Rougham witnesses have reported.

After the Michael current's flight through St Edmundsbury Cathedral, it proceeds past Woolpit and goes on to skirt spooky Colesville Grove in Bradfield St George. It is difficult to imagine how the workings and electromagnetic properties of the St Michael ley may be unconnected with the weird space-time anomalies reported in this region of Suffolk.

The same observation may be made regarding that most renowned episode of wierd goings-on in the Suffolk countryside—the infamous Rendlesham Forest incident of 1980. This refers to a series of reported sightings of unexplained lights and the alleged landing of a craft or multiple craft of unknown origin in Rendlesham Forest in late December 1980 just outside RAF Woodbridge. It is the most famous UFO event to have happened in Britain, ranking amongst the best-known UFO events worldwide. Along with the Berwyn Mountain UFO incident,[79] it has been compared to the Roswell UFO incident of 1947 in the United States, and is sometimes referred to as "Britain's Roswell." Rendlesham Forest is owned by the Forestry Commission and consists of about 5.8 square miles of coniferous plantations, interspersed with broadleaved belts, heathland and wetland areas. It is located 8 miles east of the town of Ipswich.

The incident occurred in the vicinity of two former military bases—RAF Bentwaters, which is just to the north of the forest, and RAF Woodbridge which extends into the forest from the west and is bounded by the forest on its northern and eastern edges. The forest begins at the east end of the base runway or about 0.3 miles to the east of the East Gate of RAF Woodbridge. It extends east about 1 mile and ends at a farmer's field. The multiple UFO events that occurred there are collectively known as the Bentwaters-Woodbridge-Rendlesham Forest Case. Most people nowadays simply refer to it as the Bentwaters case.

At the time of the events, both bases were being used by the United States Air Force and were under the command of wing commander Colonel Gordon E. Williams. The base commander was Colonel Ted Conrad, and his deputy was Lieutenant Colonel Charles I. Halt. Halt's memo to the Ministry of Defence on the incident, and his personal involvement in the second night of the sightings, has given the case credibility. The bases were reported to have a large stockpile of nuclear weapons; Woodbridge was the home of the 67th Aerospace Rescue and Recovery Squadron. The unit was subject only to the authority of the Department of Defense in Washington, D.C

The extraordinary events of Woodbridge-Bentwaters would begin on December 26, 1980, at around 2:00 a.m. (mis-reported as the 27th by Halt). At this time a security patrol saw strange coloured lights from a glowing metallic object apparently descending into nearby Rendlesham Forest near the East Gate of RAF Woodbridge. Receiving permission to check out the strange sightings, the servicemen followed the lights into the forest. Their initial interpretation was that a military or commercial aircraft had made a crash landing. As they approached, the object moved through the trees and "the animals on a nearby farm went into frenzy." The patrol was shocked and frightened to see a saucer-like craft manned by small, large-headed beings, which seemed to be suspended from the bottom of the craft by a type of beam. The beings appeared to be busy, possibly making some type of repair. They seemed at first to be unaware of the three men watching their activities. The

---

[79] treated in depth in *The Landing Lights of Magonia: UFOs, Aliens and the Fairy Kingdom*, AUP, 2018

guards, maintaining a safe distance from the craft and its beings, were almost transfixed by the activities at the glowing object. They radioed to the base headquarters, reported what they were seeing and requested emergency help.

Almost immediately assistance arrived with a fully equipped armed unit, which included senior officers of the base. Later, there would be reports, off the record, that witnesses who ventured closest to the craft encountered strange anomalies. Among these were "reality-bending" effects like time displacement and surreal atmospheric conditions. Also, there were allegations that some of the senior officers were able to communicate with the beings, which floated in bubbles around a triangular-shaped craft. The craft was said to have appeared from a type of low-lying cloud. It left three impressions in the ground that were visible the next day. Shortly after 4 a.m. local police were called to the scene but reported that the only lights they could see were those from the Orford Ness lighthouse, some miles away on the coast.

After daybreak on the morning of the 26th, servicemen returned to a small clearing near the eastern edge of the forest and found three small impressions in a triangular pattern, as well as burn marks and broken branches on nearby trees. Plaster casts of the imprints were taken and have been shown in television documentaries. At 10.30 a.m. the local police were called out again, this time to see the impressions on the ground, which they thought could have been made by an animal.

Several servicemen and Halt returned to the site again in the early hours of 28 December 1980 (reported as the 29th by Halt). Their equipment detected radiation in the depressions and on the near side of a tree, although the significance of the readings they obtained is disputed. Halt recorded the events on a micro-cassette recorder. During this investigation a flashing light was seen across the field to the east, almost in line with a farmhouse. However, some claim that this could have been light from the lighthouse, which is visible further to the east in the same line of sight. Later, starlike lights were seen in the sky to the north and south, the brightest of which seemed to beam down a stream of light from time to time.

There are claims that the incident was videoed by the USAF but, if so, the resulting tape has not been made public. The British Ministry of Defence (MoD) denied that the event posed any threat to national security and, thus, was never investigated as a security matter. Later evidence indicated that there was a substantial MoD file on the subject, which led to claims of a cover-up. Some interpreted this as part of a larger pattern of official information suppression concerning the true nature of unidentified flying objects, by both the United States and British governments. Deputy Base Commander Halt was of this opinion. Another was former NATO head and UK Chief of the Defence Staff Lord Peter Hill-Norton, who stated that whatever happened at this USAF base was necessarily of national security interest. However, when the file was released in 2001 it turned out to consist mostly of internal correspondence and responses to inquiries from the public. Sceptics note that the lack of any in-depth investigation in the publicly released documents is consistent with the MoD's earlier statement that they never took the case seriously.

(E109

DEPARTMENT OF THE AIR FORCE
HEADQUARTERS 81ST COMBAT SUPPORT GROUP (USAFE)
APO NEW YORK 09755

REPLY TO ATTN OF: CD

13 Jan 81

SUBJECT: Unexplained Lights

TO: RAF/CC

1. Early in the morning of 27 Dec 80 (approximately 0300L), two USAF security police patrolmen saw unusual lights outside the back gate at RAF Woodbridge. Thinking an aircraft might have crashed or been forced down, they called for permission to go outside the gate to investigate. The on-duty flight chief responded and allowed three patrolmen to proceed on foot. The individuals reported seeing a strange glowing object in the forest. The object was described as being metalic in appearance and triangular in shape, approximately two to three meters across the base and approximately two meters high. It illuminated the entire forest with a white light. The object itself had a pulsing red light on top and a bank(s) of blue lights underneath. The object was hovering or on legs. As the patrolmen approached the object, it maneuvered through the trees and disappeared. At this time the animals on a nearby farm went into a frenzy. The object was briefly sighted approximately an hour later near the back gate.

2. The next day, three depressions 1 1/2" deep and 7" in diameter were found where the object had been sighted on the ground. The following night (29 Dec 80) the area was checked for radiation. Beta/gamma readings of 0.1 milliroentgens were recorded with peak readings in the three depressions and near the center of the triangle formed by the depressions. A nearby tree had moderate (.05-.07) readings on the side of the tree toward the depressions.

3. Later in the night a red sun-like light was seen through the trees. It moved about and pulsed. At one point it appeared to throw off glowing particles and then broke into five separate white objects and then disappeared. Immediately thereafter, three star-like objects were noticed in the sky, two objects to the north and one to the south, all of which were about 10° off the horizon. The objects moved rapidly in sharp angular movements and displayed red, green and blue lights. The objects to the north appeared to be elliptical through an 8-12 power lens. They then turned to full circles. The objects to the north remained in the sky for an hour or more. The object to the south was visible for two or three hours and beamed down a stream of light from time to time. Numerous individuals, including the undersigned, witnessed the activities in paragraphs 2 and 3.

CHARLES I. HALT, Lt Col, USAF
Deputy Base Commander

The Halt Memo

The "Halt memo," the first piece of primary evidence concerning the affair, was made available publicly and unclassified in the US under its Freedom of Information Act in 1983. Halt reconstructed the UFO incidents from memory, and inadvertently mis-stated the dates on which they had occurred. The first incident in the forest actually took place around 3 a.m. on December 26th; the second incident began late on the evening of December 27th and continued into the early morning hours of the 28th. The 2-week delay between the incident and the report and, possibly, the effect of time-distortion phenomena on witnesses' mental faculties might account for errors in recalling dates and times.

When this memo was declassified, it sparked widespread media interest and public excitement about the Bentwaters sightings. UFO debunkers, most notably James McGaha, dismissed the mysterious light in the woods as the periodic flashing of nearby Orford Ness lighthouse. Colonel Halt strenuously objected to this explanation, saying in one interview, "The lighthouse was visible the whole time … it was readily apparent, and it was 30 to 40 degrees off to our right …" In other words, both the lighthouse and the unidentified light in the woods were observed simultaneously and were clearly distinguishable as two, widely-separated sources of light.

Dr David Clarke has investigated the background to this memo and the MoD's reaction to it. His interviews with the personnel involved confirmed the cursory nature of the investigation made by the MoD, and failed to find any evidence for any other reports on the incident made by the USAF or UK authorities, apart from the Halt memo.

In 1984, a copy emerged of what became known as the "Halt Tape." Unfortunately, because it had been dubbed on an old machine, much of its background conversations could not be made out. The US Sci Fi Channel acquired the original recording, which documents Halt and his patrol investigating a UFO sighting in Rendlesham Forest in December 1980. This cleaned up version not only reveals much more of the background conversations but features names that could not be heard on the poor-quality 1984 dub.

The Scottish researcher James Easton succeeded in obtaining the original witness statements made for Col. Halt by Fred A. Buran, Airman First Class John Burroughs, Airman Edward N. Cabansag, Master-Sergeant J.D. Chandler and Staff-Sergeant Jim Penniston. These documents describe the sightings of strange lights. Penniston, for instance, states that: "directly to the east [of East Gate] about 1½ miles in a large wooded area... a large yellow glowing light was emitting above the trees. In the centre of the lighted area directly in the centre ground level, there was a red light blinking on and off 5 to 10 sec intervals. And a blue light that was being for the most part steady."

Burroughs, Penniston and Cabansag drove into the forest in search of the source of the lights. They heard strange noises, too. Burroughs reported a noise "like a woman was screaming" and also that "you could hear the farm animals making a lot of noises." Halt heard the same noises two nights later.

In a CNN interview in January 2008 Burroughs said: "The livestock around the barn seemed to be going crazy." It is claimed that such noise could also have been made by Muntjac deer in the forest, which are known for their loud, shrill bark when alarmed. Cabansag said: "We figured the lights were coming from past the forest since nothing was visible when we passed through the woody forest. We would see a glowing near the beacon light, but as we got closer we found it to be a lit-up farmhouse. We got to a vantage point where we could determine that what we were chasing was only a beacon light off in the distance." Burroughs' statement also states that: "We could see a beacon going around so we went towards it. We followed it for about two miles before we could [see] it was coming from a lighthouse." The witnesses were unnerved by their experience and believed that they had witnessed something, as Buran expresses it, "out of the realm of explanation."

Penniston's statement is the only one that positively identifies a mechanical object as the source of the lights. He states that he was within 160 feet of the object and "it was definitely mechanical in nature." Penniston has subsequently claimed that, contrary to his statement at the time, he actually encountered a landed craft in the forest, which he circled, touched and made notes of for 45 minutes, although there is no corroborating evidence of this from other witnesses. John Burroughs apparently contradicts this in a separate interview in Robert Stack's *Unsolved Mysteries*. He states that after suddenly encountering the craft on the ground, "We all hit the ground, and it went up into the trees." Penniston has shown on television a notebook in which he claims to have made real-time notes and sketches of the object. The notebook is headed with the date 27 December and the time 12:20 (00:20 GMT), which does not accord with the date and time given by the other witnesses for the incident, although the date does accord with Halt's memo. Penniston claims that he saw the object at a different landing site from the one investigated by Halt, much closer to RAF Woodbridge. This is inconsistent with his initial assessment that the light source was a mile and a half from East Gate.

Suffolk Constabulary has a record, dated 26 December 1980, of a report from the law Enforcement Desk of RAF Woodbridge, stating that: "We have a sighting of some unusual lights in the sky. We have sent some unarmed troops to investigate. We are terming it as a U.F.O. at present." The police investigated this report and the result is recorded as follows: "Air Traffic Control West Drayton checked. No knowledge of aircraft. Reports received of aerial phenomena over Southern England during the night. Only lights visible this area was from Orford lighthouse. Search made of area – negative."

The police would also have been aware of other reports by local folk of unusual phenomena observed that night. During the evening of the 26th a resident of Sudbourne, a village approximately 6 miles to the northeast of Rendlesham Forest, reported a mysterious shape (like an upturned mushroom) in the sky above his garden.

Ian Ridpath has speculated that the report of "aerial phenomena" referred to the re-entry of the Soviet Cosmos 749 satellite's final stage rocket, which was widely seen over Southern England shortly after 9 p.m. on the evening of the 25th. A letter in the police file notes that one of the constables returned to the site in daylight in case he had missed something. There was nothing to be seen and remains unconvinced that the occurrence was genuine. The immediate area was swept by powerful light beams from a landing beacon at RAF Bentwaters and the Orford Ness lighthouse. Ridpath said that from personal experience, at night, in certain weather and cloud conditions, these beams are very pronounced and can cause strange visual effects. He investigated the incident in 1983, initially for BBC TV's *Breakfast Time* news programme. An article of his published by the *Guardian* on 5 January 1985 did much to discredit the accounts of the UFO sightings at Rendlesham. Ridpath asked local forester Vince Thurkettle about the flashing light, and he indicated that it originated from the lighthouse at Orford Ness. At that time, this lighthouse was the second brightest in Britain with an intensity of 5 million candelas.

In the Halt tape, one can hear an unidentified airman call out, "There it is again ... there it is," with an interval of 5 seconds, the same frequency at which the Orford Ness lighthouse flashes. Thurkettle saw the alleged "landing marks" and believed them simply to be old "rabbit diggings" covered with pine needles. USAF photographs of the marks discovered by researcher Georgina Bruni were sent to the MoD by Lord Hill-Norton in 2001 and released under the Freedom of Information Act in 2007. Moreover, the supposed burn marks in the trees were actually axe cuts made by foresters that indicated the trees were ready to be felled. To give further food for thought, a meteor "almost as bright as the full Moon" was spotted over southern England at exactly the time of the initial reports of a bright object landing in the forest, according to Dr John Mason who collects reports of meteor sightings for the British Astronomical Association.

The *Halt Affidavit*—in June 2010, Halt, then in retirement, signed a notarised affidavit, in which he again summarised what had happened and re-stated that he believed the event to have been extraterrestrial in nature and that it had been covered up by both the UK and US:

> *I believe the objects that I saw at close quarter were extraterrestrial in origin and that the security services of both the United Kingdom and the United States have attempted—both then and now—to subvert the significance of what occurred at Rendlesham Forest and RAF Bentwaters by the use of well-practiced methods of disinformation.*

Halt also dismissed claims that he and his men had confused a UFO with a lighthouse beam:

> *While in Rendlesham Forest, our security team observed a light that looked like a large eye, red in colour, moving through the trees. After a few minutes this object began dripping something that looked like molten metal. A short while later it broke into several smaller, white-coloured objects which flew away in all directions. Claims by sceptics that this was merely a sweeping beam from a distant lighthouse are unfounded; we could see the unknown light and the lighthouse simultaneously. The latter was 35 to 40-degrees off where all of this was happening.*

In 2010 base commander Colonel Ted Conrad provided a statement about the incident to Dr David Clarke of Sheffield Hallam University, UFO adviser to the UK National Archives. Conrad stated, "We saw nothing that resembled Lieutenant Colonel Halt's descriptions either in the sky or on the ground," and, "We had people in position to validate Halt's narrative, but none of them could." In an interview, Conrad criticised Halt for the claims in his affidavit, saying "he should be ashamed and embarrassed by his allegation that his country and Britain both conspired to deceive their citizens over this issue. He knows better."

Conrad also disputed the testimony of Sergeant Jim Penniston, who claimed to have touched an alien spacecraft; he said that he interviewed Penniston at the time and he had not mentioned any such occurrence. Conrad also suggested that the entire incident might have been a hoax.

Halt's partial response to this was:

> *Ted Conrad is either having memory problems, has his head in the sand or continuing the cover up. Even his son has admitted to family talk substantiating the incident... Through the years Conrad has made conflicting statements about the events. First he stated he never went out to look in the sky. Then stated he never saw anything. Apparently he doesn't remember talking to me on his radio* [about seeing a UFO sending down beams of light onto the base]... *Remind Conrad of his article in the OMNI Magazine dated March 1983...*
>
> *In the article he describes the first incident in detail and concludes 'those lads saw something, but I don't know what it was.' Now he's smearing those involved. It's pretty clear there was a very intense confrontation with something in the forest. Does Conrad want to talk about how the airmen were then subjected to mind control efforts using drugs and hypnosis by British and American authorities? Yes, Burroughs and Penniston have issues that relate to the events...*

The 1983 OMNI article cited by Halt contains this account attributed to Conrad:

> *Colonel Ted Conrad the base commander... recalls five Air Force policemen spotted lights from what they thought was a small plane descending into the forest. Two of the men tracked the object on foot and came upon a large tripod-mounted craft. It had no windows but was studded with brilliant red and blue lights. Each time the men came within 50 yards of the ship, Conrad relates, it levitated six feet in the air and backed away. They followed it for almost an hour through the woods and across a field until it took off at 'phenomenal speed.'*
>
> *Acting on the reports made by his men, Colonel Conrad began a brief investigation of the incident in the morning. He went into the forest and located a triangular pattern ostensibly made by the tripod legs... he did interview two of the eyewitnesses and concludes, 'Those lads saw something, but I don't know what it was.'*

Admiral Lord Hill-Norton, the former Chief of the UK Defence Staff, argued that an incident like this at a nuclear weapons base was necessarily of national security interest. As a member of the House of Lords, Lord Hill-Norton asked the Government: "Whether they are aware of any involvement by Special Branch in the investigation of the 1980 Rendlesham Forest incident." Baroness Symons of Vernham Dean gave the reply that "Special Branch officers may have been aware of the incident but would not have shown any interest unless there was evidence of a potential threat to national security. No such interest appears to have been shown." Hill-Norton commented: "Either large numbers of people were hallucinating, and for an American Air Force nuclear base this is extremely dangerous, or what they say happened did happen, and in either of those circumstances there can only be one answer, and that is that it was of extreme defence interest."

It is not surprising that Hill-Norton regarded the incidents as "of extreme defence interest," considering that while most of the publicity has focused on reports of a landed UFO in Rendlesham Forest, another UFO was apparently observed hovering above the Bentwaters Weapons Storage Area (WSA). This facility, the most sensitive and heavily-guarded section of the base, consisted of closely-spaced, reinforced concrete bunkers—known on base as "hot row"—in which lower-yield tactical nuclear bombs were believed to be stored. Reportedly, the UFO directed laser-like beams of light down into it, penetrating beneath the surface, in the early hours of 26 December 1980 before departing the vicinity at great speed. Sensationally, eyewitnesses also reportedly observed three small humanoid beings dressed in silvery overalls glide down from the craft in a beam of light and land in front of wing commander Colonel Williams. They looked like children: 3-4 feet tall with large heads and catlike eyes.

Although the UFO's activities at the site have never been officially confirmed by the Pentagon, investigator Robert Hastings[80] has stated that three of his ex-Royal Air Force sources, one a retired colonel, confirm that they took place. Another source, a retired U.S. Air Force officer who once worked for NATO's nuclear weapons security program, told Hastings that following the UFO incident at the WSA two of the weapons were removed from one of the bunkers shortly after the incident and shipped to the U.S. on board a C-5A Galaxy cargo aircraft for inspection.

Colonel Halt briefly alluded to the incident during a 1991 *Unsolved Mysteries* television program. "We could very clearly see [the UFO]… I noticed other beams of light coming down from the same object, falling on different places on the base. My boss was standing in his front yard in Woodbridge and he could see the beams of light falling

---

[80] Hastings, R., *UFOs & Nukes: Extraordinary Encounters at Nuclear Weapons Sites*, CreateSpace Independent Publishing Platform, 2017

down, and the people in the Weapons Storage Area and other places on the base also reported the lights." During an interview with journalist A.J.S. Rayl in May 1997, Halt returned to the topic:

> [After leaving the woods, our search team] *crossed the farmer's field past his house and across the road, stumbled through a small stream, and went out into a large plowed field. Somebody noticed several objects in the sky to the north—three objects clearly visible with multiple-colored lights on them. The objects appeared elliptical and then they turned full round, which I thought was quite interesting. All three doing that. They were stationary for awhile and then they started to move at high speed in sharp angular patterns as though they were doing a grid search.*
>
> *About that same time, somebody noticed a similar object* [in the southern sky]. *It was round—did not change shape—and at one point it appeared to come toward us at a very high speed. It stopped overhead and sent down a small pencil-like beam, sort of like a laser beam. It was an interesting beam in that it stayed—it was the same size all the way down the beam. It illuminated the ground about ten feet from us and we just stood there in awe wondering whether it was a signal, a warning, or what it was. We really didn't know. It clicked-off as though someone threw a switch, and the object receded, back up into the sky. Then it moved back toward Bentwaters, and continued to send down beams of light, at one point near the weapons storage facility. We knew that because we could hear the chatter on the* [two-way] *radio.*

Halt told the *Huffington Post* that what he and the others experienced in the forest was under intelligent control:

> *The military has nothing to do with it, other than the cover-up, but I can tell you, there is some type of superior intelligence that can change size, change shape, do funny things. What I saw, I'm firmly convinced, didn't have anything that we know or could relate to, inside it. Maybe they're not a being as we know, maybe they're an entity that just has intelligence, and we just can't relate to it.*

Staff Sergeant James Penniston and Airman 1st Class John Smith (alias) can evidently relate to "it." The pair encountered the alien ship a few hours after Penniston had had Christmas dinner with his family.

Under hypnosis in September 1994, Penniston described the appearance of blue and red lights at the Bentwaters East Gate at 2.00 a.m. He saw a white light and a large disc-shaped craft with raised symbols on its surface and equipped with triangular landing gear. He reportedly reached out and touched the symbols and received binary code information. The decoded message was "Explain. Mission. Purpose": the mission being "Contact."

Penniston claimed that the "craft" came from our future and was occupied by time travellers, not extraterrestrials. The occupants told him they needed people to interpret the lights. He was told that there were many interpreters. Human interpreters such as Penniston, he was told, might come from a bloodline that carries memory files locked inside genes that are necessary for communications between mankind and our future selves. The future Earth "time travellers" said they needed something connected with chromosomes from the interpreters, which they take from abductees. They can only travel back into the past; future travel is impossible. They need sufficient speed to make the time travel possible. They can go back a maximum of 40,000-50,000 years; any further they might not be able to return. They said that they have been coming to Earth for 30,000-40,000 years. They took nothing from Penniston because they were interrupted. Penniston was not supposed to understand the program but by touching the symbols he activated them. They explained that they have a physical problem trying to sustain their children. To address this, they use us not like breeding stock but like band-aids. They take foetuses when necessary.

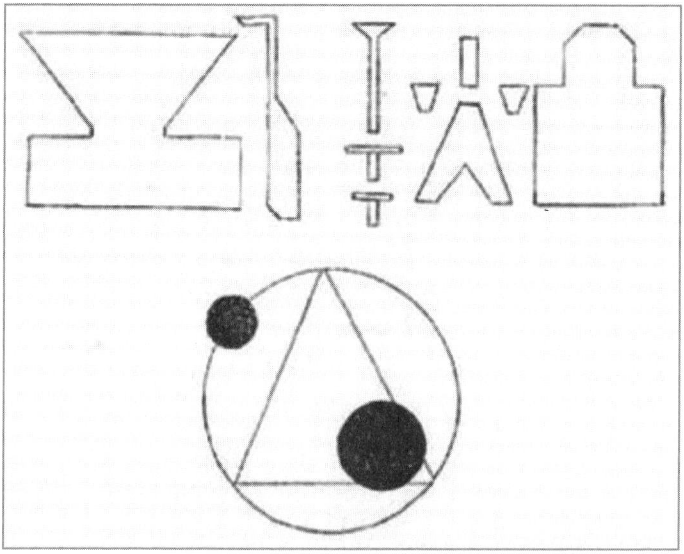

The symbols on the Rendlesham UFO described by Staff Sergeant Penniston

The object flew away after their brief encounter. Sgt. Penniston's report made shortly after the incident contains no mention of physically encountering an unknown craft or of interacting with it. This report and associated sketches are neither signed nor dated, nor are they representative of AF Form 1169, Statement of Witness.

One of the photos from the Bentwaters landing showed the insectoid type of greys (EBE Type II). Eyewitnesses described them as 1.5 metres tall wearing what appeared to be nylon-coated pressure suits with no helmets. They had claw like hands with 3 digits and an opposable thumb. One struggles to reconcile these all too familiar "greys" descriptions with what one might expect time travellers from Earth's future to look like!

The description tallies with the U.S. Government's MJ-12's SOM1-01 Special Operations Manual, which I referenced in an earlier work for AUP.[81] It describes the EBE Type II "grey" as a bipedal humanoid entity, height 3ft 5in to 4ft 2in, 25lbs-50lbs in weight. The head is proportionately larger than humans, the cranium being much larger and elongated. The eyes are very large and slanted, black with no whites and nearly wrap around the skull with a noticeable brow ridge. The skull has a slight peak that runs over the crown. The nose is two small slits that sit high over a slit-like mouth. There are no external ears. The skin is pale bluish-grey, being darker on the back of the creature. The face and body are hairless.

As noted earlier, there is abundant evidence that "grey" aliens are robotic servants made by super-intelligent beings whose origins are inevitably open to question. In the case of Penniston's experience, however, there is apparently no mystery as to the identity of the human-like occupants in the Rendlesham forest craft. They told the young serviceman that they were indeed humans, albeit from our far future. They explained to Penniston that they made journeys into the past to find pliant subjects who could assist in their "research" efforts to counter problems trying to sustain their children and, thus, prolong the continuation of human life on earth tens of thousands of years in the future. Certainly, their declaration that to attain these goals requires using present day humans as "band-aids" and the abduction of foetuses paints a picture of a future earth with few if any redeeming features.

There were many stories told by the men who were present that night at Rendlesham. One of the most remarkable concerned an underground theatre where soldiers were interrogated, debriefed, sworn to secrecy and threatened. The morning after the most pronounced

---

[81] ibid, *The Landing Lights of Magonia*

activity, a type of "men-in-black" scenario occurred. Several of the men were whisked away by the MIBs and escorted to the underground facility. Oddly enough, during the debriefing programme they were reportedly shown a number of motion picture films of different UFO recoveries around the world.

*

We have traced the serpents' flightpaths between Land's End and Hopton. Of course, that is not the absolute extent of their journeys. Neither of the currents began its life in Cornwall nor ended it in Norfolk. Electromagnetism does not behave like that; it has no beginning or end. It just *is*. Our studies reveal that the St Michael ley is a component part of the etheric earth's spinning torus, a stunningly beautiful creation of cosmic geometry that embodies the divine principle of "Mater into Matter." The ability of the five Platonic solids to "transmute into each other" and, at the same time, be "dissimilar to one another but capable of arising out of one another's disintegration" allows the earth's crystalline structure to function as a vehicle in which Universal Consciousness forms into Light, Light into Geometric Form, and Geometric Form into Matter.

Long ago, men of learning and deep esoteric insight moulded the landscape along the ley so that through ritual and prayers one might maintain a deep and loving relationship with the inner earth's spiritual life force, which was bequeathed to mankind by its first teachers, the "Sun-Men." At sacred centres such as Glastonbury, Silbury Hill and Avebury men and women gave thanks for the knowledge of these cosmic laws—the "Ancient Wisdom"—by worshipping the Sun in the heavens and the inner Light within the divine self. Neither burned brighter than the other.

In their prayers and meditations, the faithful did not neglect to honour the invisible caretakers of Nature, the elemental folk of the fairy kingdom without whose toil our planet would be a lifeless rock. The Golden Proportion relationship between the Michael and Mary line and the location of Carroll's first reading of his Wonderland fantasy reveals that the Fairy Queen figure of Alice has a special relationship with the two dragons and all the other wild and wonderful creatures that occupy the "Underground" world.

White Eagle emphasised that Carroll was guided to tell his story by the sylphs. The creatures of fairyland, aware that with the dawning of the industrial age humankind was on a path that would fracture its traditional ties to nature, resolved to remind mortals that the search for mystical truth is not trumped by relentless pursuit of material gain. In Lewis Carroll they found their muse.

His two masterpieces of children's literature (I obviously never grew up; approaching seventy, I re-read them several times each year) are, in essence, a plea from the citizens of the etheric that there is so much more to the business of living life on our beautiful planet than one can ever imagine. Do we not see in phrases such as "mirthful, changeable and eccentric… capable of assuming human form… accept human beings into their communities," distinct correspondences with the many and varied characters with whom Alice shared her adventures in the Wonderland Looking Glass worlds? And in the Red Queen's remark to Alice: "If you want to get somewhere else [here], you must run at least twice as fast as that," do we not get a feel that the world of the sylphs is every bit as real as our own, albeit ruled by an entirely different kind of physics?

Michael and Mary power the Gateways along the ley. Alice, while daydreaming about making a daisychain and, later, playing with balls of wool with Dinah the family cat, finds two doorways to the invisible which she has the courage to explore.

In Alice, we see a reflection of one's inner goddess. She combines the feminine qualities of softness, grace, intuitiveness and patience, together with the child's innate belief that anything is possible. At a deep level of understanding we learn within Carroll's pages that it is in exercising these qualities one has the possibility to find a Golden Key to a Secret Garden of one's own.

Michael, Mary and Alice are in this together, inspiring one's instinctive thirst for quest adventure, ever signposting the curious and the inquisitive to new lessons in inner learning and opportunity. The only qualifications necessary are love and respect for nature, a strong sense of belief and a healthy respect for the eccentric and the absurd.

A wise and very dear friend once told me: "Believe in the invisible and it will make itself known." I, for one, am happy to give it a try.

Eye-witness description of Rendlesham Forest UFO, December 1980

St Margaret's Church, Hopton-on-Sea, 1866

A Welsh slate "Flower of Life" crystal grid, a symbol of the Earth and its crystal form

The complete list of locations dowsed by Miller and Broadhurst on the Michael and Mary flows (21 nodes in bold)	
Michael	**Mary**
Cornwall	
Carn-Lês-Boel	**Carn-Lês-Boel**
Penlee	Ailsa Holy Well
St Michael's Mount	St. Buryan Church
Leedstown	Blind Fiddler menhir
Truro	Boscawen-Un stone circle
St Michael Penkevil	Drift Reservoir
Carwynnen Quoit	St Mary's Church, Penzance
Foxhole	**St Michael's Mount**
Saint Mewan Beacon	Perranuthnoe Church
Gover Valley	Rosudgeon Methodist Chapel
Resugga Castle	Germoe Church,
St Austell	Godolphin Church,
Saint Neot village	Black Rock
Draynes hamlet	St Crewenna Church, Crowan village
Sharptor	Calvadnack Hill
Henwood	Stithians Reservoir
St Cleer Church and Holy Well	St Stithians Parish Church
Siblyback Reservoir	Devoran Church
Upton Cross	Old Kea Church
Darley Ford	St Michael Penkevil Church
Plushabridge	Ruan Lanihorne Church
Bray Shop	Golden Mill at Tregony
Stoke Climsland Church	Grampound
St Bartholomew's, Lostwithiel	Trenowth Estate
The Hurlers and Cheesering Quoit, and Stowe's Pond "fort"	**Resugga Castle**
	St Stephens Church
	Roche Rock
	Luxulyan Church
	Lanlivery Church near Bodmin
	St Bartholomew's Church, Lostwithiel
	Boconnoc Estate
	The Hurlers and Cheesering Quoit
	Langstone Downs
	St Cleer Church and Holy Well Upton Cross
	Treveny Quoit
	Bearah Tor

	North Hill Church
	Lezant, over River Tamar into Devon
	Roche Rock
	St Clear
Devon	
Sydenham Damerel	Dunterton Church, Tavistock
Horsebridge	Milton Abbot, Tavistock
St. Michael of the Rock, Brentor	Quither Common
North Brenton	**Church of St. Michael, Brentor**
Lydfold	Mary Tavy
Lydford Gorge via Tunnel Falls, Pixie Glen and the Devil's Cauldron	St Mary's Parish Church, Mary Tavy
Lydford Church	St Mary the Virgin Ch., Throwleigh
Lydford Castle	Holy Trinity Church, Gidleigh dedicated to Blessed Mary
Across wild Dartmoor to Widgery Tor, Great Links Tor and over Okement River to Yes Tor	Holy Trinity Church, Drewsteignton ("The Druids' Town on the Teign")
Lower Halstock Farm	Spinster's Rock dolmen, Drewsteignton
Ninestones Circle, Belstone Tor	Castle Drogo, Drewsteignton
South Zeal to crossroads at Five Stone Cross	Fingle Bridge over River Teign, Drewsteignton
Whiddon Down	Iron Age hill fort, Prestonbury Castle
St Andrew's Church, Hittisleigh	Woolston Castle, Moretonhampstead
Church of St Andrew, Colebrooke	St Mary's Church, Dunsford
Crediton Church, formally Church of the Holy Cross and Mother of Him who Hung Thereon. Built on site of Crediton's cathedral dedicated to St Mary	St Mary the Virgin Church, Tedburn St Mary
St Michael and All Angels Church, Cheriton Fitzpaine, nr. Crediton	**Crediton Parish Church**
St Michael's Church at Cadbury Castle where a dragon guards hidden treasure	St Boniface's Well, Chapel Downs and Beacon Church, Crediton
St Peter's Church, Tiverton	St Mary the Virgin Church, Upton Hellions
Sampford Peverell	St Mary the Virgin Church, Calverleigh
Wellington Monument obelisk	St Mary the Virgin Church, Washfield
Black Down Hills on Devon/Somerset border	St John the Baptist Church, Cove

	Huntsham Castle earthwork
	Holcombe Rogus
Somerset	
Blagdon Hill, Taunton	St Peter's Church, Greenham
Wellington Monument	Church of St Margaret, Thorne St Margaret
Creech St Michael Church	Church of St Peter and St Paul at Runnington, Langford Budville
Church of St Nicholas, Corfe village	Church of All Saints in Nynehead
Stoke St Mary, Taunton	St Giles Church, Bradford on Tone
Church of St Michael at Orchard Portman, Taunton	All Saints Church, Trull, dedicated to St Michael with dragon window
Durston	Church of St George in Ruishton
St Michael Church at hamlet of North Newton, Bridgewater	**St Michael's Church, Creech St Michael**
Ruins of St Michael Church on Burrow Mump	Church of St Peter & St Paul, North Curry ("the cathedral of the moors"), with impressive octagonal tower
St Michael's Church, Othery	St Gregory Church, Stoke St Gregory
Street	**St Michael Church Burrow Mump**
Greylake Bridge, Greylake	Church of the Holy Cross, Middlezoy
Holy Trinity Church, Walton	Church of St Mary the Virgin, Moorlinch, at foot of Knoll Hill
Passes through Holy Thorn at Glastonbury	Church of the Blessed Virgin Mary, Shapwick, formerly under patronage of Glastonbury Abbey
Wearyall Hill, Glastonbury	**Glastonbury Tor**
Glastonbury Abbey grounds, via Lady Altar	Fair Field and walled enclosure of King Arthur's Court
St George's Chapel in St John's Ch.	**Chalice Well Gardens**
Chalice Well gardens	Chalice Hill
Glastonbury Tor and St Michael's tower	Chilkwell Street into Glastonbury Abbey grounds, to eastern end of ruined Edgar Chapel
St Mary's Church, North Wootton	current divides into two streams at the site of King Arthur's tomb and rejoins at St Mary's Chapel
Church of St John the Baptist, Pilton, founded according to legend by St Joseph of Arimathea	Mary crosses the altar in the crypt and passes through west wall and nearby Abbot's Kitchen
Church of St Peter and St Paul, Shepton Mallet	Mary leaves Abbey, enters glade near Edgarley and flows to earthworks at Ponter's Ball
Church of St Aldhelm, Doulting,	Church of St Andrew, West Bradley

where two dragons peer down from its interior arch	
Church of St Michael, Stoke St Michael	King's Hill nr. East Pennard
Holy Trinity Church, Coleford	Beard Hill, nr. East Compton
St Andrew's Church, Mells	Passes through small earthwork called Small Down Knoll shaped like a giant arrowhead
Church of St Mary Magdalene, Great Elm	Church of St Mary the Virgin, Batcombe
Frome	Mary crosses River Frome near lost village at Marston and passes into Wiltshire
Church of St Lawrence, Rode	
Devil's Bed and Bolster long barrow, Beckington parish	
Wiltshire	
Church of St James, Trowbridge	Chapel at Yarnbrook
Bowerhill housing estate at Melksham	Semington village
Prehistoric hill fort Oliver's Castle	**Bowerhill housing estate at Melksham**
crossed the Wansdyke earthwork to Bishops Canning Down to Cherhill via the White Horse	Bromham church
Windmill Hill	**Oliver's Castle**
Avebury Henge, 150 mile half-way point of Michael and Mary line	St Mary's Church, Bishops Canning
West Kennet stone avenue	crosses Wansdyke (Michael and Mary running 60 yards apart)
Cheriton Hill on the Ridgeway	Tumulus on the other side of Bishops Cannings Down
The Sanctuary circle (node where the two currents form a Celtic Cross) -	The Sanctuary circle
The Obelisk	West Kennet Long Barrow
The Cove stones	Swallowhead Spring
Ogbourne St George (node at nearby conical mound)	western side of Silbury Hill
Ogbourne St George Church	crosses Kennet at foot of Waden Hill
Ogbourne St Andrew - node at a large prehistoric mound	**Avebury Henge, passing directly through the 2 massive entry stones at the end of Kennet Avenue**
passes 50 yards from Merlin's Mound at Marlborough College and	The Obelisk then the Cove stones

flows into the Chapel	
proceeds to valley of River Kennet	St Mary's Church, Winterbourne Monckton
St George's Church, Preshute	**Windmill Hill**
Manton	Long Stones at Avebury Trusloe
Lockeridge Dean	Tumulus next to Beckhampton Road
	Passes through Waggon and Horses Inn
	Ogbourne St George
	Ogbourne St Andrew
	Former villages of Upham and Snap
	crosses Ridgeway at Fox Hill
	St John the Baptist Ch., Bishopstone
Oxfordshire and (Berkshire)	
St Michael's Church at Aldbourne (Berkshire)	White Horse Hill over and on to St Mary's Church at Uffington
Passes through two tumuli at South Fawley (Berkshire)	passes along the Vale of the White Horse and flows through Church of Holy Cross at Sparsholt
Churn Knob round barrow and Blewburton Hill hillfort	St Andrew's Church, Letcombe Regis
South Moreton and its mound	All Saints Church, East Lockinge
through a "Fairy Mound" next to All Saints Church, North Moreton	St Augustine's Church, East Hendred
Sinodun Hill	St Mary's Church, East Hendred
St Mary's Church, Long Wittenham	Harwell
St Michael's Church, Clifton Hampden	All Saints Church, Didcot (previously dedicated to St Michael)
St Peter's Church at Marsh Baldon	**Sinodun Hill**
St Mary's Church at Garsington	Dorchester Abbey
All Saints Church, Cuddesdon	St Nicholas' Church, Brightwell Baldwin
Rycote Chapel	St Margaret's Church, Lewknor
	St Peter and St Paul, Aston Rowant
	St Leonard's Church, Cuxham
	St Andrew's Church, Chinnor
Buckinghamshire, Hertfordshire, Bedfordshire, Cambridgeshire, Suffolk and Norfolk	
St Mary's Church at Haddenham	Church of St Mary the Virgin, Weston Turville
the ruined folly of Dinton Castle	St Michael and All Saints Church, Aston Clinton
Hartwell House and Stone Church	All Saints Church, Buckland

Church of Holy Trinity, Walton	All Saints Church, Marsworth
Aylesbury	St Nicholas Church, Great Kimble
St. James the Great Church, Bierton	St Mary's Church, Ivinghoe
All Saints Church, Hulcott	Ivinghoe Beacon hillfort
St Mary's Church, Mentmore	Whipsnade Park Zoo
All Saints Church at Slapton	St Mary Magdalene Church, Whipsnade
Church of St Mary the Virgin at Eaton Bray	Luton Hoo
St Giles Church at Totternhoe	St Mary's Church, King's Walden
Dunstable Priory Church	St Marton's Church, Preston
Wauluds Bank earthwork, Luton via Icknield Way	former Templar Priory, Temple Dinsley
Deacon Hill off Icknield Way	St Ippolyts Church, Ippolyts
Ickleford	Templar Priory site, Wymondley
Letchworth	old Church of St Ethelreda, Graveley
St Mary's Church, Baldock	Holy Trinity Church, Weston
Royston and Royston Cave (former Templar location)	St Mary's Church, Clothall
St Mary's Church, Ickleton	St Mary's Church, Wallington
St Botolph Church, Hadstock (Essex)	**Royston**
St Mary's Church, Withersfield	All Saints Church, Melbourn
All Saints Church, Great Thurlow	All Saints Church, Foxton
Church Of Saint Margaret's, Stradishall	Saint Margaret's Church, Newton
All Saints Church, Wickhambrook	St Mary's Church, Great Shelford
Private church in grounds of Ickworth House	Wandlebury Ring hillfort
Masonic Lodge in Chequers Square, Bury St Edmunds	St Mary-the-Less Church, Westley Waterless
Bury St Edmunds Abbey	Church of St. Mary, Dullingham
St Nicholas Church, Rushbrooke	Church of St. Mary, Stetchworth
St Georges's Church, Bradfield St George	St Peter's Church, Little Ditton
All Saints Church, Drinkstone	All Saints Church, Kirtling
St Mary's Church, Woolpit	Kirtling Manor, guardian of two dragon statues
St Mary's Church, Wetherden	St Mary's Church, Lidgate
St Andrew's Church, Cotton	St Mary's Church, Ousden
St Andrew's Church, Wickham Skeith	All Saints Church, Barrow
St Mary's Church, Thornham Magna	Saint Nicholas Church, Little Saxham
St Mary's Church, Yaxley	Westley

Church of St Peter and St Paul, Eye	Angel Hill, Bury St Edmunds
St Peter and St Paul's Church, Hoxne	**Bury St Edmunds Abbey**
St Mary's Church, nr. Syleham Manor on bank of River Waveney	Holy Innocents Church, Great Barton
Church of St Andrew, Weybread	St Mary's Church, Pakenham
St Mary Magdalene Church, Withersdale	St George's Church, Stowlangtoft
South Elmham Hall (bishops' palace)	St Mary's Church, Langham
St Peter's Church, South Elmham	St Mary's Church, Walsham le Willows
Mettingham Castle	St Margaret Church, Wattisfield
St Michael's Church, Beccles	St Mary's Church, Rickinghall
St Mary's Church, Aldeby, Beccles	St Mary of Pity, Burgate
All Saints Ch., Wheatacre, Beccles	St Mary's Church, Brome
Somerleyton Marshes	St Nicholas Church, Oakley
Somerleyton Hall	St Andrew's Church, Scole
St Mary Church, Somerleyton Park	St George's Church, Shimpling
St Margaret's Church, Hopton-on-Sea	St Mary's at Pulham St Mary
	All Saints Church, Alburgh
	St Mary's Church, Denton
	St Mary's Church, Ditchingham
	Church of St Michael, Broome
	St Margaret's Church, Hales
	neglected church on the Raveningham Estate
	Maypole Green, Toft Monks
	St Mary's Church, Haddiscoe
	St Mary the Virgin, Ashby St. Mary
	St Margaret's Church, Hopton-on-Sea

Note: Of the approximate 380 locations, 175 are on the Michael flow and 205 on Mary. 64 locations are at St Mary, St Margaret or St Mary Magdalene churches, and 21 on (dragon-slayer) St Michael or St George churches. The feminine (Goddess) aspect of the 364-mile Michael and Mary line is more significantly emphasised than the male aspect by a ratio of approximately 7:2.

Sunrise at Glastonbury Tor

Bibliography

Andrews, C., *The New Circlemakers: Insights into the Crop Circle Mystery*, Virginia Beach, VA: 4th Dimension Press, 2nd ed., 2009.

Andrews, C., with Spignesi, J., *Crop Circles: Signs of Contact*, Franklin Lakes, NJ: New Page Books, 2003.

Baring, A., and Cashford, J., *The Myth of the Goddess: Evolution of an Image,* Penguin, 1993.

Bartholomew, A. (Ed.)., Crop Circles: Harbingers of World Change, Gateway, 1991.

Bohm, D., *Wholeness and the Implicate Order*, Great Britain. Routledge, 1980.

Bond, F., *The Gate of Remembrance*, Oxford, Blackwell, 1919.

—, *The Company of Avalon*, Oxford, Blackwell, 1924.

Bord, J., *Real Encounters with Little People*, London. Michael O'Mara Books Limited, 1997.

—, *The Secret Country*, St. Albans. Granada Publishing Limited, 1974.

—, with Bord C., *Mysterious Britain*, St. Albans. Granada Publishing Limited, 1974.

Briggs, K., *A Dictionary of Fairies*, London. Penguin Books, 1977.

Bulwer-Lytton, E., *Vril: the Power of the Coming Race*, Whitefish, Montana. Kessinger Publishing LLC, 2005. (First published 1871).

Campbell, J., *The Gaelic Otherworld*, Glasgow. James Maclehose and Sons, 1900.

Carroll, L., *Alice's Adventures in Wonderland*, Macmillan, London, 1865.

—, *Through the Looking Glass*, Macmillan, London, 1872.

Cathie, B., *The Energy Grid*, Illinois. Adventures Unlimited Press, 1990.

—, *The Harmonic Conquest of Space*, Illinois. Adventures Unlimited Press, 1998.

Coats, C., *Living Energies,* Gateway, 1996.

Cohen, M., *Lewis Carroll: A Biography*, Alfred A. Knopf, 1995.

Colqoun, I., *The Living Stones*, Peter Owen, 1957.

Conan Doyle, A., *The Coming of the Fairies*, London. Hodder & Stoughton, 1922.

Cooke, G., *Sun-Men of the Americas*, Liss, Hampshire. The White Eagle Publishing Trust, 1983.

—, with Cooke, I., *The Light in Britain*, Liss, Hampshire. The White Eagle Publishing Trust, 1971.

Corliss, W., (comp.), *Science Frontiers: Some anomalies and curiosities of nature*, Glen Arm, MD: Sourcebook Project, 1994.

Dames, M., *The Avebury Cycle*, Thames and Hudson, London, 1977 and 1996.

Devereux, P., *Earth Lights*, Wellingborough. Turnstone Press Limited, 1982.

—, *Places of Power*, London. Blandford Press, 1990.

—, *Spirit Roads*, London. Collins & Brown, 2003.

—, *Symbolic Landscapes: The Dreamtime Earth and Avebury's Open Secrets*, Glastonbury. Gothic Image Publications, 1992.

Devereux, P. & Pennick, N., *Lines on the Landscape*, Robert Hale, 1989.

Eason, C., *A Complete Guide to Fairies & Magical Beings*, Judy Piatkus (Publishers) Limited, London. 2001.

Elder, I., *Celt, Druid, and Culdee*, London, 1962.

Evans-Wentz, W., *The Fairy Faith in Celtic Countries*, The Lost Library, Glastonbury, 2010.

Forbes, J. & Campbell, I., *Giants, Myths and Megaliths*, William Chudley and Son, 1973.

Furlong, D., *Illuminating the Shadow: Transmuting the Dark Side of the Psyche*, Atlanta Books, 2016.

—, *The Keys to the Temple*, Piatkus Books, 1997.

Gardner, E., *Fairies: A Book of Real Fairies*, London. The Theosophical Publishing House, 1945.

Gillings, M. and Pollard, J., *Avebury*, Bloomsbury Publishing, London, 2004.

Glickman, M., *Crop Circles*, Glastonbury, Somerset: Wooden Books, 2005.

—, Crop Circles: *The Bones of God*, Berkeley, CA: Frog Books, 2009.

Graddon, N., *The Landing Lights of Magonia: UFOs, Aliens and the*

Fairy Kingdom, Adventures Unlimited Press, 2018.

—, *Otto Rahn and the Quest for the Grail*, Kempton, Illinois, Adventures Unlimited Press, 2008.

Hall, M., *Orders of the Quest*, Philosophical Research Society, 1949.

—, *The Secret Teachings of All Ages*, Philosophical Research Society, Inc., Los Angeles, 1928.

Haselhoff, E., *Dispersion of energies in worldwide crop formations*, Physiologia Plantarum, vol. 111, 2001, pp. 123-4; Haselhoff, 2001, pp. 71-81.

—, *The Deepening Complexity of Crop Circles: Scientific Research & Urban Legends*, Frog Ltd, 2001.

Hastings, R., *UFOs & Nukes: Extraordinary Encounters at Nuclear Weapons Sites*, CreateSpace Independent Publishing Platform, 2017.

Hesemann, M., *UFOs: the Secret History*, New York: Marlowe and Company, 1998.

—, *The Cosmic Connection: Worldwide Crop Formations and ET Contacts*, Gateway Books, Bath, 1996.

Howe, L., *Glimpses of Other Realities, Volume II: High Strangeness*, New Orleans. Paper Chase Press, 1998.

—, *Mysterious Lights and Crop Circles*, New Orleans, Paper Chase Press, 2000.

Janssen, B., *The Hypnotic Power of Crop Circles*, Enkhuizen: Frontier Publishing, 2004

Jung, C., *Flying Saucers: A Modern Myth of Things Seen in the Sky*, London. Ark Paperbacks edition, 1987.

—, *The Spirit in Man, Art, and Literature*, Princeton University Press, 1966.

Keightley, T., *Fairy Mythology, volume 2*, Amsterdam. VAMzzz Publishing, 2015.

Kirk, R., *The Secret Commonwealth of Elves, Fauns and Fairies*, New York. Dover Publications, Inc. edition, 2008.

Levengood, W. & Talbott, N., (1999). *Dispersion of energies in worldwide crop formations*, Physiologia Plantarum. 105 (4): 615–24 Physiologia Plantarum. 92 (2): 356–63.

MacManus, D., *The Middle Kingdom: the faerie world of Ireland*, Buckinghamshire. Colin Smythe Limited, 1973.

Maltwood, K., *The Enchantments of Britain or King Arthur's Round Table of the Stars*, Victoria Printing and Publishing Co., 1944.

McLellan, A., *The Lost World of Agarthi: the Mystery of Vril Power*, Souvenir Press, 1982.

Michell, J., *City of Revelation*, Abacus, 1973.

—, *New Light on the Ancient Mystery of Glastonbury*, Thrift Books, 1990.

—, *The Dimensions of Paradise*, Inner Traditions, 2008.

—, *The Earth Spirit: Its Ways, Shrines and Mysteries*, Thames and Hudson, 1975.

—, *The Face and the Message*, Gothic Image Publications, 2002.

—, *The Flying Saucer Vision*, London. Abacus, 1974.

—, *The New View Over Atlantis*, London. Thames and Hudson, 1983.

Michell, J. and Rhone, C., *Twelve Tribe Nation*, Inner Traditions, 1991.

Miller, H. & Broadhurst, P., *The Sun and the Serpent,* Pendragon Press, Launceston, Cornwall, 1989.

Narby J., *The Cosmic Serpent*, Weidenfield & Nicholson, 1999.

Pennick, N., *Celtic Sacred Landscapes*, Thames & Hudson, 1996.

—., *The Ancient Art of Geomancy*, Thames and Hudson, 1979.

Preston, K., *The British Zodiac Circle – Northern Earth Mysteries Group Newsletter No. 1* (1979).

Pringle, L., *Crop Circles: The Greatest Mystery of Modern Times*, London: Thorsons, 1999.

—, *Crop Circles: Art in the Landscape*, London: Frances Lincoln Ltd., 2010.

Reiser, O., *This Holyest Erthe: The Glastonbury Zodiac and King Arthur's Camelot*, Perennial Books, London, 1974.

Roberts, A. (Ed.)., *Glastonbury: Ancient Avalon, New Jerusalem*, Rider, 1978.

Silva, F., *Secrets in the Fields: The Science and Mysticism of Crop Circles*, Charlottesville, VA: Hampton Roads Publishing Company, 2002.

Snelling, R., *The Planetary Matrix*, Spiritual Genesis Books 2013.

—, *The Atlantis Line*, 2017.

Spence, L., *The Mysteries of Britain*. London. Senate, 1994.

Talbot, M., *Mysticism and the New Physics*, London. Arkana, 1993.

—, *The Holographic Universe*, London. Harper Collins, 1996.

Thomas, A., *Vital Signs: A complete guide to the crop circle mystery and why it is not a hoax*, Seaford, East Sussex: SB Publications, 2nd ed., 2002.

Underwood, G., *The Patterns of the Past*, Abelard-Schuman Ltd, 1973.

Vallée, J., *Passport to Magonia*, Brisbane. Daily Grail Publishing, 2014.

—, *UFOs: The Psychic Solution*, St. Albans. Panther Books Ltd, 1977.

Watkins, A., *Alfred Watkins of Hereford*, London: Garnstone, 1972.

Watkins, A., *The Old Straight Track: Its Mounds, Beacons, Moats, Sites and Mark Stones*, 1925.

White Eagle Publishing Trust, *White Eagle on Divine Mother: the Feminine & the Mysteries*, 2004.

Woolf, J., *The Mystery of Lewis Carroll: Understanding the Author of Alice in Wonderland*, London: Haus Books, 2010.

Get these fascinating books from your nearest bookstore or directly from: Adventures Unlimited Press

www.adventuresunlimitedpress.com

COVERT WARS AND BREAKAWAY CIVILIZATIONS
By Joseph P. Farrell

Farrell delves into the creation of breakaway civilizations by the Nazis in South America and other parts of the world. He discusses the advanced technology that they took with them at the end of the war and the psychological war that they waged for decades on America and NATO. He investigates the secret space programs currently sponsored by the breakaway civilizations and the current militaries in control of planet Earth. Plenty of astounding accounts, documents and speculation on the incredible alternative history of hidden conflicts and secret space programs that began when World War II officially "ended."

292 Pages. 6x9 Paperback. Illustrated. $19.95. Code: BCCW

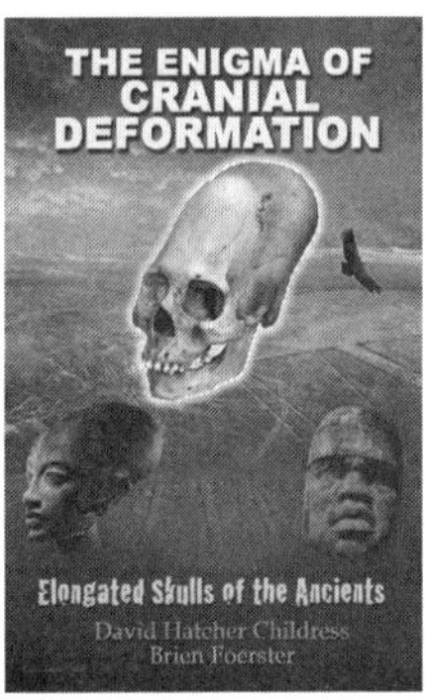

THE ENIGMA OF CRANIAL DEFORMATION
Elongated Skulls of the Ancients
By David Hatcher Childress and Brien Foerster

In a book filled with over a hundred astonishing photos and a color photo section, Childress and Foerster take us to Peru, Bolivia, Egypt, Malta, China, Mexico and other places in search of strange elongated skulls and other cranial deformation. The puzzle of why diverse ancient people—even on remote Pacific Islands—would use head-binding to create elongated heads is mystifying. Where did they even get this idea? Did some people naturally look this way—with long narrow heads? Were they some alien race? Were they an elite race that roamed the entire planet? Why do anthropologists rarely talk about cranial deformation and know so little about it? Color Section.

250 Pages. 6x9 Paperback. Illustrated. $19.95. Code: ECD

ARK OF GOD
The Incredible Power of the Ark of the Covenant
By David Hatcher Childress

Childress takes us on an incredible journey in search of the truth about (and science behind) the fantastic biblical artifact known as the Ark of the Covenant. This object made by Moses at Mount Sinai—part wooden-metal box and part golden statue—had the power to create "lightning" to kill people, and also to fly and lead people through the wilderness. The Ark of the Covenant suddenly disappears from the Bible record and what happened to it is not mentioned. Was it hidden in the underground passages of King Solomon's temple and later discovered by the Knights Templar? Was it taken through Egypt to Ethiopia as many Coptic Christians believe? Childress looks into hidden history, astonishing ancient technology, and a 3,000-year-old mystery that continues to fascinate millions of people today. Color section.

420 Pages. 6x9 Paperback. Illustrated. $22.00 Code: AOG

JACK THE RIPPER'S NEW TESTAMENT
Occultism and Bible Mania in 1888
By Nigel Graddon

This book offers evidence, for the first time, that those responsible for the Whitechapel murders were members of a hit team associated with a centuries-old European occult confederacy dedicated to human sacrifice. This was corroborated in the private papers of a Monsignor who carried out intelligence work for Pope Pius X in the run-up to the outbreak of global conflict in 1914. The priest told of the existence of a Vatican-based cabal of assassins formed by the infamous Borgias that is in alliance with a Teuton occult group formed in the 9th century. It was from within this unholy alliance that assassins travelled to London to carry out the Ripper murders to "solve a sticky problem for the British Royal Family"

302 Pages. 6x9 Paperback. Illustrated. $19.95. Code: JRNT

SECRETS OF THE HOLY LANCE
The Spear of Destiny in History & Legend
by Jerry E. Smith

Secrets of the Holy Lance traces the Spear from its possession by Constantine, Rome's first Christian Caesar, to Charlemagne's claim that with it he ruled the Holy Roman Empire by Divine Right, and on through two thousand years of kings and emperors, until it came within Hitler's grasp—and beyond! Did it rest for a while in Antarctic ice? Is it now hidden in Europe, awaiting the next person to claim its awesome power? Neither debunking nor worshiping, *Secrets of the Holy Lance* seeks to pierce the veil of myth and mystery around the Spear.

312 PAGES. 6x9 PAPERBACK. ILLUSTRATED. $16.95. CODE: SOHL

THE CRYSTAL SKULLS
Astonishing Portals to Man's Past
by David Hatcher Childress and Stephen S. Mehler

Childress introduces the technology and lore of crystals, and then plunges into the turbulent times of the Mexican Revolution form the backdrop for the rollicking adventures of Ambrose Bierce, the renowned journalist who went missing in the jungles in 1913, and F.A. Mitchell-Hedges, the notorious adventurer who emerged from the jungles with the most famous of the crystal skulls. Mehler shares his extensive knowledge of and experience with crystal skulls. Having been involved in the field since the 1980s, he has personally examined many of the most influential skulls, and has worked with the leaders in crystal skull research. Color section.

294 pages. 6x9 Paperback. Illustrated. $18.95. Code: CRSK

THE LAND OF OSIRIS
An Introduction to Khemitology
by Stephen S. Mehler

Was there an advanced prehistoric civilization in ancient Egypt? Were they the people who built the great pyramids and carved the Great Sphinx? Did the pyramids serve as energy devices and not as tombs for kings? Chapters include: Egyptology and Its Paradigms; Khemitology—New Paradigms; Asgat Nefer—The Harmony of Water; Khemit and the Myth of Atlantis; The Extraterrestrial Question; more. Color section.

272 PAGES. 6x9 PAPERBACK. ILLUSTRATED . $18.95. CODE: LOOS

VIMANA:
Flying Machines of the Ancients
by David Hatcher Childress

According to early Sanskrit texts the ancients had several types of airships called vimanas. Like aircraft of today, vimanas were used to fly through the air from city to city; to conduct aerial surveys of uncharted lands; and as delivery vehicles for awesome weapons. David Hatcher Childress, popular *Lost Cities* author, takes us on an astounding investigation into tales of ancient flying machines. In his new book, packed with photos and diagrams, he consults ancient texts and modern stories and presents astonishing evidence that aircraft, similar to the ones we use today, were used thousands of years ago in India, Sumeria, China and other countries. Includes a 24-page color section.

408 Pages. 6x9 Paperback. Illustrated. $22.95. Code: VMA

THE LOST WORLD OF CHAM
The Trans-Pacific Voyages of the Champa
By David Hatcher Childress

The mysterious Cham, or Champa, peoples of Southeast Asia formed a megalith-building, seagoing empire that extended into Indonesia, Tonga, and beyond—a transoceanic power that reached Mexico and South America. The Champa maintained many ports in what is today Vietnam, Cambodia, and Indonesia and their ships plied the Indian Ocean and the Pacific, bringing Chinese, African and Indian traders to far off lands, including Olmec ports on the Pacific Coast of Central America. opics include: Cham and Khem: Egyptian Influence on Cham; The Search for Metals; The Basalt City of Nan Madol; Elephants and Buddhists in North America; The Olmecs; The Cham in Colombia; tons more. 24-page color section.

328 Pages. 6x9 Paperback. Illustrated. $22.00 Code: LPWC

OTTO RAHN & THE QUEST FOR THE HOLY GRAIL
The Amazing Life of the Real "Indiana Jones"
By Nigel Graddon

Otto Rahn, a Hessian language scholar, is said to have found runic Grail tablets in the Pyrenean grottoes, unearthed as a result of his work in decoding the hidden messages within the Grail masterwork *Parsifal*. The fabulous artifacts identified by Rahn were believed by Himmler to include the Grail Cup, the Spear of Destiny, the Tablets of Moses, the Ark of the Covenant, the Sword and Harp of David, the Sacred Candelabra and the Golden Urn of Manna. Some believe that Rahn was a Nazi guru who wielded immense influence within the Hitler regime, persuading them that the Grail was the Sacred Book of the Aryans, which, once obtained, would justify their extreme political theories.

450 pages. 6x9 Paperback. Illustrated. Index. $18.95. Code: ORQG

THE LANDING LIGHTS OF MAGONIA
UFOs, Aliens and the Fairy Kingdom
By Nigel Graddon

British UFO researcher Graddon takes us to that magical land of Magonia—the land of the Fairies—a place from which some people return while others go and never come back. Graddon on fairies, the wee folk, elves, fairy pathways, Welsh folklore, the Tuatha de Dannan, UFO occupants, the Little Blue Man of Studham, the implications of Mars, psychic connections with UFOs and fairies. He also recounts many of the strange tales of fairies, UFOs and Magonia. Chapters include: The Little Blue Man of Studham; The Wee Folk; UFOlk; What the Folk; Grimm Tales; The Welsh Triangle; The Implicate Order; Mars—an Atlantean Outpost; Psi-Fi; High Spirits; "Once Upon a Time…"; more.

270 Pages. 6x9 Paperback. Illustrated. $19.95. Code: LLOM

ADVENTURES OF A HASHISH SMUGGLER
by Henri de Monfreid

The son of a French artist who knew Paul Gaugin as a child, de Monfreid sought his fortune by becoming a collector and merchant of the fabled Persian Gulf pearls. He was then drawn into the shadowy world of arms trading, slavery, smuggling and drugs. Infamous as well as famous, his name is inextricably linked to the Red Sea and the raffish ports between Suez and Aden in the early years of the twentieth century. De Monfreid (1879 to 1974) had a long life of many adventures around the Horn of Africa where he dodged pirates as well as the authorities.

284 Pages. 6x9 Paperback. $16.95. Illustrated. Code AHS

TECHNOLOGY OF THE GODS
The Incredible Sciences of the Ancients
by David Hatcher Childress

Childress looks at the technology that was allegedly used in Atlantis and the theory that the Great Pyramid of Egypt was originally a gigantic power station. He examines tales of ancient flight and the technology that it involved; how the ancients used electricity; megalithic building techniques; the use of crystal lenses and the fire from the gods; evidence of various high tech weapons in the past, including atomic weapons; ancient metallurgy and heavy machinery; the role of modern inventors such as Nikola Tesla in bringing ancient technology back into modern use; impossible artifacts; and more.

356 pages. 6x9 Paperback. Illustrated. $16.95. code: TGOD

THE ANTI-GRAVITY HANDBOOK
edited by David Hatcher Childress

The new expanded compilation of material on Anti-Gravity, Free Energy, Flying Saucer Propulsion, UFOs, Suppressed Technology, NASA Cover-ups and more. Highly illustrated with patents, technical illustrations and photos. This revised and expanded edition has more material, including photos of Area 51, Nevada, the government's secret testing facility. This classic on weird science is back in a new format!

230 pages. 7x10 paperback. Illustrated. $16.95. code: AGH

ANTI–GRAVITY & THE WORLD GRID

Is the earth surrounded by an intricate electromagnetic grid network offering free energy? This compilation of material on ley lines and world power points contains chapters on the geography, mathematics, and light harmonics of the earth grid. Learn the purpose of ley lines and ancient megalithic structures located on the grid. Discover how the grid made the Philadelphia Experiment possible. Explore the Coral Castle and many other mysteries, including acoustic levitation, Tesla Shields and scalar wave weaponry. Browse through the section on anti-gravity patents, and research resources.

274 pages. 7x10 paperback. Illustrated. $14.95. code: AGW

ANTI–GRAVITY & THE UNIFIED FIELD
edited by David Hatcher Childress

Is Einstein's Unified Field Theory the answer to all of our energy problems? Explored in this compilation of material is how gravity, electricity and magnetism manifest from a unified field around us. Why artificial gravity is possible; secrets of UFO propulsion; free energy; Nikola Tesla and anti-gravity airships of the 20s and 30s; flying saucers as superconducting whirls of plasma; anti-mass generators; vortex propulsion; suppressed technology; government cover-ups; gravitational pulse drive; spacecraft & more.

240 pages. 7x10 Paperback. Illustrated. $14.95. Code: AGU

THE TIME TRAVEL HANDBOOK
A Manual of Practical Teleportation & Time Travel
edited by David Hatcher Childress

The Time Travel Handbook takes the reader beyond the government experiments and deep into the uncharted territory of early time travellers such as Nikola Tesla and Guglielmo Marconi and their alleged time travel experiments, as well as the Wilson Brothers of EMI and their connection to the Philadelphia Experiment—the U.S. Navy's forays into invisibility, time travel, and teleportation. Childress looks into the claims of time travelling individuals, and investigates the unusual claim that the pyramids on Mars were built in the future and sent back in time. A highly visual, large format book, with patents, photos and schematics. Be the first on your block to build your own time travel device!

316 pages. 7x10 Paperback. Illustrated. $16.95. code: TTH

ANCIENT ALIENS ON THE MOON
By Mike Bara

What did NASA find in their explorations of the solar system that they may have kept from the general public? How ancient really are these ruins on the Moon? Using official NASA and Russian photos of the Moon, Bara looks at vast cityscapes and domes in the Sinus Medii region as well as glass domes in the Crisium region. Bara also takes a detailed look at the mission of Apollo 17 and the case that this was a salvage mission, primarily concerned with investigating an opening into a massive hexagonal ruin near the landing site. Chapters include: The History of Lunar Anomalies; The Early 20th Century; Sinus Medii; To the Moon Alice!; Mare Crisium; Yes, Virginia, We Really Went to the Moon; Apollo 17; more. Tons of photos of the Moon examined for possible structures and other anomalies.
248 Pages. 6x9 Paperback. Illustrated.. $19.95. Code: AAOM

ANCIENT ALIENS ON MARS
By Mike Bara

Bara brings us this lavishly illustrated volume on alien structures on Mars. Was there once a vast, technologically advanced civilization on Mars, and did it leave evidence of its existence behind for humans to find eons later? Did these advanced extraterrestrial visitors vanish in a solar system wide cataclysm of their own making, only to make their way to Earth and start anew? Was Mars once as lush and green as the Earth, and teeming with life? Chapters include: War of the Worlds; The Mars Tidal Model; The Death of Mars; Cydonia and the Face on Mars; The Monuments of Mars; The Search for Life on Mars; The True Colors of Mars and The Pathfinder Sphinx; more. Color section.
252 Pages. 6x9 Paperback. Illustrated. $19.95. Code: AMAR

ANCIENT ALIENS ON MARS II
By Mike Bara

Using data acquired from sophisticated new scientific instruments like the Mars Odyssey THEMIS infrared imager, Bara shows that the region of Cydonia overlays a vast underground city full of enormous structures and devices that may still be operating. He peels back the layers of mystery to show images of tunnel systems, temples and ruins, and exposes the sophisticated NASA conspiracy designed to hide them. Bara also tackles the enigma of Mars' hollowed out moon Phobos, and exposes evidence that it is artificial. Long-held myths about Mars, including claims that it is protected by a sophisticated UFO defense system, are examined. Data from the Mars rovers Spirit, Opportunity and Curiosity are examined; everything from fossilized plants to mechanical debris is exposed in images taken directly from NASA's own archives.
294 Pages. 6x9 Paperback. Illustrated. $19.95. Code: AAM2

ANCIENT TECHNOLOGY IN PERU & BOLIVIA
By David Hatcher Childress

Childress speculates on the existence of a sunken city in Lake Titicaca and reveals new evidence that the Sumerians may have arrived in South America 4,000 years ago. He demonstrates that the use of "keystone cuts" with metal clamps poured into them to secure megalithic construction was an advanced technology used all over the world, from the Andes to Egypt, Greece and Southeast Asia. He maintains that only power tools could have made the intricate articulation and drill holes found in extremely hard granite and basalt blocks in Bolivia and Peru, and that the megalith builders had to have had advanced methods for moving and stacking gigantic blocks of stone, some weighing over 100 tons.
340 Pages. 6x9 Paperback. Illustrated.. $19.95 Code: ATP

ROSWELL AND THE REICH
The Nazi Connection
By Joseph P. Farrell

Farrell has meticulously reviewed the best-known Roswell research from UFO-ET advocates and skeptics alike, as well as some little-known source material, and comes to a radically different scenario of what happened in Roswell, New Mexico in July 1947, and why the US military has continued to cover it up to this day. Farrell presents a fascinating case sure to disturb both ET believers and disbelievers, namely, that what crashed may have been representative of an independent postwar Nazi power—an extraterritorial Reich monitoring its old enemy, America, and the continuing development of the very technologies confiscated from Germany at the end of the War.

540 pages. 6x9 Paperback. Illustrated. $19.95. Code: RWR

SECRETS OF THE UNIFIED FIELD
The Philadelphia Experiment, the Nazi Bell, and the Discarded Theory
by Joseph P. Farrell

Farrell examines the now discarded Unified Field Theory. American and German wartime scientists and engineers determined that, while the theory was incomplete, it could nevertheless be engineered. Chapters include: The Meanings of "Torsion"; Wringing an Aluminum Can; The Mistake in Unified Field Theories and Their Discarding by Contemporary Physics; Three Routes to the Doomsday Weapon: Quantum Potential, Torsion, and Vortices; Tesla's Meeting with FDR; Arnold Sommerfeld and Electromagnetic Radar Stealth; Electromagnetic Phase Conjugations, Phase Conjugate Mirrors, and Templates; The Unified Field Theory, the Torsion Tensor, and Igor Witkowski's Idea of the Plasma Focus; tons more.

340 pages. 6x9 Paperback. Illustrated. $18.95. Code: SOUF

NAZI INTERNATIONAL
The Nazi's Postwar Plan to Control Finance, Conflict, Physics and Space
by Joseph P. Farrell

Beginning with prewar corporate partnerships in the USA, including some with the Bush family, he moves on to the surrender of Nazi Germany, and evacuation plans of the Germans. He then covers the vast, and still-little-known recreation of Nazi Germany in South America with help of Juan Peron, I.G. Farben and Martin Bormann. Farrell then covers Nazi Germany's penetration of the Muslim world including Wilhelm Voss and Otto Skorzeny in Gamel Abdul Nasser's Egypt before moving on to the development and control of new energy technologies including the Bariloche Fusion Project, Dr. Philo Farnsworth's Plasmator.

412 pages. 6x9 Paperback. Illustrated. $19.95. Code: NZIN

ANTARCTICA AND THE SECRET SPACE PROGRAM
By David Hatcher Childress

David Childress, popular author and star of the History Channel's show *Ancient Aliens*, brings us the incredible tale of Nazi submarines and secret weapons in Antarctica and elsewhere. He then examines Operation High-Jump with Admiral Richard Byrd in 1947 and the battle that he apparently had in Antarctica with flying saucers. Through "Operation Paperclip," the Nazis infiltrated aerospace companies, banking, media, and the US government, including NASA and the CIA after WWII. Does the US Navy have a secret space program that includes huge ships and hundreds of astronauts?

392 Pages. 6x9 Paperback. Illustrated. $22.00 Code: ASSP

ANCIENT ALIENS & SECRET SOCIETIES
By Mike Bara

Did ancient "visitors"—of extraterrestrial origin—come to Earth long, long ago and fashion man in their own image? Were the science and secrets that they taught the ancients intended to be a guide for all humanity to the present era? Bara establishes the reality of the catastrophe that jolted the human race, and traces the history of secret societies from the priesthood of Amun in Egypt to the Templars in Jerusalem and the Scottish Rite Freemasons. Bara also reveals the true origins of NASA and exposes the bizarre triad of secret societies in control of that agency since its inception. Chapters include: Out of the Ashes; From the Sky Down; Ancient Aliens?; The Dawn of the Secret Societies; The Fractures of Time; Into the 20th Century; The Wink of an Eye; more.

288 Pages. 6x9 Paperback. Illustrated. $19.95. Code: AASS

AXIS OF THE WORLD
The Search for the Oldest American Civilization
by Igor Witkowski

Polish author Witkowski's research reveals remnants of a high civilization that was able to exert its influence on almost the entire planet, and did so with full consciousness. Sites around South America show that this was not just one of the places influenced by this culture, but a place where they built their crowning achievements. Easter Island, in the southeastern Pacific, constitutes one of them. The Rongo-Rongo language that developed there points westward to the Indus Valley. Taken together, the facts presented by Witkowski provide a fresh, new proof that an antediluvian, great civilization flourished several millennia ago.

220 pages. 6x9 Paperback. Illustrated. $18.95. Code: AXOW

LEY LINE & EARTH ENERGIES
An Extraordinary Journey into the Earth's Natural Energy System
by David Cowan & Chris Arnold

The mysterious standing stones, burial grounds and stone circles that lace Europe, the British Isles and other areas have intrigued scientists, writers, artists and travellers through the centuries. How do ley lines work? How did our ancestors use Earth energy to map their sacred sites and burial grounds? How do ghosts and poltergeists interact with Earth energy? How can Earth spirals and black spots affect our health? This exploration shows how natural forces affect our behavior, how they can be used to enhance our health and well being.

368 pages. 6x9 Paperback. Illustrated. $18.95. Code: LLEE

THE MYSTERY OF U-33
By Nigel Graddon

The incredible story of the mystery U-Boats of WWII! Graddon first chronicles the story of the mysterious U-33 that landed in Scotland in 1940 and involved the top-secret Enigma device. He then looks at U-Boat special missions during and after WWII, including U-Boat trips to Antarctica; U-Boats with the curious cargos of liquid mercury; the journey of the Spear of Destiny via U-Boat; the "Black Subs" and more. Chapters and topics include: U-33: The Official Story; The First Questions; Survivors and Deceased; August 1985—the Story Breaks; The Carradale U-boat; The Tale of the Bank Event; In the Wake of U-33; Wrecks; The Greenock Lairs; The Mystery Men; "Brass Bounders at the Admiralty"; Captain's Log; Max Schiller through the Lens; Rudolf Hess; Otto Rahn; U-Boat Special Missions; Neu-Schwabenland; more.

351 Pages. 6x9 Paperback. Illustrated. $19.95. Code: MU33

THE COSMIC WAR
Interplanetary Warfare, Modern Physics, and Ancient Texts
By Joseph P. Farrell

There is ample evidence across our solar system of catastrophic events. The asteroid belt may be the remains of an exploded planet! The known planets are scarred from incredible impacts, and teeter in their orbits due to causes heretofore inadequately explained. Included: The history of the Exploded Planet hypothesis, and what mechanism can actually explode a planet. The role of plasma cosmology, plasma physics and scalar physics. The ancient texts telling of such destructions: from Sumeria (Tiamat's destruction by Marduk), Egypt (Edfu and the Mars connections), Greece (Saturn's role in the War of the Titans) and the ancient Americas.

436 Pages. 6x9 Paperback. Illustrated.. $18.95. Code: COSW

THE GRID OF THE GODS
The Aftermath of the Cosmic War & the Physics of the Pyramid Peoples
By Joseph P. Farrell with Scott D. de Hart

Farrell looks at Ashlars and Engineering; Anomalies at the Temples of Angkor; The Ancient Prime Meridian: Giza; Transmitters, Nazis and Geomancy; the Lithium-7 Mystery; Nazi Transmitters and the Earth Grid; The Master Plan of a Hidden Elite; Moving and Immoveable Stones; Uncountable Stones and Stones of the Giants and Gods; Gateway Traditions; The Grid and the Ancient Elite; Finding the Center of the Land; The Ancient Catastrophe, the Very High Civilization, and the Post-Catastrophe Elite; Tiahuanaco and the Puma Punkhu Paradox: Ancient Machining; The Black Brotherhood and Blood Sacrifices; The Gears of Giza: the Center of the Machine; Alchemical Cosmology and Quantum Mechanics in Stone; tons more.

436 Pages. 6x9 Paperback. Illustrated. $19.95. Code: GOG

THE SS BROTHERHOOD OF THE BELL
The Nazis' Incredible Secret Technology
by Joseph P. Farrell

In 1945, a mysterious Nazi secret weapons project code-named "The Bell" left its underground bunker in lower Silesia, along with all its project documentation, and a four-star SS general named Hans Kammler. Taken aboard a massive six engine Junkers 390 ultra-long range aircraft, "The Bell," Kammler, and all project records disappeared completely, along with the gigantic aircraft. It is thought to have flown to America or Argentina. What was "The Bell"? What new physics might the Nazis have discovered with it? How far did the Nazis go after the war to protect the advanced energy technology that it represented?

456 pages. 6x9 Paperback. Illustrated. $16.95. Code: SSBB

MAPS OF THE ANCIENT SEA KINGS
Evidence of Advanced Civilization in the Ice Age
by Charles H. Hapgood

Charles Hapgood has found the evidence in the Piri Reis Map that shows Antarctica, the Hadji Ahmed map, the Oronteus Finaeus and other amazing maps. Hapgood concluded that these maps were made from more ancient maps from the various ancient archives around the world, now lost. Not only were these unknown people more advanced in mapmaking than any people prior to the 18th century, it appears they mapped all the continents. The Americas were mapped thousands of years before Columbus. Antarctica was mapped when its coasts were free of ice!

316 pages. 7x10 paperback. Illustrated. $19.95. code: MASK

HITLER'S SUPPRESSED AND STILL-SECRET WEAPONS, SCIENCE AND TECHNOLOGY
by Henry Stevens

In the closing months of WWII the Allies assembled mind-blowing intelligence reports of supermetals, electric guns, and ray weapons able to stop the engines of Allied aircraft—in addition to feared x-ray and laser weaponry. Chapters include: The Kammler Group; German Flying Disc Update; The Electromagnetic Vampire; Liquid Air; Synthetic Blood; German Free Energy Research; German Atomic Tests; The Fuel-Air Bomb; Supermetals; Red Mercury; Means to Stop Engines; more.

335 Pages. 6x9 Paperback. Illustrated. $19.95. Code: HSSW

PRODIGAL GENIUS
The Life of Nikola Tesla
by John J. O'Neill

This special edition of O'Neill's book has many rare photographs of Tesla and his most advanced inventions. Tesla's eccentric personality gives his life story a strange romantic quality. He made his first million before he was forty, yet gave up his royalties in a gesture of friendship, and died almost in poverty. Tesla could see an invention in 3-D, from every angle, within his mind, before it was built; how he refused to accept the Nobel Prize; his friendships with Mark Twain, George Westinghouse and competition with Thomas Edison. Tesla is revealed as a figure of genius whose influence on the world reaches into the far future. Deluxe, illustrated edition.

408 pages. 6x9 Paperback. Illustrated. Bibliography. $18.95. Code: PRG

THE ENCYCLOPEDIA OF MOON MYSTERIES
Secrets, Anomalies, Extraterrestrials and More
By Constance Victoria Briggs

Our moon is an enigma. The ancients viewed it as a light to guide them in the darkness, and a god to be worshipped. Did you know that: Aristotle and Plato wrote about a time when there was no Moon? Several of the NASA astronauts reported seeing UFOs while traveling to the Moon?; the Moon might be hollow?; Apollo 10 astronauts heard strange "space music" when traveling on the far side of the Moon?; strange and unexplained lights have been seen on the Moon for centuries?; there are said to be ruins of structures on the Moon?; there is an ancient tale that suggests that the first human was created on the Moon?; Tons more. Tons of illustrations with A to Z sections for easy reference and reading.

152 Pages. 7x10 Paperback. Illustrated. $19.95. Code: EOMM

OBELISKS: TOWERS OF POWER
The Mysterious Purpose of Obelisks
By David Hatcher Childress

Some obelisks weigh over 500 tons and are massive blocks of polished granite that would be extremely difficult to quarry and erect even with modern equipment. Why did ancient civilizations in Egypt, Ethiopia and elsewhere undertake the massive enterprise it would have been to erect a single obelisk, much less dozens of them? Were they energy towers that could receive or transmit energy? With discussions on Tesla's wireless power, and the use of obelisks as gigantic acupuncture needles for earth, Chapters include: Megaliths Around the World and their Purpose; The Crystal Towers of Egypt; The Obelisks of Ethiopia; Obelisks in Europe and Asia; Mysterious Obelisks in the Americas; The Terrible Crystal Towers of Atlantis; Tesla's Wireless Power Distribution System; Obelisks on the Moon; more. 8-page color section.

336 Pages. 6x9 Paperback. Illustrated. $22.00 Code: OBK

HESS AND THE PENGUINS
The Holocaust, Antarctica and the Strange Case of Rudolf Hess
By Joseph P. Farrell

Farrell looks at Hess' mission to make peace with Britain and get rid of Hitler—even a plot to fly Hitler to Britain for capture! How much did Göring and Hitler know of Rudolf Hess' subversive plot, and what happened to Hess? Why was a doppleganger put in Spandau Prison and then "suicided"? Did the British use an early form of mind control on Hess' double? John Foster Dulles of the OSS and CIA suspected as much. Farrell also uncovers the strange death of Admiral Richard Byrd's son in 1988, about the same time of the death of Hess.

288 Pages. 6x9 Paperback. Illustrated. $19.95. Code: HAPG

HIDDEN FINANCE, ROGUE NETWORKS & SECRET SORCERY
The Fascist International, 9/11, & Penetrated Operations
By Joseph P. Farrell

Farrell investigates the theory that there were not *two* levels to the 9/11 event, but *three*. He says that the twin towers were downed by the force of an exotic energy weapon, one similar to the Tesla energy weapon suggested by Dr. Judy Wood, and ties together the tangled web of missing money, secret technology and involvement of portions of the Saudi royal family. Farrell unravels the many layers behind the 9-11 attack, layers that include the Deutschebank, the Bush family, the German industrialist Carl Duisberg, Saudi Arabian princes and the energy weapons developed by Tesla before WWII.

296 Pages. 6x9 Paperback. Illustrated. $19.95. Code: HFRN

THRICE GREAT HERMETICA & THE JANUS AGE
By Joseph P. Farrell

What do the Fourth Crusade, the exploration of the New World, secret excavations of the Holy Land, and the pontificate of Innocent the Third all have in common? Answer: Venice and the Templars. What do they have in common with Jesus, Gottfried Leibniz, Sir Isaac Newton, Rene Descartes, and the Earl of Oxford? Answer: Egypt and a body of doctrine known as Hermeticism. The hidden role of Venice and Hermeticism reached far and wide, into the plays of Shakespeare (a.k.a. Edward DeVere, Earl of Oxford), into the quest of the three great mathematicians of the Early Enlightenment for a lost form of analysis, and back into the end of the classical era, to little known Egyptian influences at work during the time of Jesus.

354 Pages. 6x9 Paperback. Illustrated. $19.95. Code: TGHJ

ROBOT ZOMBIES
Transhumanism and the Robot Revolution
By Xaviant Haze and Estrella Eguino,

Technology is growing exponentially and the moment when it merges with the human mind, called "The Singularity," is visible in our imminent future. Science and technology are pushing forward, transforming life as we know it—perhaps even giving humans a shot at immortality. Who will benefit from this? This book examines the history and future of robotics, artificial intelligence, zombies and a Transhumanist utopia/dystopia integrating man with machine. Chapters include: Love, Sex and Compassion—Android Style; Humans Aren't Working Like They Used To; Skynet Rises; Blueprints for Transhumans; Kurzweil's Quest; Nanotech Dreams; Zombies Among Us; Cyborgs (Cylons) in Space; Awakening the Human; more. Color Section.

180 Pages. 6x9 Paperback. Illustrated. $16.95. Code: RBTZ

BIGFOOT NATION
A History of Sasquatch in North America
By David Hatcher Childress

Childress takes a deep look at Bigfoot Nation—the real world of bigfoot around us in the United States and Canada. Whether real or imagined, that bigfoot has made his way into the American psyche cannot be denied. He appears in television commercials, movies, and on roadside billboards. Bigfoot is everywhere, with actors portraying him in variously believable performances and it has become the popular notion that bigfoot is both dangerous and horny. Indeed, bigfoot is out there stalking lovers' lanes and is even more lonely than those frightened teenagers that he sometimes interrupts. Bigfoot, tall and strong as he is, makes a poor leading man in the movies with his awkward personality and typically anti-social behavior. Includes 16-pages of color photos that document Bigfoot Nation!

320 Pages. 6x9 Paperback. Illustrated. $22.00. Code: BGN

MEN & GODS IN MONGOLIA
by Henning Haslund

Haslund takes us to the lost city of Karakota in the Gobi desert. We meet the Bodgo Gegen, a god-king in Mongolia similar to the Dalai Lama of Tibet. We meet Dambin Jansang, the dreaded warlord of the "Black Gobi." Haslund and companions journey across the Gobi desert by camel caravan; are kidnapped and held for ransom; withness initiation into Shamanic societies; meet reincarnated warlords; and experience the violent birth of "modern" Mongolia.

358 Pages. 6x9 Paperback. Illustrated. $18.95. Code: MGM

PROJECT MK-ULTRA
AND MIND CONTROL TECHNOLOGY
By Axel Balthazar

This book is a compilation of the government's documentation on MK-Ultra, the CIA's mind control experimentation on unwitting human subjects, as well as over 150 patents pertaining to artificial telepathy (voice-to-skull technology), behavior modification through radio frequencies, directed energy weapons, electronic monitoring, implantable nanotechnology, brain wave manipulation, nervous system manipulation, neuroweapons, psychological warfare, satellite terrorism, subliminal messaging, and more. A must-have reference guide for targeted individuals and anyone interested in the subject of mind control technology.

384 pages. 7x10 Paperback. Illustrated. $19.95. Code: PMK

LIQUID CONSPIRACY 2:
The CIA, MI6 & Big Pharma's War on Psychedelics
By Xaviant Haze

Underground author Xaviant Haze looks into the CIA and its use of LSD as a mind control drug; at one point every CIA officer had to take the drug and endure mind control tests and interrogations to see if the drug worked as a "truth serum." Chapters include: The Pioneers of Psychedelia; The United Kingdom Mellows Out: The MI5, MDMA and LSD; Taking it to the Streets: LSD becomes Acid; Great Works of Art Inspired and Influenced by Acid; Scapolamine: The CIA's Ultimate Truth Serum; Mind Control, the Death of Music and the Meltdown of the Masses; Big Pharma's War on Psychedelics; The Healing Powers of Psychedelic Medicine; tons more.

240 pages. 6x9 Paperback. Illustrated. $19.95. Code: LQC2

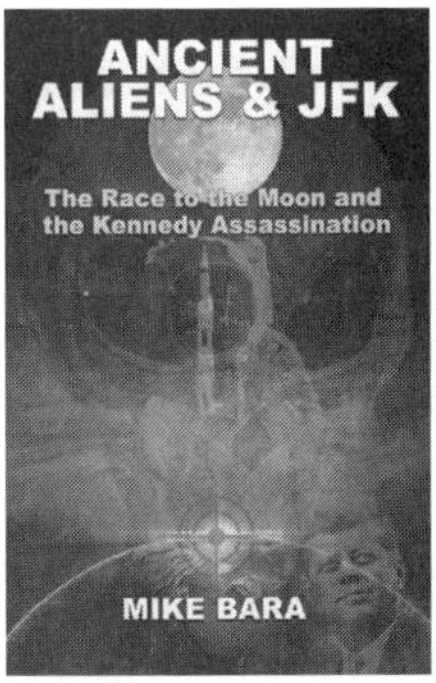

ANCIENT ALIENS AND JFK
The Race to the Moon & the Kennedy Assassination
By Mike Bara

Relying on never-before-seen documents culled from the recent Kennedy assassination papers document dump, Bara shows the secret connections between key assassination figures like Oswald, LBJ, and highly placed figures inside NASA who had reasons to want Kennedy dead. Bara also looks into the bizarre billion-dollar Treasury bonds that Japanese businessmen attempted to deposit in a Swiss bank that had photos of Kennedy and the Moon on them. Is the wealth of the Moon being used as collateral by the USA? The book will dig deeply into Kennedy's silent war with shadowy Deep State figures who were desperate to shut down his Disclosure agenda. Also: the Apollo mission; "Apollo 20," and more. Includes 8-page color section.

248 Pages. 6x9 Paperback. Illustrated. $19.95. Code: AAJK

HIDDEN AGENDA
NASA and the Secret Space Program
By Mike Bara

Bara delves into secret bases on the Moon, and exploring the many other rumors surrounding the military's secret projects in space. On June 8, 1959, a group at the ABMA produced for the US Department of the Army a report entitled Project Horizon, a "Study for the Establishment of a Lunar Military Outpost." The permanent outpost was predicted to cost $6 billion and was to become operational in December 1966 with twelve soldiers stationed at the Moon base. Does hacker Gary Mackinnon's discovery of defense department documents identifying "non-terrestrial officers" serving in space? Includes an 8-page color section.

346 Pages. 6x9 Paperback. Illustrated. $19.95. Code: HDAG

THE ANTI-GRAVITY FILES
A Compilation of Patents and Reports
Edited by David Hatcher Childress

In the tradition of *The Anti-Gravity Handbook* and *the Time-Travel Handbook* comes this compilation of material on anti-gravity, free energy, flying saucers and Tesla technology. With plenty of technical drawings and explanations, this book reveals suppressed technology that will change the world in ways we can only dream of. Chapters include: A Brief History of Anti-Gravity Patents; The Motionless Electromagnet Generator Patent; Mercury Anti-Gravity Gyros; The Tesla Pyramid Engine; Anti-Gravity Propulsion Dynamics; The Machines in Flight; More Anti-Gravity Patents; Death Rays Anyone?; The Unified Field Theory of Gravity; and tons more. Heavily illustrated. 4-page color section.

216 pages. 8x10 Paperback. Illustrated. $22.00. Code: AGF

SECRET MARS: The Alien Connection
By M. J. Craig

While scientists spend billions of dollars confirming that microbes live in the Martian soil, people sitting at home on their computers studying the Mars images are making far more astounding discoveries... they have found the possible archaeological remains of an extraterrestrial civilization. Hard to believe? Well, this challenging book invites you to take a look at the astounding pictures yourself and make up your own mind. *Secret Mars* presents over 160 incredible images taken by American and European spacecraft that reveal possible evidence of a civilization that once lived, and may still live, on the planet Mars... powerful evidence that scientists are ignoring! A visual and fascinating book!

352 Pages. 6x9 Paperback. Illustrated. $19.95. Code: SMAR

ORDER FORM

10% Discount When You Order 3 or More Items!

ADVENTURES UNLIMITED

One Adventure Place
P.O. Box 74
Kempton, Illinois 60946
United States of America
Tel.: 815-253-6390 • Fax: 815-253-6300
Email: auphq@frontiernet.net
http://www.adventuresunlimitedpress.com

ORDERING INSTRUCTIONS

- ✓ Remit by USD$ Check, Money Order or Credit Card
- ✓ Visa, Master Card, Discover & AmEx Accepted
- ✓ Paypal Payments Can Be Made To: info@wexclub.com
- ✓ Prices May Change Without Notice
- ✓ 10% Discount for 3 or More Items

SHIPPING CHARGES

United States

- ✓ Postal Book Rate { $4.50 First Item; 50¢ Each Additional Item
- ✓ POSTAL BOOK RATE Cannot Be Tracked! Not responsible for non-delivery.
- ✓ Priority Mail { $7.00 First Item; $2.00 Each Additional Item
- ✓ UPS { $9.00 First Item (Minimum 5 Books); $1.50 Each Additional Item

NOTE: UPS Delivery Available to Mainland USA Only

Canada

- ✓ Postal Air Mail { $19.00 First Item; $3.00 Each Additional Item
- ✓ Personal Checks or Bank Drafts MUST BE US$ and Drawn on a US Bank
- ✓ Canadian Postal Money Orders OK
- ✓ Payment MUST BE US$

All Other Countries

- ✓ Sorry, No Surface Delivery!
- ✓ Postal Air Mail { $19.00 First Item; $7.00 Each Additional Item
- ✓ Checks and Money Orders MUST BE US$ and Drawn on a US Bank or branch.
- ✓ Paypal Payments Can Be Made in US$ To: info@wexclub.com

SPECIAL NOTES

- ✓ RETAILERS: Standard Discounts Available
- ✓ BACKORDERS: We Backorder all Out-of-Stock Items Unless Otherwise Requested
- ✓ PRO FORMA INVOICES: Available on Request
- ✓ DVD Return Policy: Replace defective DVDs only

ORDER ONLINE AT: www.adventuresunlimitedpress.com

10% Discount When You Order 3 or More Items!

Please check: ✓

☐ This is my first order ☐ I have ordered before

Name
Address
City
State/Province Postal Code
Country
Phone: Day Evening
Fax Email

Item Code	Item Description	Qty	Total

Please check: ✓

Subtotal ▶
Less Discount-10% for 3 or more items ▶

☐ Postal-Surface — Balance ▶
☐ Postal-Air Mail (Priority in USA) — Illinois Residents 6.25% Sales Tax ▶
Previous Credit ▶
☐ UPS (Mainland USA only) — Shipping ▶
Total (check/MO in USD$ only) ▶

☐ Visa/MasterCard/Discover/American Express

Card Number:
Expiration Date: Security Code:

✓ SEND A CATALOG TO A FRIEND: